# Terrorism and Disaster Management

*Preparing Healthcare Leaders
for the New Reality*

# Terrorism and Disaster Management

*Preparing Healthcare Leaders
for the New Reality*

Edited by K. Joanne McGlown

ACHE Management Series
Health Administration Press

Chicago, IL

Your board, staff, or clients may also benefit from this book's insight. For more information on quantity discounts, contact the Health Administration Press Marketing Manager at (312) 424-9470.

08    07    06    05    04         5    4    3    2    1

**Library of Congress Cataloging-in-Publication Data**

Terrorism and disaster management: preparing healthcare leaders for the new reality
    / edited by K. Joanne McGlown.
        p. cm.
    Includes bibliographical references and index.
    ISBN 1-56793-218-5
        1. Terrorism—Health aspects. 2. Bioterrorism—Health aspects. 3. Emergency management. I. McGlown, K. Joanne.

RC88.9.T47R47 2004
362.18—dc22

                                                            2003067556

The paper used in this publication meets the minimum requirements of American National Standard for Information Sciences—Permanence of Paper for Printed Library Materials, ANSI Z39.48-1984. ∞™

Acquisitions manager: Audrey Kaufman; project manager: Joyce Sherman; layout editor: Amanda Karvelaitis; cover designer: Betsy Pérez

Health Administration Press
A division of the Foundation
    of the American College of
    Healthcare Executives
One North Franklin Street
Suite 1700
Chicago, IL 60606
(312) 424-2800

# Contents

# Preface

"The only time you must not fail is the last time you try."

—*Anonymous*

"Bioweapons...are cheap, easy to make, and easy to use. In the coming years, they will become very much a part of our lives...[E]xisting defenses against these weapons are dangerously inadequate, and when biological terror strikes, as I'm convinced it will, public ignorance will only heighten the disaster."

—*Ken Alibek, Prologue to* Biohazard *(2000)*

"America is one killer organism away from a living nightmare that threatens all we hold dear. The question isn't whether we will face a terrorist attack with a deadly viral or bacterial weapon, but when and where—and how devastating it will be."

—*Michael Osterholm,* Living Terrors *(Osterholm and Schwartz 2000)*

The events of one day—September 11, 2001—changed our country in many ways, but the warnings and discussions of potential terrorism on our own soil, of future threats of biowar and plagues, of massive earth changes, or of thermonuclear war have existed for decades. The need for medical care is the one constant element in the aftermath of any disaster, whether treating the physically wounded or sick, the scared, or those suffering from the many psychological traumas that bring the "walking wounded" in for care. Healthcare leaders who choose a path of awareness and prepare for the threats around them benefit greatly when their communities are threatened and their facilities are able to respond effectively.

During the last three decades, the field of emergency management has evolved as a respected profession. Emergency managers are managers of disasters—coordinators of the dance—orchestrating the preparedness for, response to, recovery from, and mitigation against future events. Drabek and Hoetmer (1991) write that emergency management is "the discipline and profession of applying science, technology, planning and management to deal with extreme events that can injure or kill large numbers of people, do extensive damage to property, and disrupt community life."

Emergency management calls on all aspects of a community to participate equally in ensuring the community is prepared.

A failure to prepare breeds disorganization, lack of coordination, and total confusion, conditions in which terrorists thrive. It is our new reality that terrorism drastically increases the need for preparedness, the urgency for interoperability, and the flexibility to address masses in need with very limited and stressed resources. Terrorism poses an equal-opportunity threat, and every community is at risk.

The concept of communitywide preparedness systems is new to most patient care organizations. Although most have prepared and tested disaster plans, healthcare organizations often operate in isolation, and their disaster plans reflect this inclination (AHA 2002). Hospital administrators, public health practitioners, and other health professionals are now called on to deliver. It is imperative that we meet the challenge.


## CHALLENGES TO MAINTAINING A STATE OF PREPAREDNESS

Many issues stress our ability to prepare for and perform in disasters. The most frequent pressures are the following:

- *Inadequate staff and professional resources.* The American Hospital Association (AHA 2002) reports that 62 percent of all hospitals and 79 percent of urban hospitals are at or over emergency department (ED) capacity, and a severe shortage of nurses (projected to be in excess of 800,000 by 2020); pharmacists; laboratory technicians; respiratory therapists; and, increasingly, physicians is already compromising access to healthcare services. Lack of staff coupled with increasing acuity levels and shrinking resources confound a disaster situation in which a single healthcare facility will most likely experience morbidity and mortality at proportional rates similar to the area as a whole.
- *Lack of appropriate equipment and supplies.* Most urban hospitals report a lack of medical equipment, in appropriate volumes and of the right type, to handle the large increase of patients expected from a bioterrorist incident. For this reason, the hospital grant programs of the Centers for Disease Control and Prevention (CDC) and Health Resources and Services Administration (HRSA) have

provided funding to cover these deficiencies. In addition, as health-care facilities have transitioned to just-in-time (JIT) inventories for medical/surgical supplies, pharmaceuticals, foodstuffs, linens, and other items, their incapacity in a disaster response is guaranteed. The facility can provide only limited service once supplies are depleted.

- *Technology dependence.* Most healthcare facilities have failed to main-tain a backup or manual procedure for tasks that are currently com-puterized or technology driven. Without redundant systems and adequate supplies and equipment to survive a long-term disaster event, our ability to serve the public or recover from a technology failure is jeopardized.
- *Lack of financial resources or reimbursement.* Few hospitals are in a financial position to spend money on items or procedure imple-mentation that do not add to the bottom line. Financial disaster assistance is available for some healthcare facilities for mitigation and response, but guidelines and restrictions regarding obtaining such assistance are stringent (see Chapter 13 for more information on federal disaster reimbursement).

### Expectation of the Public

The public expects that a hospital's doors will always be open, that care will be available for them when they need it, and that hospital staff will be competent and prepared to handle any threat or disastrous event. They expect that we are ready. However, the responsibilities for preparedness must be shared with the public.

We are failing to educate the public in many areas, which may later jeopardize our ability to provide timely service and to ensure our health-care facilities are safe and secure. We must encourage the use of family physicians or ambulatory care clinics, instead of EDs, for minor illnesses; educate the public to understand the risks of contaminants on clothing and the necessity to decontaminate an exposed individual prior to en-tering the ED or hospital; and inform the public and media of changes in security or visitation rules designed to protect patients, staff, and the facility. By increasing public education and awareness, the community will be better prepared to respond appropriately in a mass casualty event.

However, healthcare leaders often struggle to know how to begin. The questions heard most frequently are, "How does the system work, and where does my facility fit in?"; "Who is in charge, and what do they expect of me?"; and "What do I need to do first?" These questions and more are answered throughout this book.

## ABOUT THIS BOOK

This book is written for the healthcare administrator, manager, or leader responsible for the preparedness of his or her facility, employees, and staff in any disaster situation. The chapters focus on planning and preparedness, with a special emphasis on issues of terrorism. The authors have attempted to address questions that are often raised when discussing this topic.

As this book goes to press, the federal government and the emergency management community are in the midst of the largest reorganization in history, and each of their agencies and support services is in flux. These massive changes and revised organizational functions are addressed, and many charts and tables are provided to clarify the confusing web of governmental and agency direction, control, and oversight that could derail the best planning efforts. Some unique topics, such as federal disaster reimbursement for the healthcare industry and the legal and ethical issues surrounding disaster planning and preparedness, shed new light, and checklists and tools are provided for guidance. We must be prepared every day, and it is our hope that this book will answer questions to ease this task.

Schwartz writes in *Living Terrors: What America Needs to Know to Survive the Coming Bioterrorist Catastrophe* (Osterholm and Schwartz 2000, xiii–xiv) that "when people are too complacent you do have to sound an alarm.... [T]his [is] a topic worth getting scared about, [but it should be] fear with a purpose—scaring us into taking action." I hope this book will provide you with the purpose and desire to take action for the future that awaits us.

### Chapter Summaries

*Chapter 1. Preparing Your Healthcare Facility for Disaster*

K. Joanne McGlown, Ph.D., M.H.H.A., R.N., CHE, introduces the threat of disasters, the need for preparedness, and our new responsibility to prepare in the post-9/11 world. This chapter summarizes organizational and community issues affecting preparedness of the healthcare delivery sectors.

### Chapter 2. The New Threat: Weapons of Mass Effect

Jerry L. Mothershead, M.D., FACEP, describes the various weapons of mass effect and unique preparedness challenges for healthcare providers related to these threats. Biological and chemical agents, and traits of the diseases or illness they cause, are presented.

### Chapter 3. Disaster Planning for Terrorism

Dr. Mothershead presents the basics of disaster planning for healthcare facilities. Techniques and tools include the hazard vulnerability analysis and the threat and risk analysis; an overview of emergency operations planning is also provided. The importance of education and training through drills and exercises is highlighted.

### Chapter 4. Understanding and Implementing Standards and Guidelines for Emergency Management

Peter W. Brewster introduces the reader to standards and guidelines from a variety of government and private organizations that affect healthcare industry preparedness for disaster and terrorism. An overview of the "all hazards" concept, comprehensive emergency management, the Integrated Emergency Management System, the Incident Command System, and other critical emergency management concepts are presented. The role of the Joint Commission on Accreditation of Healthcare Organizations is highlighted.

### Chapter 5. Protecting the Healthcare Population and Facility

Barbara Vogt, Ph.D., and John H. Sorensen, Ph.D., bring their expertise from Oak Ridge National Laboratory to this overview of personal protective equipment, decontamination, sheltering issues, and evacuation for healthcare personnel and facilities.

## Chapter 6. Preparedness Issues for Populations with Special Needs

Avagene Moore, CEM, discusses the unique issues related to preparing special populations with medical concerns (e.g., the mentally, physically, and sensory challenged; children; the homebound; those receiving home health care) for disasters.

## Chapter 7. Understanding the Government's Role in Emergency Management

Donna F. Barbisch, D.H.A., M.P.H., CRNA, and Connie J. Boatright, M.S.N., R.N., present an overview of all aspects of the federal emergency management system and agencies that serve the states and local communities. Recent initiatives of CDC and HRSA to fund healthcare preparedness for bioterrorism are discussed, and components of the Department of Veterans Affairs' emergency management planning are highlighted.

## Chapter 8. Public Health Aspects of Weapons of Mass Destruction

Eric K. Noji, M.D., M.P.H., provides an overview of the critical role of the U.S. Public Health Service and CDC and future preparedness goals for the country. The Strategic National Stockpile (formerly known as the National Pharmaceutical Stockpile) is discussed.

## Chapter 9. Obtaining and Maintaining Local Interoperability

The concept of interoperability is at the core of successful emergency planning and response at any level. John D. Hoyle, Sr., LFACHE, provides an overview of medical and community interoperability and the importance of seamless operation for the healthcare provider.

*Chapter 10. Integrating Civilian and Military Medical Resources and Response Capabilities*

Dr. Barbisch presents the role of the military, military processes, and access to military assets to support state and local response in disasters. The National Disaster Medical System is described.

*Chapter 11. Legal and Ethical Considerations in Disaster Situations*

William R. Wayland, Jr., J.D., M.S.H.H.A., discusses various standards and laws that may affect the way healthcare organizations prevent, prepare for, respond to, and recover from a disaster situation. Individual rights, confidentiality, the Emergency Medical Treatment and Active Labor Act, the Joint Commission on Accreditation of Healthcare Organizations, and the Homeland Security Act are highlighted. Marjorie H. Brant, J.D., provides an overview of ethics in medical and healthcare preparedness and disaster situations. A summary of the codes of ethics of various healthcare organizations and agencies are highlighted.

*Chapter 12. Availability of Disaster Assistance from the Federal Emergency Management Agency*

The Federal Emergency Management Agency's guidelines for providing disaster assistance to the healthcare community are complex and often misunderstood. Ernest B. Abbot, Esq., clearly describes the assistance available and how healthcare services and facilities may qualify.

*Chapter 13. Lessons from the Israeli Experience*

The most current "lessons" for the healthcare and medical communities often come from countries at war. The unique challenges faced by professionals in the Israeli healthcare system through decades of violence and threat have uniquely prepared them to share their experience and knowledge with those who wish to be prepared. Jakov Adler, M.D., describes the Israeli healthcare system, the challenges facing its healthcare delivery process (prehospital and hospital based), and the steps it has taken to prepare for both chemical and biological warfare.

## A WORD ABOUT TERMINOLOGY

As government planning for homeland security is in flux, so are the terms for common works that will prevail in print for a few years. Efforts have been made to use the most current terms; for example, the former National Pharmaceutical Stockpile is currently known as the Strategic National Stockpile. To help the reader navigate the "alphabet soup" of emergency management, Appendix A provides an alphabetical listing of most of the acronyms used throughout this book.

## ACKNOWLEDGMENTS

There are a number of people without whose support and guidance this book would not have been possible. I have been blessed with many great friends and colleagues who have been willing to share their knowledge. They have opened doors to provide a very unique glimpse of the realities of this world and of our future in it. It is impossible to thank everyone I would like to; however, a few people must not be ignored for their specific contribution to this book and to my life.

*J. Thomas Stanley*—a gifted and successful author, who first encouraged and inspired my interest in writing.

*Audrey Kaufman, Helen Fry, and Joyce Sherman*—Audrey is the most gracious editor an author could ask for, who gently prodded, encouraged, and pushed to get this book into print. Helen Fry's insight and excellent technical writing skills enriched this book and brought "order to the chaos" for an enormous amount of information undergoing constant change. Joyce pushed and pulled toward final production with a tenacity and passion rarely seen. Thanks to each of you for believing in this project and believing I was the one to deliver it for you.

*The Girls of Summer*—for your friendship, humor, and faith that the knowledge we have is worth sharing. You are each brilliant leaders, and you support me and so many others in our efforts to improve this tiny planet we call home.

*James O. Page and Jakov Adler*—my mentors. For more than 20 years you have each shared your expertise and knowledge and through your support have expanded my experiences in ways that have altered my life.

*Jim Self*—Your love completes me. (AERC.)

Finally, I wish to dedicate these pages to my parents, John and Kathlyn, whose patience, unconditional love, and sense of humor paved the way for me to be. And to my very large and unique family, this book is for you. As Dr. Michael Osterholm (Osterholm and Schwartz 2000, xii) wrote to his family in the Acknowledgments section of *Living Terrors: What America Needs to Know to Survive the Coming Bioterrorist Catastrophe*, "I never want you to have to experience the hell of a bioterrorism attack. For you alone, every effort put into this book and all my other activities addressing this issue are worth it."

*Isaiah 6:8*

—*K. Joanne McGlown, Ph.D.,*
*M.H.H.A., R.N., CHE*
McGlown-Self Consulting
Montevallo, Alabama

## REFERENCES

Alibek, K. 2000. *Biohazard: The Chilling True Story of the Largest Covert Biological Weapons Program in the World—Told from the Inside by the Man Who Ran It.* New York: Random House.

American Hospital Association (AHA). 2002. "Cracks in the Foundation: Averting a Crisis in America's Hospitals." Report. Chicago: AHA.

Drabek, T. E., and G. J. Hoetmer, eds. 1991. *Emergency Management: Principals and Practice for Local Government.* Washington, DC: International City/County Management Association.

Osterholm, M. R., and J. Schwartz. 2000. *Living Terrors: What America Needs to Know to Survive the Coming Bioterrorist Catastrophe.* New York: Delacorte Press.

# PART I

*Understanding the Growing
Threat of Terrorism*

### CHAPTER ONE

# Preparing Your Healthcare Facility for Disaster

K. Joanne McGlown

The number of natural disasters, the people affected by them, and the economic costs associated with them have been steadily increasing since the 1950s. The number of people affected by natural disasters in the last 50 years equals about two-thirds of the world's population and exceeds the number killed in disaster-related incidents by 500-fold. Climate changes, global warming, sea-level rise, and changes in societal actions (such as increased development, deforestation and clear-cutting, migration of the population to coastal areas, and the filling in of floodplains) may contribute to future calamities as well. Presidential disaster declarations, which averaged 35 per year from 1976 to 2002, are routinely sought for events that exceed state capabilities (FEMA 2003).

No healthcare facility, nor any aspect of the healthcare community, is immune to disasters, and yet the healthcare system is called on to respond, be available, and be prepared for whatever emerges. *Preparedness* is a state of readiness to respond to a disaster, crisis, or any other type of emergency situation. The Federal Emergency Management Agency (FEMA) further defines it as "the leadership, training, readiness and exercise support, and technical and financial assistance to strengthen citizens, communities, state, local and tribal governments, and provisional emergency workers as they prepare for disasters, mitigate the effects of

K. Joanne McGlown, Ph.D., M.H.H.A., R.N., CHE, is chief executive officer of McGlown-Self Consulting in Montevallo, Alabama; a medical consultant with Battelle Memorial Institute in Crystal City, Virginia; and adjunct professor at University of Alabama at Birmingham.

disasters, respond to community needs after a disaster and launch effective recovery efforts" (Haddow and Bullock 2003, 116). No emergency management organization can function without a strong preparedness capability—a capability built through planning, training, and exercises—nor can a healthcare facility.

## UNDERSTANDING THE NEW RESPONSIBILITY OF PREPAREDNESS

A 2003 report from the General Accounting Office (GAO) states that four of five hospitals (81 percent) have a written emergency response plan that specifically addresses bioterrorism, and it also states that 18 percent are developing one (U.S. GAO 2003a). Checklist 1.1 at the end of this chapter outlines some general concepts required for a successful emergency planning process for any healthcare facility or entity. However, preparedness is more than having a plan, and disaster planning differs from the principles that guide management of an event.

Assessing hazards in local areas; basing plans on these hazard assessments; preparing staff; coordinating with the community; and ensuring readiness through drills, exercises, education, and training are imperative. (See Chapter 4 for more information on how to conduct a hazard vulnerability analysis.) An all-hazards approach to emergency management ensures effective and consistent response to any disaster or emergency that threatens the citizens and communities of a state, and the four phases of comprehensive emergency management—preparedness, response, recovery, and mitigation—are the foundation of the all-hazards approach (NEMA 2002).

Planning for terrorism differs from anything healthcare organizations have yet undertaken. And although the probability of an occurrence in any one city or town is low, the risks nationwide are incredibly high. The more common weapons of terrorism (e.g., explosives) are visible; however, biological and chemical terrorism are invisible enemies.

The bacteria and viruses that terrorists unleash may not be the same as those we deal with daily. Most medical providers have never seen a patient with tularemia, brucellosis, or anthrax; caregivers do not know how these diseases present in patients nor how to appropriately protect themselves or others. These are unknown entities to medical providers and thus are easily dismissed. As with most disasters, the threat must "hit close to home" and affect your community directly before action is taken. Yet your organization may not have time to internalize the risk before the community is affected.

## PREPARING THE HEALTHCARE FACILITY: ORGANIZATIONAL ISSUES

Nations that have dealt with terrorism for decades have developed a "disaster culture" in which preparedness is of primary importance and becomes part of the daily operation of healthcare facilities. Changing the culture is one of the hardest goals to accomplish in any organization, but the American healthcare industry is lacking a vital disaster culture. The effort to change begins with solid leadership from dedicated chief executive officers (CEOs) and administrators.

### Role of JCAHO in Preparedness

Internally, through its Environment of Care standards and intents, and externally, through resources, documents, and education programs, the Joint Commission on Accreditation of Healthcare Organizations (JCAHO) has spearheaded much of the recent internal disaster-preparedness effort in the healthcare industry. The December 2001 special issue of *Joint Commission Perspectives* is considered a classic publication that assisted healthcare facilities early in their preparedness initiatives. Chapter 4 further discusses various standards, regulations, and guidelines that should be considered within an organization's emergency management program; and a number of valuable tools, from JCAHO and other organizations, are listed in the web and print references in the appendices of this book.

## INTEGRATING INTERNAL PREPARATIONS

Although integrated planning requires involvement of the external community in your facility plans, healthcare facilities must first be internally integrated. Without a seamless team response, the facility will be unable to assist the outside community.

Response requirements are not always predictable and smooth. Disasters may damage the physical structure of a healthcare facility, as has happened in previous earthquake and flooding events, and the damage must be addressed while staff are responding to the external community disaster (O'Toole, Mair, and Inglesby 2002). In addition, the healthcare facility may be compromised because of failures to the infrastructure, such as the loss of electrical power, water systems, and communication lines. A thorough internal disaster plan should address contingency "work arounds" for all possible damage to the facility.

A number of aspects of integrated preparedness are addressed below, and Checklist 1.2 at the end of the chapter provides a more detailed listing for healthcare facility preparedness, both internally and in relation to the community and external environment.

## Communications

Adequate disaster response requires instant and multifaceted communications networks that are reliable and flexible. However, a mere forecast of a disaster can overwhelm vital communication services, and in most disasters, the communication lines are the first to overload or fail. Redundant phone systems, broadcast fax capability, and the ability to increase the number of dedicated wireless phones within the healthcare system should rank high on the facility's communication to-do list.

A hospital's first alert or notification of an event may be via public television or radio broadcasts, requiring that hospitals mobilize for an event of which they have little knowledge. As with any community, warnings provide critical information that empowers people at risk to take action to save lives, reduce losses, and speed recovery. The extra time from an early warning allows improved preparedness and activation of services. Unfortunately, our national warning system—the Emergency Alert System—does not reach all people at risk, and the warning capability for many natural disasters is inadequate or may go unheeded.

### Testing Capabilities

The U.S. GAO (2003a) reports that less than half of the hospitals surveyed for bioterrorism preparedness in early 2003 had conducted drills or exercises simulating a bioterrorism incident. Although staff training in biological agents was widespread, hospital participation in drills was less common.

The drills, training, and exercises that test plans and abilities and spearhead organizational improvement are among the most important aspects of disaster preparedness. The primary benefit of exercises is to reveal areas needing improvement. When disasters are not threatening, drills and exercises allow participants to make corrective actions to ensure all systems are ready when needed. A description of the primary types of exercises can be found in Chapter 3.

## Mental Health Preparedness

For every one physical casualty caused by a terrorism incident, there are an estimated 4 to 20 psychological victims (Warwick 2002). In the aftermath of the 9/11 attacks, the psychiatric department at St. Vincent's Catholic Medical Center—just one of the many healthcare facilities in the affected New York area—provided counseling and support to more than 7,000 people and received more than 10,000 calls to their help line during the first two weeks following the disaster (Rosuck 2002).

Hospitals and healthcare services should make provisions for accommodating and managing the substantial acute mental health needs of the community when a natural disaster or terrorist event occurs (JCAHO 2003). Psychological casualties often include those who are treating the physically affected—healthcare providers. For this reason, departments such as nursing, human resources, and social work as well as the chaplaincy, organizational development, and mission staff should be included in mental health planning sessions. Specifically, your organization plan should address the provision of nutritional, housing, spiritual, psychological, and other psychosocial needs and integrate these with the community plan. A triage system for behavioral health must consider the following people:

- Survivors, those who lost a loved one, rescue workers, and people who witnessed the events
- Those who lost a home, business, or job as a result of the event
- Anyone else who was deeply affected

## Benchmarking Organization Preparedness

Healthcare facilities can internally assess and broadly "eyeball" levels of preparedness based on assessment data, plans, human resources information, equipment, training, and performance during exercises and actual incidents. Self-assessments, exercises, and procedures for comparison with other facilities are important tools (IAEM 2003). To get accurate data, however, readiness must be evaluated by objective parties against prospectively established standards. A thorough assessment includes evidence of readiness maintained over time.

Readiness is not defined by the creation of a plan or by its periodic testing. To improve preparedness efforts, actions must be documented and efforts made to learn from mistakes and strengthen weaknesses. The current lack of standardized methodologies to compare the events of one facility to those of another, to compare activities among different types of disaster events, or to compare those taking place in different locations hampers the best assessment efforts. Sidebar 1.1 provides one research solution that attempts to deal with this challenge.

Yet despite the lack of a standardized assessment tool, much is still to be learned from the experiences of hospitals that have implemented emergency management plans in real-world situations. Sidebar 1.2 provides several lessons learned from these situations.

### Automated Tools for Assistance

A plethora of new tools and models is emerging to assist communities in preparing their healthcare sector for response. Two such tools are listed below.

The National Guard Bureau's *Automated Exercise and Assessment System*, a free software program, is easily deployed on personal computers and can be used to test community readiness for incidents involving weapons of mass destruction. Communities receive immediate feedback on command decisions, observe the consequences of those decisions, and receive response assessments on multiple levels. Using their actual resources, a participating community can survey and enter those resources into the software's database and for the next 12 to 14 hours work through one of 11 different scenarios with up to 41 different roles for participants.

**Sidebar 1.1. The Utstein Template: A Research Solution**

The ability to measure readiness and improvement in preparedness efforts or response has been stifled from a lack of a universally accepted, organized methodology for standardized, objective evaluations of the interventions applied in dealing with disasters. Without these, the conversion of data into important information that promotes the prevention of future events or mitigation of the effects, should they occur, will not be forthcoming—making it impossible to learn from our experiences.

The Utstein Template and Guidelines is a research methodology designed by the Task Force on Quality Control of Disaster Management, the World Association of Disaster and Emergency Medicine (WADEM), and the Nordic Society for Disaster Medicine (TFQCDM/WADEM 2003). Edited for publication by Drs. K. O. Sundnes and M. L. Birnbaum, this work is supported by six collaborating organizations, including the World Health Organization and the United Nations Department of Humanitarian Affairs. The template introduces a structural framework for investigating the medical and public health aspects of disasters, ensuring appropriate design, conduct, and reporting for evaluation and research.

"This structural framework includes (1) a standardized, universal set of definitions; (2) a conceptual model for disasters; (3) indicators and standards; (4) descriptions of 14 basic societal functions bound together by a coordination and control function; and (5) a disaster response template and two research templates. The templates are to be used in the design, conduct, analysis, and reporting of research and/or evaluations of interventions directed at preventing hazards from becoming a disaster-producing event, mitigating the effects of such an event on the affected society, and/or responses to a disaster."

*Source*: The Task Force on Quality Control of Disaster Management and the World Association of Disaster and Emergency Medicine (TFQCDM/WADEM). 2003. "Health Disaster Management: Guidelines for Evaluation and Research in the Utstein Style. Volume I: Conceptual Framework of Disasters," Chapter 1: Introduction. *Prehospital and Disaster Medicine* 17 (3, Suppl.): 1–24.

The Weill/Cornell Mass Prophylaxis/Vaccination Campaign Staffing Model, created in 2003 by Hupert and Cuomo of the Department of Public Health at Weill Medical College of Cornell University, is described as an interactive planning tool designed to "estimate the number and type of staff required to operate [mass prophylaxis] clinics" to provide a community with critical medical supplies in an efficient and timely fashion. The model will provide as output the number of sites and types of staff required to complete an inoculation campaign in a selected time frame. It allows planners to formulate realistic mass prophylaxis contingency

**Sidebar 1.2. Case Examples: Hospital and Healthcare Lessons Learned**

We benefit from real events. By examining the experiences of other healthcare organizations and the actions taken, valuable lessons are learned. The following reports summarize some of the lessons learned from healthcare facilities in recent disasters.

*Hurricanes Dennis and Floyd, Eastern Seaboard, summer 1999*. Pitt County Memorial Hospital (North Carolina) was completely isolated, lost electrical power intermittently, lacked water, and experienced failure of the pressurized water system. It established an external connection to its water supply, and tankers from 18 fire departments provided water. An on-site well provided an alternate water source. Having adequate fuel filters on hand to keep rental generators going and an extra fuel oil truck were important (Carpenter 2001).

*Northridge earthquake, Los Angeles, January 1994*. Granada Hills Community Hospital flooded when a 2,500-gallon reserve water tank ruptured on the roof. Departing from its disaster plan, the facility was required to take a spontaneous approach to quickly evacuate and salvage equipment and supplies. "Have some very basic task assignments drawn up so that when you do have community volunteers, you don't turn them away," said Richard Colon, director of environmental services and food services at Granada Hills. "It frees up your staff to do other things" (Carpenter 2001).

*Murrah Federal Building bombing; Oklahoma City, Oklahoma; April 1995*. A huge influx of victims, overeager volunteers, and the media created problems for local hospitals. The local hospital representatives interviewed for the article warn others to "be watchful of the media—they arrived inside ambulances or in cars carrying patients. One crew purchased lab coats and stethoscopes and snuck in to film interviews" (Carpenter 2001). This infiltration of the media led to a total facility lockdown. Based on experiences at the Murrah Federal Building, a preauthorized visitors list is recommended, and it is suggested that media and volunteers be escorted to their designated areas and kept there (Carpenter 2001). A citywide medical disaster plan with standardized communications and terminology should be fully integrated and include every emergency medical service agency, emergency department, hospital, pharmacy, and supplier. After the Oklahoma City bombing, unsolicited donations came by the truckloads, including medical supplies. The Oklahoma Hospital Association estimated that wasted medical supplies totaled more than $1.5 million. It is thus recommended that such offerings be anticipated and planned for (O'Toole, Mair, and Inglesby 2002).

***Ice storm, Maine, January 1998***. Inches of ice placed the VA Medical Center (Togus) on emergency generators for 90 hours. Barrels of oil were shuttled in, and emergency generators were trucked in and rotated among outbuildings. Electricity needs were paramount, and with only one electrical outlet per room and in key spots throughout the facility, those needs were not met. The lesson is to prepare for long, sustained power outages that can force the organization into an entirely new routine (Carpenter 2001). Powerless for four weeks, the staff of St. Mary's Regional Medical Center (Lewiston) used empty hallways to house the elderly with medical needs, home care patients, and those on oxygen tanks or dialysis. Staff also provided care at shelters. The Maine Hospital Association created a storm clearinghouse to help members deal with personnel, supply, and equipment shortages (Weinstock 1998).

Taking care of little details ahead of time pays off. Jeannie Cross, assistant vice president of the Healthcare Association of New York State, recommends stocking up on D-cell batteries for flashlights and making sure the hospital association has cell-phone numbers of its members. "A regular phone number [landline system] does no good if the phone lines are down," stated Cross.

***Red River flooding; Grand Forks, North Dakota; April 1997***. Staff ripped up the parking lot at Altru Health System, dug up the dirt, and piled it up to keep the water out as long as possible. Staff shared that "laying the groundwork for evacuation, thinking innovatively and remembering to keep in contact with the city emergency operations center and other agencies might be all a hospital facility manager could do to prepare for such a huge disaster" (Carpenter 2001).

***Midair collision; Zion, Illinois; February 2001***. A plane crash into the roof of a five-story cancer treatment facility forced the evacuation of 54 patients. "I don't think anybody across the country knows that the fire department takes over your building in case of disaster," stated Michael White, vice president in charge of the facilities and security departments, "you're somewhat at their mercy." Local fire officials set up command posts to guard against a fire outbreak and to control access (Carpenter 2001).

**Wildfires; Flagler County, Florida; summer 1998**. Four huge fires forced evacuation of all 43,000 residents of Flagler County, including Florida's Memorial Hospital, which evacuated patients to two other facilities in its system. Hospital officials reported that "In a crisis, there's no such thing as being over prepared.

*continued on following page*

plans for their target populations. Healthcare organizations can access this tool at www.ahrq.gov/research/biomodel.htm (Hupert and Cuomo 2003).

## PREPARING THE HEALTHCARE FACILITY: COMMUNITY ISSUES

Internal preparedness must be accomplished while strengthening community and external ties. The adage that "all disasters are local" is true in every case, as the initial response will be performed at the local level.

The GAO identified the following nine critical entities required for planning to ensure a coordinated response:

1. Emergency medical services
2. Fire services
3. Hazardous materials teams
4. Law enforcement
5. Hospitals
6. Laboratories
7. State and local government agencies
8. Public and private utilities
9. Public health

However, as of summer 2003, only 40 percent of hospitals reported contacting all nine entity types in developing their plans (U.S. GAO 2003a).

Despite this alarming statistic, the U.S. emergency management systems are becoming recognized as among the best in the world. Some efforts that facilitated this trend are the following:

- Emphasis on building partnerships among disciplines and across sectors, including the private sector and media
- Development and application of new technologies to provide the tools needed to be successful
- Emphasis on communication to partners, the public, and the media
- Focus on prevention as the cornerstone of emergency management

These same approaches are the cornerstone of excellence in healthcare facility preparedness and community interoperability.

## Building Critical Partnerships

Healthcare facilities have only recently concerned themselves with building partnerships among disciplines, across sectors, or with the private sector and media in relation to disaster preparedness. Nor have they often addressed the barriers to communication with partners, the public, or the media in disasters. This changed dramatically following the events of 9/11, which ushered in strong programs at the federal and state level to address preparedness.

One of the most important changes proposed to the nation's healthcare system, and one that is long overdue, is the critical benchmarking established in the Centers for Disease Control and Prevention (CDC 2003) grant process. This mandates development of regional plans for responding to bioterrorism, other infectious diseases, and other public health threats and emergencies.

Hospitals and other healthcare facilities have long formed mutual-aid agreements (although most are informal "handshake" agreements) with surrounding facilities and services to cover potential disasters. However, the sharing of knowledge, agreements to mutually plan, and agreements to share resources in case of disaster were rarely practiced prior to 2002.

State emergency management agencies encourage the development of mutual-aid agreements to enhance overall emergency preparedness, response, and recovery capabilities. The key to regional planning and mutual-aid agreements is centralizing specialized assets, equipment, and overall response capabilities to provide maximum accessibility to all local government within the region at the time they are needed. Regional planning also includes outreach to bordering states that may share similar threats (NEMA 2002).

Having formal mutual-aid agreements in place prior to a disaster ensures a quicker and more efficient response (NEMA 2002). Verbal agreements of the past may work for small businesses where resources are not critical nor delivery imperative. However, for large vendors with many clients, the informal agreement may actually harm the healthcare facility.

State preparedness surveys have revealed that many healthcare facilities—in some cases, entire regions—are depending on support from a single vendor for a critical item. In one case, the primary vendor for the area was found to be the sole provider for certain services or materials to more than 40 facilities (Missouri Hospital Association 2002). In a disaster, the loyalty and service delivery will go first to clients with whom the vendor holds formal agreements. Those who conduct business on a handshake have exactly that left, because the vendor has no binding agreement to produce.

It is imperative that healthcare administrators seek information on the number of additional facilities to which a single vendor is contracted to provide materials or services in disasters. If you perceive they are overloaded, they are. Seek agreements with additional providers.

### Multistate Planning

As important as regionalized planning is among intrastate facilities, so too is multistate planning among contiguous states. The federal Emergency Management Assistance Compact (EMAC), initiated in 1992, facilitated the first efforts at interstate assistance among emergency management organizations, a process that also benefits the delivery of healthcare services.

EMAC is a national interstate mutual-aid agreement that allows states to share resources during times of disaster. Signatories include 47 states, 2 territories, and the District of Columbia. Components include training, standardized response protocols, and activation review. Legally binding agreements are signed that address the critical issues of liability, workers' compensation coverage, and reimbursement of expenses. Intrastate mutual-aid agreements, whereby all local jurisdictions would have established agreements to provide resources and assistance in time of need, are also being encouraged. If adopted, this would cease the practice of handshake agreements and move the industry toward improved preparedness. These may even become a future prerequisite for eligibility to receive federal homeland-security funding (NEMA 2002).

## Applying New Technologies

A plethora of new technologies has flooded the emergency management market. New and improved personal protective equipment (PPE) for responders and the mass population, early warning devices for the detection of chemical agents or notification of the public, computerized and wireless alert notices, and sophisticated computer models to estimate the plume projection of hazardous materials are only a few of the new refinements and items available. The current emphasis being placed on homeland security will bring future benefits for the healthcare delivery system as new items for responder information and protection emerge.

## Emphasizing Communication

One of the most difficult and frustrating aspects in the movement toward interoperability at the federal, state, and local levels has been information sharing. A recent report of the U.S. GAO (2003b) states that "no level of government perceived the process [of information sharing] as effective, particularly when sharing information with federal agencies. Information on threats, methods, and techniques of terrorists is not routinely shared; and the information that is shared is not perceived as timely, accurate, or relevant." Federal officials have not yet established comprehensive processes and procedures to promote sharing with state and local agencies.

With the lack of a centralized national communications system, an aging telecommunications infrastructure, cellular networks, and crashes from viruses attacking primary computer components, the communication among local providers and responders—which is supported by basic technology and processes—is that much more critical. A fax broadcast service for emergency mass communication, emergency e-mail, or wireless network notification services are increasing in popularity; redundant systems, manual work-arounds, or other basic alternatives are imperative. Having a telephone that does not plug into the wall is crucial when power fails, as is maintaining batteries and updated emergency contact lists, including numbers for cell or mobile phones, beepers, and wireless contact information.

## Focusing on Prevention

According to K. O. Sundnes and M. L. Birnbaum (TFQCDM/WADEM 2003, 39), "prevention is the aggregate of approaches and measures taken to ensure that human actions, or natural phenomenon, do not cause or result in the occurrence of an event related to the identified or unidentified hazard." It has no relationship to decreasing the amplitude, intensity, scale, and/or magnitude of an event. Although many natural disasters are impossible to prevent, some man-made events could be eliminated, and the effects of all these events could be decreased with preparedness.

Aspects of preparedness the healthcare community must address include the following:

- Risk analysis and hazards vulnerability analysis
- Incident management
- Surge capacity
- Protection of direct caregivers
- Provision for continuity of the daily (standard) levels of care
- Management of mental health and special-population needs
- Public education and involvement
- Redundant communications and process capabilities
- Periodic testing through communitywide drills and exercises
- Types and quantities of PPE and other protective items to be stocked
- Decontamination capabilities
- Regulations and standards that direct or mandate action

Progressive improvement in our ability to respond effectively and efficiently to disasters is imperative. Many factors have a profound influence on the occurrence of events and their effects. Because of the challenges and barriers we face, healthcare managers must be knowledgeable, flexible, and eager to engage in their community-preparedness efforts. With internal and external efforts, disaster readiness and service to our communities will be improved.

## REFERENCES

Anderson, B., J. Dilling, P. Mann, and A. Moore. 1996. *Emergency Planning for Assisted Living Facilities*. Silverdale, WA: Emergency Training & Consulting, International.

Carpenter, D. 2001. "Be Prepared! Coping with Floods, Fires, Quakes and Other Disasters." *Health Facilities Management* 14 (4): 20–22.

Centers for Disease Control and Prevention (CDC). 2003. "Continuation Guidance for Cooperative Agreement on Public Health Preparedness and Response for Bioterrorism—Budget Year Four." [Online report; retrieved 8/03.] http://www.bt.cdc.gov /planning/continuationguidance/index.asp.

Federal Emergency Management Agency (FEMA). 2003. "Total Major Disaster Declarations." [Online information; retrieved 12/2/03.] www.fema.gov/library/dis_ graph.shtm.

Gibson, L. 1998. "Fire Escape: Florida Wildfires Put Hospital System's Evacuation Plan to the Test." *Hospitals & Health Networks* 72 (20): 36–38.

Haddow, G. D., and J. A. Bullock. 2003. *Introduction to Emergency Management*. Burlington, MA: Elsevier Science.

Hupert, N., and J. Cuomo. 2003. Mass Prophylaxis/Vaccination Campaign Staffing Model. [Online information; retrieved 8/03 from AHA web site, http://www .hospitalconnect.com/aha/key-issues/disaster_readiness.] Ithaca, NY: Weill Medical College of Cornell University.

International Association of Emergency Managers (IAEM). 2003. "DHS Secretary Ridge Explores Measuring Preparedness." *IAEM Bulletin* 20: 8.

Joint Commission on Accreditation of Healthcare Organizations (JCAHO). 2001. "Emergency Management in the New Millennium." Special issue. *Joint Commission Perspectives* 21 (12): 1–23.

———. 2003. *Health Care at the Crossroads: Strategies for Creating and Sustaining Community-wide Emergency Preparedness Systems*. [Online report; retrieved 12/9/03.] http://www.jcaho.org/about+us /public+policy+initiatives/emergency+preparedness.pdf.

Landesman, L. Y., ed. 1996. *Emergency Preparedness in Health Care Organizations*. Oak Brook Terrace, IL: Joint Commission on Accreditation of Healthcare Organizations.

Missouri Hospital Association. 2002. *Emergency Preparedness Needs Assessment for Hospitals and Ambulatory Surgical Centers*. Report, October. Jefferson City, MO: Missouri Hospital Association.

National Emergency Management Association (NEMA). 2002. *If Disaster Strikes Today: A Governor's Primer on All-Hazards Emergency Management*. Report. Lexington, KY: NEMA.

O'Toole, T., M. Mair, and T. V. Inglesby. 2002. "Shining Light on 'Dark Winter'." *Clinical Infectious Diseases* 34 (7): 972–83.

Rosuck, J. 2002. "Mental Health Effects of Terrorism." *Psychiatric News* Jan. 4: 4–5.

Task Force on Quality Control of Disaster Management and the World Association of Disaster and Emergency Medicine (TFQCDM/WADEM). 2003. "Health Disaster Management: Guidelines for Evaluation and Research in the Utstein Style. Volume I: Conceptual Framework of Disasters," edited by K. O. Sundnes and M. L. Birnbaum. *Prehospital and Disaster Medicine* 17 (3, Suppl.): 1–177.

U.S. General Accounting Office (GAO). 2003a. *Hospital Preparedness: Most Urban Hospitals Have Emergency Plans but Lack Certain Capacities for Bioterrorism Response*. Report No. GAO-03-924, August.

———. 2003b. "Efforts to Improve Information Sharing Need to be Strengthened." *GAO Highlights*. Report No. GAO-03-0760. [Online report; retrieved 8/03.] http://www.gao.gov/cgi-bin/getrpt?AO-03-760.

Warwick, M. C. 2002. "Psychological Effects of Weapons of Mass Destruction. *Missouri Medicine* 99 (1): 15–16.

Weinstock, M. P. 1998. "Icy 'Disaster' Turns Hospitals into Both Victims and Refugees." *AHA News* January.

# Checklists

## CHECKLIST 1.1. A SUCCESSFUL EMERGENCY PLANNING PROCESS

❏ Commitment and leadership from the top of the organization: The CEO, or equivalent, must be the champion for preparedness, setting an example for all employees and being the purveyor of the growth of a "disaster culture" in the organization.

❏ An organizational need and desire to "do the right things": A mandated plan, for the sake of meeting mandated requirements, is a useless tool. It will not be followed, is rarely developed as a facility-specific entity, and will fail to meet the needs of the facility. The desire for preparedness must be inherent within the organization.

❏ A facility-specific disaster plan: Plans that address appropriate responses to the needs of your facility are not transferable to your neighbor's facility, nor to other types of healthcare facilities.

❏ Input from the organization as a whole: Management and staff must participate to create staff ownership and pride in the plan and to ensure that all areas of concern and need are appropriately addressed.

❏ Integration with the community: Coordination with and understanding of community resources and assistance are critical.

❏ Delineated support functions: Authority and coordination, roles and responsibilities, and the ability to find and access needed resources must be addressed in detail.

*Source*: Adapted from Anderson, B., J. Dilling, P. Mann, A. Moore. 1996. *Emergency Planning for Assisted Living Facilities*. Silverdale, WA: Emergency Training & Consulting, International. Used with permission.

## CHECKLIST 1.2. FACILITY PREPAREDNESS FOR TERRORISM

### I. Emergency Management Team and Planning

1. Designate an emergency management or disaster planning team in each facility and the community that
   ❏ Consists of all disciplines that will respond to the disaster

- ❏ Is represented by all standard and support departments (create an internal call list of team members, with all contact numbers)
- ❏ Designates and understands the healthcare facility's role in the community emergency management team and response
- ❏ Understands the medical functions and their interconnectivity in a federalized response

2. Define the work of the emergency management team and the work to be accomplished.
   - ❏ Conduct an internal hazards vulnerability analysis (HVA)
   - ❏ Prioritize threats and risks, and establish a plan to address each
   - ❏ Conduct a community and area HVA
   - ❏ Develop production time lines for each HVA issue addressed
   - ❏ Assess community programs and processes for current disaster response, and identify weaknesses and gaps in service
   - ❏ Plan for alternative delivery methods and routes for delivery of supplies, personnel, or other needs
   - ❏ Review all relevant disaster-response plans, and ensure that appropriately designated staff are familiar with their content and strategies
   - ❏ Know the community's local or regional emergency management plans, command structures, and contacts in each organization
   - ❏ Determine secondary and backup processes and programs, and identify need for redundant systems

3. Assess and test power and backup systems.
   - ❏ Identify all patient care needs in a power failure; prepare to use manual systems for a prolonged time
   - ❏ Develop a staffing support system for critical tasks during power or infrastructure failures
   - ❏ Understand the capabilities of the area emergency operations center (EOC) for communication and service should the area be without power for extended lengths of time
   - ❏ Preidentify special needs and services that the healthcare facility will require from the community or area services in a power failure; have a clear understanding of capabilities and limitations available in the local area
   - ❏ Assess strengths and vulnerabilities of internal technology, communications, information, and data systems
   - ❏ Ensure manual access to automated systems (e.g., medication dispensing) in power failures

4. Establish an internal command center in each healthcare facility.
   ❏ Prepare staff and volunteers via incident command system standards and protocols for seamless response
   ❏ Practice setting up and operating the center frequently
   ❏ Involve ham or volunteer radio operators in EOC operations; you may elect to have an on-site HAM operator to ensure continual communications

## II. Communications Systems

❏ Establish internal and external lines of communications (to medical staff, personnel, responding agencies, and public health authorities) with appropriate and redundant technology; develop a call list of external team members and contact numbers.

❏ Establish collaborative strategies for communicating with neighboring hospitals, civic leaders, law enforcement, public health authorities, and emergency response agencies.

❏ Assess routine staffing and emergency call-up plans, and ensure they are supported with communication and transportation strategies.

❏ Maintain ongoing primary and redundant communication systems.

❏ Inform staff of how you will communicate with them when off duty and what is expected of them in disasters; if a call chain is to be used for staff activation from home, make certain that alternate means of reaching each person are available.

❏ Communications systems for influx of large volumes of calls must be predetermined, tested often, and designed to meet the needs of all Emergency Support Functions of the National Response Plan.

❏ Ensure adequate internal communication systems and prepare for failures of vital equipment (e.g., cell phones and pagers); develop alternative delivery systems, including runners.

## III. Communications, Alerts, and Warnings

❏ Coordinate all activities through the area command center, emergency management agency, or EOC.

❏ Know the alert systems and sources for alert information in your area.

❏ Incorporate the community warning system into your facility disaster planning.
❏ Link the community command center or EOC to each healthcare provider in your area.

## IV. Community Integration

❏ Develop strong relationships with other healthcare organizations and providers.
❏ Develop personal and professional relationships with providers through a continual planning process.
❏ Plan and conduct communitywide drills often, taking into account input from all sectors of the community.
❏ Establish formal memoranda of understanding and agreements with critical providers of services.
❏ Establish ties with counterparts at other healthcare organizations (e.g., incident commanders, pharmacists, laboratory directors, administrators) to better know each other and understand the plans of respective facilities.
❏ Quantify pharmaceutical and antibiotic supplies, both at central and satellite facilities; routinely update this list.
❏ Participate in the development of a coalition of hospitals that are geographically close to share supplies, pharmaceuticals, and staff under a clear chain of command.
❏ Assess strengths and vulnerabilities of the community's internal technology, communications, and information and data systems, and know how these interact with healthcare facility systems or providers.
❏ Ensure that appropriate healthcare professionals from all agencies are aware of the importance of reporting unusual disease presentations, clusters, and atypical patterns of hospital use, and know the mechanisms for reporting.

## V. Disaster Preparedness

❏ Ensure preparedness to operate independently and be self-sufficient for up to 72 hours minimum.

❑ Assess routine staffing and emergency call-up plans, and ensure that these are supported with communication and transportation strategies; update the roster of essential personnel.

❑ Develop work-arounds or substitutions for any services and supplies you anticipate may not be available or may be inaccessible for delivery.

❑ Consider developing a volunteer safety service team to assist with safety, security, and crowd control if professional help is not available.

❑ Coordinate the preestablishment of an areawide licensure or certification approval system for local physicians, nurses, and other professional staff; establish a system to quickly evaluate essential credentials for temporary or volunteer professional staff; establish a community or area database to track and verify certification of medical personnel.

❑ Develop a community or area volunteer service (e.g., Citizens Corp), and provide training and education and determine tasks for these teams in disasters to strengthen the overall response.

❑ Ensure that the community is prepared to receive the Strategic National Stockpile in the event of a massive medical emergency; personnel needed for unloading, warehousing, security, and medication distribution should be preidentified; personnel should be trained and prepared in their roles and the processes tested in every drill event.

❑ Prepare for mass-fatality management of deaths occurring inside the facility and in the community; bodies or body parts must be identified, cataloged, and refrigerated, and contaminated remains must be identified and secured for proper disposal.

## VI. Drills and Exercises

❑ Conduct both internal and external drills and exercises.

❑ Participate in all communitywide disaster drills and exercises when requested.

❑ Focus external drills on the role of the facility to respond to community needs in concert with emergency medical services and other emergency responders.

❑ Clearly define the roles of first-responder agencies in various types of disaster events (e.g., Which department takes the lead in decontamination of victims? Will this be done in the field or at the hospital only? Will there be assistance from outside agencies if decontamination capability is established outside the emergency department?).

❑ Conduct a communitywide tabletop exercise to include the most difficult tasks such as lockdown or quarantine of the town, a facility, or an area.

❑ Drill multiple aspects of the plan at a time to provide an opportunity for the healthcare facility to realistically test interoperability with other community responders.

❑ Include the establishment and operation of various shelters to provide care in a community; test medical overflow shelters or temporary structures.

❑ Plan with community providers to treat a large number of patients (hundreds to thousands).

❑ Test evacuation plans for the area, including the evacuation of the healthcare facilities.

❑ Test shelter-in-place provisions throughout the healthcare delivery system.

❑ Assess mutual-aid pacts and cooperative agreements for mass-casualty treatment capability.

*Sources*: This checklist was developed by K. J. McGlown, with additional information from the following: JCAHO. 2001. "The Power of Preparation." Special issue, entitled "Emergency Management in the New Millennium." *Joint Commission Perspectives* 21 (12): 13–15; JCAHO. 2001. "Responding Effectively in the Midst of a Natural Emergency." Special issue, entitled "Emergency Management in the New Millennium." *Joint Commission Perspectives* 21 (12): 22–23.

## CHECKLIST 1.3. SUCCESSFUL DRILLS AND EXERCISES

❑ Involve employees from all departments in planning an exercise; incorporate their suggestions and ideas for specific actions to be tested and examined.

❑ Exercise emergency plans a minimum of twice a year, with a variety of internal and external events; various types of exercises can keep preparedness issues before staff year-round.

❑ Fully integrate exercises to involve all area healthcare facilities and providers.

❏ Test the communication and notification links within the organization and those from the organization to the external community at large.
❏ Test internal systems.
  a.   Notifying key personnel
  b.   Setting up the command post
  c.   Assessing internal damage to the physical plant and the impact on patient care delivery
  d.   Preparing the emergency department (ED) to identify, process, and care for large groups of patients (establish alternate emergenct care locations in case the ED is destroyed or contaminated)
  e.   Testing capacity and ability to clear beds as needed
  f.   Implementing victim tracking and documentation
  g.   Determining equipment and supplies available for activation (test delivery of items to ED or central care points)
  h.   Establishing a triage center outside the ED
  i.   Securing all ED operations and access points into the department
  j.   Securing all entrances to the facility
  k.   Establishing media control and public relations procedures
  l.   Activating secondary call and standby for patient care services (e.g., surgery, burn unit, pediatrics, etc.)
  m.   Testing communications with the area emergency operations center and other external responding agencies; testing backup systems of various types
❏ Practice the stand-down of the exercise, testing the return to normalcy. These actions include adjustment of staff schedules and call coverage, communications required, and reporting processes.
❏ Critique the exercise. Have outside experts evaluate your effectiveness; request comments from all participating organizations.
❏ Conduct a "results oriented" evaluation process, and address (among others) the following major aspects of disaster preparedness:
  a.   Alert systems
  b.   Mobilization
  c.   Direction and control
  d.   Facilities
  e.   Communications
  f.   Exposure of responders

    g.   Monitoring of environment

    h.   Public information

    i.   Media information and rumor control

    j.   Special populations/schools

    k.   Reception or mass-casualty receiving centers

    l.   Traffic and access

    m.  Medical services, transportation, facilities, and equipment

❏ Develop corrective action plans from the gaps between performance and expectations.

❏ Provide timely feedback to staff to reinforce lessons learned.

❏ Take corrective actions on gaps identified from the exercise; document all actions taken.

❏ Write the final "after action" report of the exercise, including findings and corrective action taken; share results with decision makers and those with a need to know.

*Sources*: Landesman, L. Y., ed. 1996. *Emergency Preparedness in Health Care Organizations*. Oak Brook Terrace, IL: Joint Commission on Accreditation of Healthcare Organizations; Haddow, G. D., and J. A. Bullock. 2003. *Introduction to Emergency Management*. Burlington, MA: Elsevier Science.

### CHAPTER TWO

# The New Threat:
# Weapons of Mass Effect

Jerry L. Mothershead

T he phrase *weapons of mass destruction* has been well known among the emergency management community since 1995, and it has become a household word since the tragic events of 2001. As codified in public law, a weapon of mass destruction (WMD) is defined as (U.S. Congress 1996)

> any weapon or device that is intended, or has the capability, to cause death or serious bodily injury to a significant number of people through the release, dissemination, or impact of (A) toxic or poisonous chemicals or their precursors; (B) a disease organism; or (C) radiation or radioactivity.

Variations of this definition have been used by other federal agencies and professional organizations. The Department of Defense, for example, prefers the acronym CBRNE to denote chemical, biological, radiological, nuclear, and [high-yield] explosives (U.S. DoD 2001). The phrase *weapons of mass effect* (WME) has recently appeared in the homeland security lexicon, and many consider it to be a more appropriate description

Jerry L. Mothershead, M.D., FACEP, is physician advisor for the Medical Readiness and Response Division at Battelle Memorial Institute in Hampton, Virginia; senior medical consultant for the Navy Medicine Office of Homeland Security; and commander (ret.) of the Medical Corps of the United States Navy.

of these horrific devices, considering the motivations of those who would seek to use them.

All of these materials have the potential to cause large numbers of casualties if used in sufficient quantity against an unprotected population. However, physical destruction does not occur equally among these weapons and, in fact, would only occur in those agents whose primary mechanism of effect was explosive release. Furthermore, radiological devices in and of themselves would more likely produce massive contamination, with the concomitant disruption of routine operations in those contaminated areas, for variable lengths of time until cleanup operations could be completed. The only common feature of all these weapons is their ability to produce widespread effects on a community against which they might be used. These effects may be destructive. They may also be primarily seen in the health (including mental health) and well-being of individuals residing in those communities. Because prime motivations of any terrorist in using such weapons would be to disrupt the very fabric of society, to create mistrust of the governmental leadership, and to cause terror, the consequences to the community at large may be equally as grave as those of victims directly affected by WME. These overarching psychological effects make these weapons even more horrific than any actual physical damage they might cause and lend support to the use of the phrase *weapons of mass effect* when describing them.

## WEAPONS OF MASS EFFECT

This chapter provides a basic overview of the major categories of terrorist weapons that could produce widespread death, disability, destruction, and panic. The five basic categories of weapons of mass effect are

1. chemicals,
2. biological pathogens and toxins,
3. radioactive material,
4. nuclear devices, and
5. nonconventional high-yield explosives.

More specific details on any and all of these may be found in the literature, and the appendices to this book provide some sources of further information available on the Internet.

## Chemical Weapons

Chemical agents fall into the following three categories:

1. Chemicals developed specifically for use in combat operations
2. Chemicals used widely in industry but adaptable for use by the military
3. Chemicals used exclusively in industrial settings but having the potential to cause widespread contamination or serious disability if accidentally or intentionally released

Chemical and other agents are listed by type, common name, and use in Tables 2.1. and 2.2. Patient symptoms and antidotes for each category of agent are provided in Table 2.3.

### Military Chemical Weapons

Military chemical weapons include nerve agents and vesicants. *Nerve agents*, first developed by German scientists in the 1930s, are closely related chemically to organophosphate insecticides. They cause injury and death by binding with the enzyme acetylcholine esterase, which is required for the degradation of one of the body's natural neurotransmitters, acetylcholine. Subsequent excesses in acetylcholine at nerve endings, neuromuscular junctions, and the central nervous system initially produce respiratory and gastrointestinal difficulties; mental status changes; and, eventually, seizures, coma, and respiratory arrest. The release of the nerve agent sarin in the Tokyo, Japan, subway system in 1995 resulted in 11 deaths and several hundred injuries and sent more than 5,000 individuals seeking treatment to local hospitals (Okumura et al. *n.d.*). The antidotes atropine and praladoxime chloride, if given in sufficient amounts in a timely manner, reduce the effects of these agents and may be life saving.

*Vesicants* evolved from legitimate chemotherapeutic agents used in cancer therapy. Although several different types of vesicants were developed, the most commonly known are the mustard agents lewisite and phosgene. These agents act by alkylating proteins within cells. The clinical results are intense pain and the development of severe chemical burns, with large blister (bullae) formation. Inhaled, they produce similar effects on the bronchial tree, with resultant noncardiogenic pulmonary edema.

## TABLE 2.1. CATEGORIES OF CHEMICAL AND OTHER AGENTS

| Category of Agents | Common and/or Chemical Name |
| --- | --- |
| **Chemical Agents** | |
| Nerve agents | Tabun (ethyl N, N-dimethylphosphoramidocyanidate), sarin (iso-propylmethylphosphanofluoridate), soman (pinacolyl methyl phosphonofluoridate), GF (cyclohexylmethylphosphonofluoridate), VX (o-ethyl-[S]-[2-diisopropylaminoethyl]-methylphosphonothiolate |
| Blood agents | Hydrogen cyanide, yanogen chloride |
| Blister agents (vesicants) | Lewisite (an aliphatic arsenic compound, 2-chlorovinyldichloroar-sine), nitrogen and sulfur mustards, phosgene oxime |
| **Other Agents** | |
| Heavy metals | Arsenic, lead, mercury |
| Volatile toxins | Benzene, chloroform, trihalomethanes |
| Pulmonary agents | Phosgene, chlorine, vinyl chloride |
| Incapacitating agents | BZ (3-quinuclidinyl benzilate) |
| Pesticides, persistent and nonpersisent | |
| Dioxins, furans, and polychlorinated biphenyls (PCBs) | |
| Explosive nitro compounds and oxidizers | Ammonium nitrate combined with fuel oil |
| Flammable industrial gases and liquids | Gasoline, propane |
| Poisonous industrial gases, liquids, and solids | Cyanides, nitriles |
| Corrosive industrial acids and bases | Nitric acid, sulfuric acid |

Mustard agents were used during World War I and were responsible for more casualties than any other nonconventional weapon used during the conflict, primarily due to temporary or permanent blindness. Ninety-five percent of mustard-agent casualties survived, but most required lengthy hospitalizations. These agents were also used during the Iran-Iraq War (Sidell et al. 1997). Other effects in survivors include bone marrow suppression with susceptibility to infections and a long-term increase in

## TABLE 2.2. CHEMICAL WARFARE AGENTS BY TYPE

| Military Chemical Weapons | Dual Use Chemical Agents | Toxic Industrial Chemicals and Materials |
| --- | --- | --- |
| **Nerve Agents** | **Vesicants** | **Incapacitating and Riot-Control Agents** |
| Sarin | Mustard | Ester of glycollic acid (Agent 15) |
| Soman | Sulfur | Anticholinergic 3-quinulidinyle benzi- |
| Tabun | Nitrogen | late (BZ) |
| Cyclosarin (GF) | Lewisite | Chlorobenzylidenemalononitrile (CS) |
| O-ethyl S-(2-diiso propylaminoethyl) methylphosphono- thioate (VX) | Phosgene | Chloroacetophenone (Mace) (CN) |
| | **Choking Agents** | |
| | Phosogene oxime | |
| | Chlorine | |
| | Oxides of nitrogen | |
| | Perfluroisobutylene | |
| | **Blood Agents** | |
| | Hydrogen cyanide (AC) | |
| | Cyanogen chloride (CK) | |

*Source*: U.S. Army. 1999. *Medical Management of Chemical Casualities Handbook*. Aberdeen Proving Ground, MD: U.S. Army Medical Research Institute of Chemical Defense.

cancer risk. Unlike nerve agents, no effective antidotes exist for vesicants, and treatment is supportive only.

### Dual-Use Chemical Agents

Several different chemicals that are used widely in industry were weaponized for combat use prior to the 1972 Chemical Weapons Convention.[1] These are referred to in military circles as choking and blood agents.

*Choking agents* include such chemicals as chlorine gas and phosgene, which primarily affect the respiratory system. These gases produce intense irritation of the respiratory system, with profuse secretions; a reactive bronchospasm; and respiratory compromise, including pulmonary edema and respiratory arrest.

*Blood agents*, misnamed because the mechanism of action was misunderstood, include those chemicals containing various forms of cyanide. Cyanide causes cellular death by interfering with the mitochondrial cytochrome system required for the utilization of oxygen in cellular metabolism—the cells, in effect, suffocate despite adequate delivery of oxygen to the tissues. Cyanide, known best for its use in state-sponsored

## TABLE 2.3. SYMPTOMS AND ANTIDOTES OF CHEMICAL AGENTS BY CATEGORY

| Category | Symptoms | Antidote Available |
|---|---|---|
| Nerve agents | Convulsions, muscle twitching<br>Respiratory distress, constriction<br>Gastrointestinal difficulties: increased motility, pain, diarrhea<br>Mental status change<br>Profuse, watery saliva<br>Seizures<br>Coma<br>Respiratory arrest<br>*Death: within minutes* | Atropine<br><br>Praladoxine chloride (2PAMCl)<br><br><br><br><br><br>None known |
| Vesicants | **Acute**<br>Tearing, itchy, burning eyes<br>Erythema to vesication of skin<br>Severe chemical burns<br>Pulmonary edema<br>Blindness<br><br>**Chronic (if survive)**<br>Susceptibility to infections<br>Bone marrow suppression<br>Long-term increase in cancer risk<br>Severe tissue damage<br>*Treatment: decontamination of self immediately after contact* | |
| Choking agents | Irritation of respiratory system<br>Profuse pulmonary secretions<br>Reactive bronchospasm<br>Respiratory compromise<br>Pulmonary edema<br>Respiratory arrest | |
| Blood agents | **Hydrogen cyanide (AC)**<br>Weak legs, vertigo, nausea<br>Hemorrhage, brain softening<br>Cardiac failure<br><br>**Cyanogen chloride (CK)**<br>Symptoms of AC, plus:<br>Irritation of nose, eyes, throat<br>Lacrimation<br>Convulsions, retching<br>Lung irritation<br>Dyspnea, then paralysis of respiratory center | Marginal for cyanide gas<br><br><br><br>Oxygen therapy<br>IV drugs |

TABLE 2.3. *(continued)*

| Category | Symptoms | Antidote Available |
|---|---|---|
| Toxic industrial chemicals or materials | **Acute** <br> Headache <br> Nausea <br> Respiratory failure <br> Oxygen displacement <br> Temporary or instantaneous blindness | Chemical dependent |
| | **Chronic:** <br> Tumors <br> Blood poisoning <br> Respiratory restriction <br> Leukemia <br> Sterility <br> Blindness | |

*Source*: U.S. Army. 1999. *Medical Management of Chemical Casualties Handbook*. Aberdeen Proving Ground, MD: U.S. Army Medical Research Institute of Chemical Defense.

executions and in German concentration camps, is found in many industrial settings such as mining and in household products such as rodenticides. The accidental release of methylisocyanate at the Union Carbide plant in Bhopal, India, in 1985 caused more than 3,800 deaths and at least that many casualties with long-term disabilities (Dhara 1992). Similar accidents occurred at mining sites in West Virginia at approximately the same time, but no fatalities occurred and the incidents received little publicity (Keithline 2000). Antidotes exist for cyanide intoxication but have marginal efficacy in mass encounters with cyanide gas. The margin between the threshold for symptoms and death is very small, and use of the antidotes requires intravenous administration and close monitoring, both of which would be difficult to achieve in a mass-casualty situation. Furthermore, the time required to establish hazardous-materials procedures and to extricate victims prohibits timely delivery of these medications to those who need them most.

## Toxic Industrial Chemicals and Materials

More than 155,000 highly toxic industrial chemicals (TICs) and toxic industrial materials (TIMs) are produced in or stored near communities across the United States (Chemical Sources International 2003). A *TIC* or *TIM* is any chemical substance that can render a person ineffective under normal conditions. Primarily inhalation hazards, they can also be absorbed through the skin or ingested. They are inexpensive, they can have chronic or acute effects, and their detection is limited. Examples of chemical agents, with common symptoms and available antidotes, are provided in Table 2.3.

Approximately 4 billion tons of TICs and TIMs are transported annually, and more than 60,000 incidents involving chemical spills are reported each year (Smithson 2000). Most of these are small events, producing few casualties and posing more an environmental surety nuisance than a true threat. However, significant amounts have been released, requiring expeditious and, at times, prolonged evacuation of whole communities. The most significant toxic industrial spill in North American history occurred in 1979 near Mississauga, Canada, as the result of the derailment of a train carrying several different toxic industrial materials. More than 218,000 people were evacuated, including those in several hospitals and nursing homes (Mississauga Library System 2001). The potential harm as a result of an intentional release of one of these materials against an unprotected community is obvious.

**Biological Weapons**

Since the anthrax-laden postings to members of the media and government officials in October 2001, the federal government has focused most extensively on these biological types of terrorist weapons. Biological weapons fall into two categories: pathogens and toxins. *Pathogens* are bacteria or viruses that have the potential to cause serious illness or death in plants, animals, or humans. *Toxins* are chemicals produced by living organisms.

There are literally thousands of potential pathogens, but probably less than two dozen pose a significant risk of being used by foreign nations or terrorist organizations. Contrary to what has been publicized, it requires significant education, skill, and resources to obtain sufficiently virulent samples of these pathogens, reproduce them *en masse*, stabilize them for storage and weaponization, and develop delivery systems capable of affecting large populations.

The former Soviet Union had a massive offensive program and successfully weaponized some of these pathogens by the tons. Concerns based on intelligence data have recently arisen that as many as 20 countries may have, or are pursuing development of, such weapons. This concern is heightened by the possibility that unemployed former Soviet scientists may have taken their skills, and even some samples, to these other countries (Center for Nonproliferation Studies 2002).

Another major concern with regard to biological weapons is the possibility of genetic engineering. Poliovirus has already been reproduced in a laboratory. Australian scientists, using a benign form of mousepox to develop a "birth control" vaccine, inadvertently suppressed cell-mediated immunity in research mice. Not only did the mousepox cause death among the animals, but it was also unnaturally resistant to vaccines (Jackson et al. 2001). As with many advances in modern science, there may well be a dark side to the results of biological research.

The Centers of Disease Control and Prevention (CDC), in an attempt to focus its efforts on those pathogens and toxins of greatest threat to American citizens, classified a number of agents into three categories based on a variety of criteria, including lethality, the consequential disruption to society, and ease of production (CDC 2000). These pathogens and toxins are listed in Table 2.4.

With rare exceptions, the skin is an effective barrier against infection, and even with stabilization processes, extremes of the environment and ultraviolet light kill pathogens rather quickly. Terrorists would most likely attempt an aerosol release of biological agents. Aerosolization allows a wider area of coverage over a shorter period of time. Biological agents in general produce disease by either direct tissue invasion or through derangement of physiological processes and cause either primary pulmonary/respiratory or neurological disease syndromes.

Science has developed few vaccines that protect against these weapons, and although all bacterial pathogens are susceptible to antibiotic therapy, few viruses are. Unlike chemical weapons, no antidotes exist for toxins. Compounding these challenges is the difficulty in recognizing that an attack has occurred: early manifestations of disease caused by many agents mimic common, relatively benign entities such as influenza and other viral syndrome maladies. And it is during the early phase of disease progression that medical interventions have the greatest effect. Table 2.5 lists traits of each category of disease, including transmission capability, incubation period, duration of illness, lethality, and availability of a vaccine for each disease.

TABLE 2.4. PRIORITY BIOLOGICAL AGENTS BY CATEGORY

| Category | Agents | Characteristics |
| --- | --- | --- |
| Category A—<br>High-priority<br>biological agents | Variola major (smallpox)<br>Bacillus anthracis (anthrax)<br>Yersinia pestis (plague)<br>Clostridium botulinum<br>   toxin (botulism)<br>Francisella tularensis<br>   (tularemia)<br>Filoviruses<br>• Ebola hemorrhagic fever<br>• Marburg hemorrhagic<br>   fever<br>Arenaviruses<br>• Lassa (lassa fever)<br>• Junin (Argentine hemor-<br>   rhagic fever)<br>• related viruses | Pathogens that are rarely seen in the United States and high-priority agents, including organisms that pose a risk to national security because they can be easily disseminated or transmitted person to person; cause high mortality, with a potential for major public health impact; may cause public panic and social disruption; and require special action for public health preparedness[a] |
| Category B—<br>Second-highest-<br>priority biological<br>agents | Coxiella burnetti (Q fever)<br>Brucella species (brucel-<br>   losis)<br>Burkholderia mallei (glan-<br>   ders)<br>Alphaviruses<br>• Venezuelan<br>   encephalomyelitis<br>• Eastern and western<br>   equine encephalomyelitis<br>• Ricin toxin from Ricinus<br>   communis (castor beans)<br>• Epsilon toxin of<br>   Clostridium perfringens<br>• Staphylococcus entero-<br>   toxin B | Agents that are moderately easy to disseminate; cause moderate morbidity and low mortality; and require specific enhancements of CDC's diagnostic capacity and enhanced disease surveillance<br><br>A subset of Category B agents includes pathogens that are food or water borne. These pathogens include but are not limited to Salmonella species, Shigella dysenteriae, Escherichia coli O157:H7, Vibrio cholerae, and Cryptosporidium parvum[a] |
| Category C—<br>Third-highest-<br>priority biological<br>agents | Nipah virus<br>Hantaviruses<br>Tick-borne hemorrhagic<br>   fever<br>Tick-borne encephalitis<br>   viruses<br>Yellow fever<br>Multidrug-resistant tuber-<br>   culosis | Agents include emerging pathogens that could be engineered for mass dissemination because of availability; ease of production and dissemination; and potential for high morbidity and mortality, with major health impact<br><br>Preparedness for Category C agents requires ongoing research to improve disease detection, diagnosis, treatment, and prevention. Prior knowledge of which newly emergent pathogens might be employed by terrorists is not |

TABLE 2.4. *(continued)*

| Category | Agents | Characteristics |
|----------|--------|-----------------|
|          |        | possible; therefore, linking bioterrorism preparedness efforts with ongoing disease surveillance and outbreak response activities as defined in CDC's emerging infectious disease strategy is imperative [a] |

[a] Chemical Sources International (2003).

*Note:* Chart contributed by Dr. Eric Noji (used with permission of author).

*Sources*: Centers for Disease Control and Prevention. 1998. *Preventing Emerging Infectious Diseases: A Strategy for the 21st Century*. Atlanta, GA: U.S. Department of Health and Human Services; Centers for Disease Control and Prevention. 1999. "Critical Biological Agents for Public Health Preparedness." [Online article; retrieved 11/3/03.] http://www.cdc.gov/ncidod/emergplan; Centers for Disease Control and Prevention. 2003. "Bioterrorism Agents/Diseases." [Online information; retrieved 12/1/03.] http://www.bt.cdc.gov/agent /agentlist.asp; Adapted from United States Army Medical Research Institute of Infectious Diseases (USAMRIID). 2001. "BW Agent Characteristics," Appendix C. [Online appendix; retrieved 7/03.] In *Medical Management of Biological Casualties Handbook*, 4th ed. Fort Detrick, MD: USAMRIID. http://www.usamriid.army.mil/education/bluebook.html.

## Radiological Weapons

Radioactive materials are common in the industrialized world. Radioemitters are used in a wide range of products, from smoke detectors to satellites. Under most circumstances, the quantities in these devices are low, and shielding is sufficient such that humans are exposed to more ambient radiation from the environment than from these devices.

The more common radiological sources with the potential to contaminate are cesium, cobalt, depleted uranium, iodine (radioactive), nickel-63, plutonium, thorium, and tritium. However, the source may not warrant as much concern as the delivery system. The greatest concern among terrorism experts is the use of radiological dispersal devices (RDDs). The most likely scenario in which an RDD might be used would be in the "lacing" of a conventional explosive with radioactive material. The subsequent event would disperse radioactive material over a wide area. Although it is unlikely that those individuals surviving the blast would suffer sufficient exposure to develop acute radiation syndrome, environmental contamination would be extensive, and surety measures (efforts to ensure that the environment is safe) would be expensive and time consuming. Two other scenarios are worth mentioning: the release of radioactive materials from a nuclear power plant and

TABLE 2.5. DISEASE TRAITS FROM EXPOSURE TO BIOLOGICAL AGENTS BY CATEGORY

| Category | Disease | Transmitted Person to Person | Incubation Period | Duration of Illness | Lethality | Vaccine Availability |
|---|---|---|---|---|---|---|
| A | Anthrax, inhalation | No | 1–6 days | 3–5 days | High (fatal if untreated) | Yes |
| | Pneumonic plague | High | 2–3 days | 1–6 days | Usually fatal; must treat within 12–24 hours. | Yes |
| | Botulism | No | 1–5 days | Death in 24 hours; lasts months if not lethal | High without respiratory support | Yes |
| | Viral hemorrhagic fevers | Moderate | 4–21 days | Death in 7–16 days | Zaire strain is high; Sudan strain is moderate | No |
| | Smallpox | High | 7–17 days | 4 weeks | High to moderate | Yes |
| | Tularemia | No | 2–10 days | ≥2 weeks | Moderate if untreated | Yes |
| B | Q fever | Rare | 10–40 days | 2–14 days | Very low | Yes |
| | Brucellosis | No | 5–60 days | Week to months | <5% if untreated | No |
| | Glanders | Low | 10–14 days | Death in 7–10 days in septicemic form | >50% | No |
| | Venezuelan equine encephalitis | Low | 2–6 days | Days to weeks | Low | Yes |
| | Ricin | No | 18–24 hours | Days; death in 10–12 days for ingestion | High | No |
| | Staph enterotoxin B | No | 3–12 hours | Hours | <1% | No |
| | Cholera | Rare | 4 hours–5 days | ≥1 week | Low with treatment, high without | Yes |

*Source:* Adapted from United States Army Medical Research Institute of Infectious Diseases (USAMRIID). 2001. "BW Agent Characteristics," Appendix C. [Online appendix; retrieved 7/03.] In *Medical Management of Biological Casualties Handbook*, 4th ed. Fort Detrick, MD: USAMRIID. http://www.usamriid.army.mil/education/bluebook.html.

the surreptitious placement of large quantities of radioactive material in a public place.

Reactors in the United States are of a different design than those involved with the Chernobyl IV reactor accident of 1986 in the Ukraine, and recent engineering analyses have dispelled concerns of a major breach of the reactor even from a direct strike by the largest commercial aircraft now in existence (Chapin et al. 2002). Nonetheless, the Three Mile Island Nuclear Reactor accident in Pennsylvania in 1979 showed that any such incident at a nuclear power plant would create great concern among the population located in close proximity.

Covert placement of radioactive materials occurred in Moscow, Russia, in 1995 when Chechen rebels placed a trunk containing cesium-137 in a park and alerted authorities to this fact several weeks later (GlobalSecurity.org 2002). Such covert placement could cause injury to many over longer periods of time, and the threat of such a placement, even if untrue, could create generalized anxiety among the population threatened. A significant number of incidents involving "orphan" radioemitters have also occurred in developing countries: radioactive materials are disposed of improperly and discovered accidentally, with subsequent harm to the discoverers.

## Nuclear Devices

Although nuclear weapons could be considered the big brothers of RDDs, they deserve special mention. Even small nuclear explosives produce damage over a wider area, and radioactive dust (fallout) can spread on wind currents over hundreds of miles. The current theory among terrorism experts is that nuclear weapons would probably not be used by terrorists because of the difficulty in obtaining nuclear material, the risks and difficulties to the weaponeers in producing such a device, and the relative ease of detection as compared with biological or chemical production facilities. However, this assumption may not be entirely accurate.

State-supported terrorists may be able to obtain such weapons from their sponsors, and it is possible to produce relatively small nuclear devices that could nonetheless yield widespread damage. During the Cold War, the U.S. military produced several smaller tactical nuclear weapons. For example, the Davy Crockett was a mortar-launched weapon that weighed 55 pounds. The explosive device itself was approximately 33 pounds and, if detonated as an airburst, could produce an effect 100 times that of the nitrogen fertilizer/fuel oil device that demolished the Murrah Federal Building in Oklahoma City, Oklahoma, in 1995 (Brookings Institution 1998).

### High-Yield Explosives

Of all the weapons of mass effect, high-yield explosives or incendiary devices probably cause the least anxiety. These produce sudden-impact, defined-scene incidents that are more closely related to other technological or natural disasters with which Americans are familiar. These incidents pose little threat to rescuers, and traditionally recovery operations are not hampered by the lack of personnel or resources.

The key difference in the use of high-yield explosives by terrorists is the targets of those events. Khobar Towers in Dhahran, Saudi Arabia; the American embassies in Nairobi, Kenya, and Dar es Salaam, Tanzania; the Murrah Federal Building in Oklahoma City, Oklahoma; and most recently the World Trade Center in New York and the Pentagon in Washington, DC, are testaments to the widespread damage, destruction, and death that these devices can cause. Explosive devices remain the weapons of choice for terrorists because they are relatively easy to obtain and their use garners high visibility. Furthermore, as was historically seen in Northern Ireland and is currently being experienced in Israel, frequent, smaller explosions among a population can produce longer-term psychological effects, even among those not directly affected (Bleich et al. 1991).

## RISK MANAGEMENT AND WME

The actual risks from the use of such horrific weapons by terrorists against the American population are difficult to determine. Most communities face a much greater threat from unintentional anthrogenic or natural disasters. Traditional events—those due to accident, nature, or human error—can be predicted or at least anticipated based on historical records, and the magnitude of the consequences can be estimated. For instance, the existence and location of floodplains are known, as are areas prone to tornadoes or hurricanes, and local emergency planning committees are aware of the locations and quantities of highly toxic materials. Armed with such information, engineering and administrative controls instituted as an outcome of previous disasters have greatly lessened the consequences of these events.

The key elements of effective risk management are threat and vulnerability assessments. These processes, discussed in greater detail in Chapter 3, form the backbone for risk assessment. Risk assessment drives mitigation initiatives to prioritize actions to reduce either the probability that an event will occur or lessen the consequences should it happen. Modeling and simulation are powerful tools to identify community or facility vulnerabilities to a wide range of potential threats but do little to determine the actual threat.

The WME threat is based on terrorist motive, opportunity, and availability of the weapons or agents. Little need be said concerning terrorist motivation to do harm against the United States and its citizens. Although the United States is the most open society in the world, difficulties in gaining entrance to the nation while harboring significant caches of these weapons lessen, but do not eliminate, the opportunity. It is only the lack of the availability of such weapons, or the skills and resources by which to produce them, that keeps the overall threat low. Advances in science may work against these odds in the future, however. It is generally presumed that terrorists will have the greatest difficulty in obtaining or fielding those weapons that produce the greatest threat: nuclear or biological weapons. Chemical-warfare attacks and the use of radiological dispersal devices are considered to pose an intermediate threat, and the use of conventional explosives or the intentional release of toxic industrial materials poses the greatest threat.

It is equally difficult to measure the threat against a specific community or organization. Most terrorist attacks historically were targeted against governments, the military, or industry. Although these organizations and entities remain high on terrorist lists, a trend has developed over the last decade toward attacks against the civilian population. This shift is in keeping with the prime motivation of terrorists to create terror. Although the random sniper attacks near Washington, DC, in fall 2002 did not use WME, the effect was the same: a population significantly affected by fear. Finally, extremist organizations within our borders, such as religious cults or single-issue terrorists, may target organizations traditionally not prone to such attacks. One can only imagine the overall effect on its citizens if hospitals in small towns across the United States were targeted for explosions in a random fashion over several weeks or months.

## HEALTHCARE OPERATIONS IN A WME ENVIRONMENT

Weapons of mass effect pose a particular challenge to healthcare operations not normally seen in the response to technological or natural disasters. Most American disasters have been distinguished by significant property destruction, with relatively low levels of death or significant injuries. There have been only 7 disasters in U.S. history (excluding the events of 9/11) resulting in more than 1,000 deaths (Auf der Heide 1989). The single bloodiest non-war-related day in American history occurred when the Galveston Island (Texas) hurricane of 1900 claimed between 6,000 and 8,000 lives (*Galveston County Daily News* staff 2003). The terrorist attacks against the World Trade Center and the Pentagon on 9/11 resulted in nearly 3,000 lives lost.

These are extreme, and rare, events. Most disasters in the United States have resulted in fewer than 50 deaths, with injuries on that same order of magnitude. Healthcare operations in disasters typically were marked more by a temporary mismatch between supply and demand than absolute shortages: less than 5 percent of hospitals involved in disaster response suffer either personnel or material shortages, and few healthcare facilities are directly affected by those events.

On the contrary, a widespread disaster resulting from a terrorist attack using WME could, at a time when the demand for healthcare would be at a sustained high level,

- damage, destroy, or contaminate healthcare facilities;
- produce significant healthcare personnel losses through contamination, illness (among themselves or their families), or fear; or
- result in significant and prolonged material-resource deficits in critically needed items (e.g., ventilators, negative pressure isolation rooms, antibiotics).

One need look no further than recent history to understand the potential magnitude of these gaps. Two examples that easily come to mind are the effects of Tropical Storm Allison on healthcare operations in Houston in 2000 and the consequences of the terrorist posting of anthrax-laden letters in New York; Washington, DC; and Florida in 2001. (See the case examples in Sidebar 2.1.)

Hospital capacity to handle even relatively small surges in patient loads under more routine circumstances is a cause for concern. In a study

**Sidebar 2.1. Case Examples: Tropical Storm Allison and Anthrax Mailings**

Tropical Storm Allison dumped up to 35 inches of rain over 5 days in June 2001 on Houston, Texas; killed 22 people; and left almost 15,000 people homeless and in shelters. Texas Medical Center lost all electrical power because of flooding. Two other academic medical centers, Hermann Hospital and Ben Taub Hospital, were without power and inaccessible. Shortages of ambulances and emergency medical service providers compounded the situation in which more than 500 critically ill patients in these facilities required transfer to other acute care hospitals already overwhelmed by the events (Cocanour et al. 2002).

Tropical Storm Allison was only one-third the size of a major hurricane, one that would bring storm surge and tornadic winds in addition to the rain. Consider the devastating consequences if a major hurricane were to strike Houston today: "hundreds of thousands dead, damage in the tens of billions of dollars and perhaps as many as 1 million left homeless, to say nothing of dismal long-term economics" (Berger 2002). In a Category 5 hurricane, "a dome of water, perhaps 50 miles wide and 30 feet high, would surge over nearly one-fourth of Travis County, flooding about 700,000. It would take 30 hours to evacuate this area, and as 10 percent of people traditionally don't heed evacuation warnings, and of those left behind 10 percent die in a major storm surge, the math reveals a grisly death total of 7,000" (Berger 2002). The Federal Emergency Management Agency provided a total of $5.2 million to replace medical equipment from the Texas Medical Center hospitals (Associated Press 2002).

The anthrax mailings in fall 2001 resulted in illness in 22 persons who developed anthrax—11 inhalational and 11 cutaneous—and the death of 5 persons. Although this was a "small" terrorist attack, more than 30,000 people eventually received prophylaxis by way of official recommendations, and physicians throughout the country were besieged by patients requesting prophylaxis regardless of the minimal threat. The final costs of environmental testing and surety measures may never be known. The Brentwood Postal facility in Washington, DC, was thoroughly decontaminated in a process similar to that performed at the Hart Senate Office Building. The postal facility opened more than a year after the contamination (Royce 2002). The Florida building housing the publishing business contaminated in October 2001 has never reopened.

commissioned by the American Hospital Association (The Lewin Group 2002), 62 percent of all hospital emergency departments and 79 percent of urban hospitals reported that they were functioning at or over capacity, and more than half of urban hospitals reported significant time on diversion (time during which patients had to be diverted to other hospitals) because of lack of available critical care beds in the hospitals. These hospitals report an increase in demand as high as 12 percent from 2001 to 2003.

Even if a hospital were not directly affected by a terrorist event, it could indirectly become a casualty. As was clearly demonstrated in the Tokyo sarin incident, chemically contaminated but ambulatory victims might not wait for the arrival of hazardous-materials and decontamination units at the scene. Entrance of these victims into emergency departments would threaten existing patients and staff and might force closure of the department itself.

In one 2001 study conducted in the northwest United States, only 6 percent of hospitals surveyed had the capability to manage a hypothetical sarin incident. Although 75 percent of facilities responding had some decontamination capabilities, these were minimal and certainly would not be able to handle even a moderate number of contaminated casualties. Few hospitals had personal protective equipment appropriate for responding to a chemical incident, and in those that did, the equipment was minimal (one or two respirators or masks). Only about half of the hospitals polled had antibiotic supplies sufficient to provide prophylaxis to even 50 individuals for two days (Wetter, Daniell, and Treser 2001).

Improvements may have occurred since this study was published; however, it is unlikely that funding has sufficiently improved to produce a dramatic turnaround in these results in such a short period of time. Hospitals designated as receiving facilities for accidents at nuclear power facilities are required to have appropriate equipment, training, and testing to manage small numbers of casualties from incidents at these locations, but most hospitals in the United States do not.

## OPTIMAL PREPAREDNESS OF THE HEALTHCARE SECTOR

Many chapters of this book outline an approach to preparedness and planning for a terrorist event involving WME in more detail; however, three overarching principles for optimal preparedness of the healthcare sector cannot be overemphasized: integration, testing, and resources.

### Integration

Planning and preparedness for any disaster cannot be done in isolation, nor can hospitals develop plans based on untested assumptions of what other response agencies (fire services, law enforcement, etc.) will or will not do in a disaster response. Similar agencies must plan as a unit. In the event of a large-scale catastrophe, all hospitals will be involved, and thus area facilities must plan as though they are part of a regional network.

The healthcare sector encompasses much more than hospitals. Primary care clinics and private physicians, emergency medical services, private ambulance companies, community and state public health agencies, pharmacies, veterinary clinics, urgent care centers, long-term-care facilities and hospices, funeral homes, medical vendors and warehouses, and many other business concerns have both potential roles and a stake in the success of response operations. These potential sources of staffing and material resources must be included in planning and preparation. Integration and interoperability are discussed in further detail in other chapters of this book.

## Testing

Modeling and simulation for terrorist events have historically been based on large-scale events that would rapidly overwhelm the local response system's capacity, requiring the utilization of state and federal resources. Although this may be a valid test of vertical integration (the ability to incorporate regional, state, and federal resources into local disaster operations), another rarely used approach is to determine the system's actual time-phased functional capability and capacity.

This methodology seeks to determine the resources actually required from all response sectors at a given period of time after the incident and may be of particular value because it could be used to establish the trigger required to activate and release these higher-level resources. Prospective determination of a system's capacity allows a "high-water line" with which to compare an actual event as it unfolds, allowing more accurate needs assessments and requests for assistance that drive the state and federal responses.

## Resources

It is unreasonable to expect the healthcare sector to expend resources they do not have or to amass large quantities of excess expirable supplies based on a low-probability event. Unlike the majority of emergency response organizations, the healthcare sector has historically received little or no funding from the public coffers for disaster preparedness and mitigation. The December 2003 Homeland Security Presidential Directive/HSPD-8 includes "clinical care" among its defined "first responders," and healthcare is a first-responder discipline listed in budgets for fiscal year 2004 Office of Domestic Preparedness grant monies. This will allow the healthcare sector to use the grant money for planning, organizing, equipping, training, and exercising (The White House 2003).

Recent legislation has allotted some funding to improvements in state and community public health agencies, and a small percentage of this funding is designated for traditional healthcare operations. Businesses involved with healthcare operations should gain the support of local and state governments for a share of disaster preparedness funding if the communities can reasonably expect full participation in planning for these events.

Weapons of mass effect pose a challenge that the healthcare sector has not seen in the history of this country. Federal resources are necessary; however, these events would be first and foremost local calamities, and the local healthcare system will be part of the vanguard of response. Mitigation, planning, resource procurement, education, and training are required if this critical partner in response is to be prepared for these events.

## NOTE

1. The Convention on the Prohibition of the Development, Production and Stockpiling of Bacteriological (Biological) and Toxin Weapons and on Their Destruction was signed in London; Moscow; and Washington, DC, on 10 April 1972.

## REFERENCES

Associated Press. 2002. "Feds Provide $5.5 Million for Texas Medical Center Recovery." [Online article; retrieved 3/6/02.] HoustonChronicle.com. http://www.chron.com/cs/CDA/story.hts/storm2001/1285020.

Auf der Heide, E. 1989. *Disaster Response: Principles of Preparation and Coordination*. St. Louis, MO: Mosby.

Berger, E. 2002. "Can City Weather Bigger Storms?" [Online article; retrieved 6/4/02.] *Houston Chronicle.* http://www.chron.com/cs/CDA/story.hts/storm2001/1434799.

Bleich, A., S. Kron, C. Margalit, G. Inbar, Z. Kaplan, S. Cooper, and Z. Solomon. 1991. "Israeli Psychological Casualties of the Persian Gulf War: Characteristics, Therapy, and Selected Issues." *Israeli Journal of Medical Science* 27 (11/12): 673–76.

The Brookings Institution. 1998. "The Davy Crockett." [Online article; retrieved 7/12/03.] U.S. Nuclear Weapons Cost Study Project. http://www.brook.edu/FP/projects/nucwcost /davyc.HTM.

Center for Nonproliferation Studies. 2002. "Chemical and Biological Weapons: Possession and Programs Past and Present." [Online article; retrieved 4/12/03.] Monterey Institute of International Studies. http://cns.miis.edu/research/cbw/possess.htm.

Centers for Disease Control and Prevention (CDC). 1998. *Preventing Emerging Infectious Diseases: A Strategy for the 21st Century.* Atlanta, GA: U.S. Department of Health and Human Services.

———. 1999. "Critical Biological Agents for Public Health Preparedness." [Online article; retrieved 11/3/03.] http://www.cdc.gov/ncidod/emergplan.

———. 2000. "Biological and Chemical Terrorism: Strategic Plan for Preparedness and Response. Recommendations of the CDC Strategic Planning Workgroup." *Morbidity and Mortality Weekly* 49 (RR-4): 1–4.

———. 2003. "Bioterrorism Agents/Diseases." [Online information, retrieved 12/1/03.] http://www.bt.cdc.gov/agent/agentlist.asp.

Chapin, D. M., K. P. Cohen, W. K. Davis, E. E. Kintner, L. J. Koch, J. W. Landis, M. Levenson, I. H. Mandil, Z. T. Pate, T. Rockwell, A. Schriesheim, J. W. Simpson, A. Squire, C. Starr, H. E. Stone, J. J. Taylor, N. E. Wolfe, and E. L. Zebroski. 2002. "Nuclear Safety. Nuclear Power Plants and Their Fuel as Terrorist Targets." *Science* 297 (5589): 1997–99.

Chemical Sources International, Inc. 2003. "Chem Sources—USA." Clemson, SC: Chemical Sources International, Inc.

Cocanour, C. S., S. J. Allen, J. Mazabob, J. W. Sparks, C. P. Fischer, J. Romans, and K. P. Lally. 2002. "Lessons Learned from the Evacuation of an Urban Teaching Hospital." *Archives of Surgery* 137 (10): 1141–45.

Dhara, R. 1992. "Health Effects of the Bhopal Gas Leak: A Review." *Epidemiologia e prevenzione* 14 (52): 22–31.

*Galveston County Daily News* staff. 2003. "The 1900 Storm: Galveston Island, Texas." [Online article; retrieved 6/12/03.] Galveston Newspapers Inc. and the City of Galveston 1900 Storm Committee. http://www.1900storm.com/.

GlobalSecurity.org. 2002. "Chechnya Special Weapons." [Online article; retrieved 7/12/03.] Global Security. http://www.globalsecurity.org/wmd/world/chechnya/.

Jackson, R. J., A. J. Ramsay, C. D. Christensen, S. Beaton, D. F. Hall, and I. A. Ramshaw. 2001. "Expression of Mouse Interleukin-4 by a Recombinant Ectromelia Virus Suppresses Cytolytic Lymphocyte Responses and Overcomes Genetic Resistance to Mousepox." *Journal of Virology* 75 (3): 1205–10.

Keithline, J. 2000. "Emergency Planning and Community Right-to-Know Citizen Suits: Should the Supreme Court Extend Gwaltney?" [Online article; retrieved 4/21/03.] *Washington and Lee University Law Review* Oct. 13. http://lawreview.wlu.edu/abs/Keithline.htm#N_1_.

The Lewin Group. 2002. "Emergency Department Overload: A Growing Crisis. The Results of the AHA Survey of Emergency Department (ED) and Hospital Capacity." [Online presentation slides; retrieved 7/12/03.] Presentation for the American Hospital Association, April. http://www.hospitalconnect.com/aha/press_room-info/content/EdoCrisisSlides.pdf.

Mississauga Library System. 2001. "1979 Mississauga Train Derailment." [Online article; retrieved 4/21/03.] Mississauga, Ontario, Canada: City of Mississauga. http://www.city.mississauga.on.ca/library/history/derail.htm.

Okumura, T., N. Takasu, S. Ishimatsu, S. Miyanoki, A. Mitsuhashi, K. Kumada, K. Tanaka, and S. Hinohara. (n.d.) "Report on 640 Victims of the Tokyo Subway Sarin Attack." *Annals of Emergency Medicine* 28 (2): 129–35.

Royce, L. 2002. "Anthrax Decontamination of Brentwood Facility Under Way." [Online article; retrieved 7/12/02.] CNN.com, December 14. http://www.cnn.com/2002/US/South/12/14/anthrax.decon/index.html.

Sidell, F. R., J. S. Urbanetti, W. J. Smith, and C. G. Hurst. 1997. "Vesicants." In *Textbook of Military Medicine, Part I: Medical Aspects of Chemical and Biological Warfare*, edited by R. Zajtchuk and R. F. Bellamy. Washington, DC: Borden Institute.

Smithson, A. 2000. *Ataxia: The Chemical and Biological Terrorism Threat and the US Response*. Report No. 35, October. Washington, DC: The Stimson Center.

United States Army. 1999. *Medical Management of Chemical Casualties Handbook*. Aberdeen Proving Ground, MD: United States Army Medical Research Institute of Chemical Defense.

United States Army Medical Research Institute of Infectious Diseases (USAMRIID). 2001. "BW Agent Characteristics," Appendix C. [Online appendix; retrieved 7/03.] USAMRIID. http://www.usamriid.army.mil/education/bluebook.html. In *Medical Management of Biological Casualties Handbook*, 4th ed. Fort Detrick, MD.

U.S. Congress. House of Representatives. National Security Committee, Judiciary Committee. 1996. *Defense Against Weapons of Mass Destruction Act of 1996*. Public Law 104-201. [Online information; retrieved 7/12/03.] Thomas Legislative Information. http://thomas.loc.gov/bss/d104/d104laws.html.

U.S. Department of Defense (DoD). 2001. "DoD Antiterrorism Standards." Instruction 2000.16, June 14. [Online information; retrieved 11/3/03.] http://www.dtic.mil/whs/directives/.

Wetter, D. C., W. E. Daniell, and C. D. Treser. 2001. "Hospital Preparedness for Victims of Chemical or Biological Terrorism." *American Journal of Public Health* 91 (5): 710–16.

The White House. 2003. December 17, 2003 Homeland Security Presidential Directive/HSPD-8, National Preparedness. [Online policy; retrieved 12/20/03.] http://www.whitehouse.gov/news/releases/2003/12/20031217-6.html.

# PART II

*Creating a Preparedness
Infrastructure*

CHAPTER THREE

# Disaster Planning for Terrorism

Jerry L. Mothershead

C omprehensive emergency management, although a continuous process of often-overlapping phases, is typically divided into pre-event (preparedness and mitigation) and post-event (response and recovery) activities, as shown in Figure 3.1. Some specific issues are unique or especially challenging to healthcare systems in preventing or reducing vulnerabilities to weapons of mass effect (WME) events and mitigating the effects of those events should they occur. This chapter provides insight into the pre-event phases and how hospitals can assess risk, reduce vulnerabilities, and mitigate the effects of WME events. It also touches briefly on issues of recovery and resumption of critical services.

Although preparedness for a terrorist incident involving chemical, biological, radiological, nuclear, or high-yield explosive (CBRNE) devices or agents follows the same principles used in emergency management for any catastrophic event, a community healthcare system will require more preparedness for these incidents than for natural or technological disasters. Generally, healthcare systems are ill prepared to respond to events of the magnitude that could occur with even a moderately sized CBRNE event.

---

Jerry L. Mothershead, M.D., FACEP, is physician advisor for the Medical Readiness and Response Division at Battelle Memorial Institute in Hampton, Virginia; senior medical consultant for the Navy Medicine Office of Homeland Security; and commander (ret.) of the Medical Corps of the United States Navy.

FIGURE 3.1. FOUR PHASES OF COMPREHENSIVE EMERGENCY MANAGEMENT

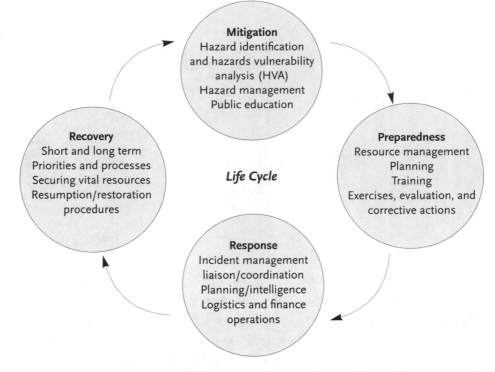

*Source*: Brewster, P. W. 2000. "CEM as Applied to NFPA 1600 Program Elements." Created for use in this book.

## ASSESSING RISK AND VULNERABILITY

*Risk* is the potential for loss or failure to perform; it is synonymous with the adverse outcomes that an organization strives to avoid. As part of the community, healthcare systems may be directly affected by an intentional (or unintentional) disaster. As part of the emergency response, they may be called on to provide response and recovery operations in the wake of a disaster that affects their community. This makes them doubly vulnerable to CBRNE events. Unlike natural disasters, with which a community usually has historical experience, few communities have had to contend with terrorist events. This produces challenges in conducting realistic risk assessments.

Risk is a function of the following three variables:

1. Probability of an event occurring
2. Consequences should it occur
3. Costs or impact (monetary or otherwise) of those consequences

An organization may analyze risk either quantitatively or qualitatively. Quantitative risk assessments use numerical values assigned to the variables being evaluated and attempt to rank hazards based on formulae. These assessments are problematic in that data used in deriving risks may be unreliable or inaccurate, probabilities are rarely accurate, and low probabilities for certain events may lead to complacency.

More reliable and much easier to perform, qualitative risk assessments are generally derived from analysis of threats, vulnerabilities, and controls. These terms are often used interchangeably, although there are slight differences. *Threats*—situations that can go wrong or that can "attack" the system—are present in every system. *Vulnerabilities* are the susceptibilities of resources to negative impacts from hazard events. They are weaknesses in system procedures, system design, implementation, physical structure, or internal controls that could be exploited to violate system security, make a system more prone to attack, or allow an attack to have a greater impact. *Controls*, or countermeasures for vulnerabilities, are derived from mitigation activities.

A risk-assessment matrix can be useful in prioritizing mitigation activities. Many formats are available, from the most simple to the very complex, and all serve the purpose well. The healthcare facilities would need to alter the list of hazards based on its specific needs and environment to increase its value as a preparedness tool. One example of a hazards vulnerability analysis (HVA) tool, with directions for its use, is shown in Figure 3.2. Using an HVA matrix, a potential threat or hazard is evaluated for probability, risk or impact, and resources to increase preparedness levels.

Issues to consider in determining probability include familiarity with the risk (a known risk), historical data, or other available projections or data. For instance, when examining the probability of a hazardous-materials incident in the community, information on existing hazardous materials, transportation routes of those materials, or other storage areas may be obtained from the local emergency planning committee or local emergency management agency. Communities should pay special attention to planning when targets of high value to terrorists exist, such as government office buildings, mass-gathering sites, healthcare facilities, financial centers, and/or historic monuments. The tool also allows users to categorize risk, including loss of life, disruption of services, loss of community trust, business continuity, or legal issues. Preparedness evaluation may include the status of current plans and agreements, presence

FIGURE 3.2. HVA TOOL WITH INSTRUCTIONS

**Hazards Vulnerability Analysis Tool**

| Type of Hazard | Historical Occurrence | Probability of Occurrence | Human Impact | Property Impact | Business Impact | Mitigation Activities | Internal Resources | External Resources | *Total* |
|---|---|---|---|---|---|---|---|---|---|
| Civil disturbance | | | | | | | | | 0.0 |
| Communications failure | | | | | | | | | 0.0 |
| Computer crime or attack | | | | | | | | | 0.0 |
| Crime, general | | | | | | | | | 0.0 |
| Dam failure | | | | | | | | | 0.0 |
| Disease (epidemic or otherwise) | | | | | | | | | 0.0 |
| Drought | | | | | | | | | 0.0 |
| Earthquake | | | | | | | | | 0.0 |
| Fire | | | | | | | | | 0.0 |
| Flooding (including tsunami) | | | | | | | | | 0.0 |
| Hardware/software failure | | | | | | | | | 0.0 |
| Landslides and subsidence | | | | | | | | | 0.0 |
| Loss of key supplier/customer | | | | | | | | | 0.0 |
| Loss of lifelines | | | | | | | | | 0.0 |
| Terrorist act or accident | | | | | | | | | 0.0 |
| Chemical agent | | | | | | | | | 0.0 |
| Biological agent | | | | | | | | | 0.0 |
| Radiological agent | | | | | | | | | 0.0 |
| Nuclear agent | | | | | | | | | 0.0 |
| Explosive (high-yield) | | | | | | | | | 0.0 |
| Transportation accident | | | | | | | | | 0.0 |
| Volcano eruption | | | | | | | | | 0.0 |
| Windstorm (including tornado) | | | | | | | | | 0.0 |
| Winter storm | | | | | | | | | 0.0 |
| Workplace violence | | | | | | | | | 0.0 |

FIGURE 3.2. (continued)

## Instructions for Completing the Hazards Vulnerability Analysis Tool

This tool examines an organization's or a community's vulnerability to the effects of various hazards. Using a scale of 0 to 5, the probability of occurrences and the impact potential are measured against mitigation activities and the resources availabe to respond to the hazard. The total is based on a formula that weighs risk heavily but provides credit for mitigation and response and recovery resources. The highest score possible is 5.0. The lower the total score, the lower the overall risk from the hazard.

### Instructions

Score each hazard based on a scale of 0 to 5, with 5 being the highest. Add or delete hazards as required based on your analysis.

Historical occurrence: Based on number of occurrences in the last 20 years. Maximum is 5. If it is a new hazard, use 0.

Probability of occurrence: Score 1 if the probability that the hazard will occur is less than 1%, 2 if less than 5%, 3 if less than 10%, 4 if less than 20%, and 5 if greater than 20%.

Impact: Based on "worst-case scenario." Score the greatest possible impact to the facility or community should a "worst-case event" occur.

Final step: Sort the Total column in descending order once scoring is completed. Planning should place emphasis on the "high risk" items first, followed by those ranked as "medium risk."

### Analysis Results

| | |
|---|---|
| High risk | Greater than 3.5 |
| Medium risk | 2.0 to 3.5 |
| Low risk | Less than 2 |

or lack of training or equipment, staffing shortages, availability of backup systems, or procedural deficiencies.

## REDUCING VULNERABILITY THROUGH MITIGATION ACTIVITIES

*Mitigation activities* or controls are any actions taken to permanently eliminate or reduce the risk of hazards to human life, property, and function. The four basic mitigation activities are as follows:

1. Deterrent controls reduce the likelihood of a deliberate attack and/or dissuade would-be attackers by making a facility less desirable as a target.
2. Preventive controls protect vulnerabilities by making an attack unsuccessful or reducing its impact.
3. Corrective controls reduce the effect of an attack.
4. Detective controls discover attacks and may trigger preventive or corrective controls.

### Combining Risk Assessments and Mitigation Initiatives

A more sophisticated method of conducting risk analysis and assessing mitigation initiatives is a failure modes and effects analysis (FMEA) (Electronic Industries Association 1971). Developed by the U.S. military in 1949 as a reliable evaluation technique to determine the effect of system and equipment failures (U.S. Armed Services 1984), FMEA systematically identifies potential system failures, their causes, and the effects on the system's operation. It is most often used to proactively assess the safety of system components and to identify design modifications and corrective actions needed to mitigate the effects of a failure on the system.

The FMEA process can be a valuable tool in improving internal preparedness for response to emergencies or disasters of any sort and has been endorsed by the Joint Commission on Accreditation of Healthcare Organizations (JCAHO). When the analysis is extended to include an assessment of the failure mode's severity and probability of occurrence, the analysis is called a failure mode, effects, and criticality analysis (FMECA). The nine-step FMECA process is shown in Checklist 3.1 at the end of this chapter.

An example of the FMECA process applied to routine hospital operations might be patient admissions through the emergency department. To admit a patient, a number of functions must occur: an accepting physician must be identified and contacted, initial orders must be provided to the accepting floor or ward, administrative and clerical work accompanying the admission must be completed, a bed and the nursing staff must be prepared to accept the patient, and the patient must be delivered to the floor or ward. A defined failure might be the inability to admit the patient within one hour of the determination that admission is warranted. By analyzing the processes involved with getting the patient admitted, failure modes can be identified (e.g., inordinate delay in preparing the patient's room), and the root cause of these failure modes can be further elucidated. If the cost of the failure mode is sufficient (e.g., patient or staff dissatisfaction), procedures may be modified, additional staff may be hired, or other actions may be taken to improve this process.

## TAKING STEPS FOR DISASTER PREPAREDNESS

Most healthcare organizations have disaster plans; however, few have disaster preparedness programs. The basic process for developing a program is shown in Checklist 3.2. A sound disaster preparedness program includes the following elements:

- Capability and capacity assessments
- Emergency operations planning
- Resource procurement and management
- Education and training
- Exercises
- Continuous quality improvement (CQI)

These elements are considered in the following sections (CQI is discussed at the end of the chapter).

### Capability and Capacity Assessments

A *capability assessment* involves determining if a process or function can be performed, whereas a *capacity assessment* provides a quantitative evaluation of that capability. A variety of professional organizations, such as

JCAHO, the National Fire Protection Association, and ASTM International (formerly the American Society for Testing and Materials), have established standards for disaster preparedness capability, but few standards exist concerning capacity.

In 1996, the Federal Emergency Management Agency (FEMA) coordinated with the International Association of Emergency Managers to develop a standardized format for disaster capability assessment, known as the Capability Assessment for Readiness (CAR) (FEMA 1997). This format categorizes emergency management readiness into 13 distinct emergency management functions. Originally developed for state and territorial assessment, the CAR has been modified for local community use and is being implemented nationally to assess county- and state-level readiness (see Table 3.1).

The Healthcare Association of Hawaii (2001) developed a version of the CAR process specifically for hospitals. The Hospital Capability Assessment for Readiness (HCAR) is available on the Internet and addresses 12 unique aspects of the hospital or healthcare environment that must be addressed in comprehensive planning for WME and all-hazards events. Although it is very similar to the CAR, the HCAR addresses topics in various categories from a strictly medical-operations vantage point and is worth examining when developing a planning tool for a healthcare facility. Summaries of the CAR and the HCAR topic areas are presented in Table 3.1.

Most healthcare emergency planners can tabulate resources and capability, but a mere cataloging of staffing pools and material assets does little to determine a healthcare organization's capacity. A time-phased approach ensures a resource will be available and accessible within the time frame needed. For example, decontamination teams that are not always available, personal protective equipment (PPE) not present at sites of use, and security personnel who must be recalled to the facility from home or remote locations all represent degradations to actual capabilities and capacities and must be included in readiness projections.

## Emergency Operations Planning

Many healthcare organizations confuse emergency operations planning with preparedness. In fact, developing an emergency operations plan (EOP) is but one component of an effective emergency management program to ensure preparedness. Healthcare organizations must develop

TABLE 3.1. FUNCTIONAL AREAS IN THE CAR AND HCAR

| CAR | HCAR[a] |
|---|---|
| | *Preface materials.* General organizational profile information, which includes type of facility, governance, accreditation or licensure type, NDMS status, helicopter capability; water utility, medical gases and emergency power generation (days on campus, type, and capacity), notification and contact lists for incident commander and section chiefs and others; warning and notification network, bed profile (by type and capabilities: staffed, negative airflow, monitored); surge capacity, by triage category |
| 1. *Laws and authorities.* Federal, state, and local issuances and any implementing regulations that (a) establish authority for development and maintenance of the emergency management program and organization and (b) define the emergency powers, authorities, and responsibilities of the chief executive officer and emergency program manager | 1. *Leadership and governance.* Presence of emergency program manager who is a member of planning committee, educated in emergency management |
| 2. *Hazard identification and risk assessment.* The process of identifying situations or conditions that have the potential of causing injury to people, damage to property, or damage to the environment and the assessment of the likelihood, vulnerability, and magnitude of incidents that could result from exposure to hazards | 2. *Hazard identification, analysis, and control.* HVA conducted in past 24 months, incorporated into emergency management plan; active program to identify, control, and mitigate hazards on campus; measurement for effectiveness of program |
| 3. *Hazard management.* Systematic management approach to eliminate hazards that constitute a significant threat within the area of responsibility or to reduce the effects of hazards that cannot be eliminated through a program of hazard mitigation | 3. *Planning and plans.* Emergency management plan is compliant with NFPA 1600 and JCAHO or other accrediting bodies. Plan is fully compliant and published throughout organization. Participates in biosurveillance activities, including reporting when requested by state department of health or other authority |
| 4. *Resource management.* Systematic development of methodologies for the prompt and effective identification, acquisition, distribution, accounting, | 4. *Direction, control, and coordination.* Facility has EOC located in secure area. EOC staff are oriented to their duties and have conducted at least one drill in last 12 months. |

*(continued on following page)*

TABLE 3.1. *(continued)*

| CAR | HCAR[a] |
|-----|---------|
| and use of medical personnel, equipment, and supplies for essential emergency functions | EOC can monitor local media, is equipped for 24/7 operation, and can sustain for minimum of five (local preference) days. EOC has at least one phone per section chief. Has formal incident command system (such as HEICS). Emergency operating procedures are coordinated with county EOC |
| 5. *Planning.* The collection, analysis, and use of information and the development, promulgation, and maintenance of the comprehensive emergency management, action, and mitigation plans | 5. *Communication and warning.* Has formal, well-articulated process for receiving and responding to warning information from public safety agencies (civil defense, emergency management agency, or government). Has access to and is part of a statewide or regional warning and notification network. Has computer access to local and area emergency operations web sites. Has access to amateur radio technology with in-house equipment or provided through licensed radio amateur in community. Includes amateur radio operators oriented to duties during emergency, participates in exercises and actual emergency events. Organization has formal, documented staff-notification and recall process that is tested at least annually |
| 6. *Direction, control, and coordination.* Development of the capability for the senior HSS officer to direct, control, and coordinate medical response and recovery operations | 6. *Operations and procedures.* Has established a formal system for management of trauma casualties. Process includes a triage officer, defined triage protocols, and necessary equipment and supplies. Defined areas for treatment by triage category. Has casualty tracking system. Has developed system for management of casualties from WMD events. Has procedures for protecting staff and facilities from effects of CBRNE agents. Has PPE for all key response staff. Can capture wastewater from decontamination. Has a specified and licensed vendor for site remediation and waste disposal |
| 7. *Communications and warning.* Development and maintenance of a reliable communications capability to alert officials and emergency response personnel, warn the public, and effectively manage response to an actual or impending emergency | 7. *Resource management.* Has operational inventory of equipment, supplies, pharmaceuticals, and other essential material to respond to a major emergency. Inventory is immediately available, maintained real-time (not just-in-time). Maintains WMD-specific pharmaceuticals with levels exceeding 200%, 300% (250-bed facility capable of influx of 500 casualties using on-campus pharmaceuticals) |

TABLE 3.1. *(continued)*

| CAR | HCAR[a] |
|-----|---------|
| 8. *Operations and procedures.* Development, coordination, and implementation of operational policies, plans, and procedures for emergency management | 8. *Logistics and facilities.* Has established system for protecting facility perimeter (lockdown) within ten minutes after notification by community agency. Staff trained in procedure, which can be accomplished without augmentation by local police. Organization has designated alternative care site(s). Has specific evacuation and relocation procedures incorporated into the emergency management plan. Written agreements exist between organization and alternative care sites |
| 9. *Logistics and facilities.* Identification, location, acquisition, distribution, and accounting for services, resources, materials, and facilities to support emergency HSS management. Logistics actions fall into one of four major categories: material management, property management, facility management, and transportation management | 9. *Public information.* Public information officer has been designated and oriented to the emergency management plan and has designated a specific location for the media within the facility |
| 10. *Training.* Assessments, development, and implementation of a training/education program for officials and emergency HSS response personnel | 10. *Orientation and training.* Orientation of staff and physicians to the emergency management program and plan and to their role and responsibilities. Emergency response personnel have been formally trained in roles and responsibilities, including use of PPE, deployment of equipment and supplies, and other key information. Training is current and includes treating casualties of WMD events |
| 11. *Exercises, evaluations, and corrective actions.* Assessment and evaluation of emergency response plans and capabilities through a program of regularly scheduled tests and exercises | 11. *Exercises.* Assessment and evaluation of emergency response plans and capabilities through a program of regularly scheduled tests and exercises compliant with JCAHO standards. Exercise or actual emergency should include influx of human casualties and test exposure to WMD agents requiring decontamination |
| 12. *Crisis communications, public education, and information.* Procedures to disseminate and respond to requests for predisaster, disaster, and postdisaster information involving employ- | 12. *Performance improvement.* Organization has specific procedure or format for conducting after-action reviews of simulated or actual emergency events. Has defined process for |

*(continued on following page)*

TABLE 3.1. *(continued)*

| CAR | HCAR[a] |
|---|---|
| ees, responders, the public, and the media. Also, an effective public education program regarding hazards affecting the area of responsibility | achieving enhanced performance based on after-action reports, observations, and findings |
| 13. *Finance and administration.* Development of finance and administrative procedures to support emergency HSS measures before, during, and after disaster events and to preserve vital records | |

[a] Adapted from "Hospital Capability Assessment for Readiness," Version 1.10. Healthcare Association of Hawaii. 2001©. Used with permission.

*Note*: CBRNE = chemical, biological, radiological, nuclear, or high-yield explosive weapons; EOC = Emergency Operations Center; HEICS = Hospital Emergency Incident Command System; HVA = hazards vulnerability analysis; NFPA = National Fire Protection Agency; JCAHO = Joint Commission on Accreditation of Healthcare Organizations; PPE = personal protective equipment; HSS = Health Service Support; NDMS = National Disaster Medical System; WMD = weapons of mass destruction

plans for two different scenarios: one in which they serve as response agencies and one in which they are also victims of the incident. If one plan alone is developed, it must address both of these circumstances. An EOP can be thought of as an executive-level or leadership guidebook to manage the consequences of a disaster. It is a concept document that describes in general terms what response operations and functions will be performed or accomplished by what department, agency, or organization and under what circumstances. It is not a detailed reference tome to be used as a standard operating procedures manual by all response personnel during actual disaster operations.

In addition to EOPs, many organizations develop adjunctive standard operating procedures or job aids. These are more detailed, job-specific or department-specific checklists that delineate duties and responsibilities of each individual or position that is part of the organization response plan. Many of the details usually seen in EOPs should rightfully be placed in these documents, which provide instructions on how to do what is necessary in support of the EOP.

Of paramount importance in EOP development for incidents involving CBRNE are 15 basic issues. These areas are described in the following sections.

*Notification.* It is imperative that hospitals and emergency departments be included in a notification system that a disaster event has occurred that may affect healthcare services. In CBRNE events, the risk to the facility multiplies. Less than 20 percent of those contaminated by industrial chemicals are subsequently decontaminated on the scene (Levitin and Siegelson 1996); thus, the potential for arrival of contaminated victims at the healthcare facility must be considered and planned for.

*Decontamination.* Who will perform decontamination, where it is to be performed, how the disposition of victims and their belongings will be handled, and how contaminated wastewater will be handled should be addressed early in the planning process. If outside resources will be required, their availability and timeliness of response must be verified. Appropriate supplies and equipment, PPE, and a process for patient flow from contaminated to clean areas must be addressed.

*Facility physical protection.* In addition to actual victims, a large number of asymptomatic, possibly exposed individuals (often referred to as "worried well") may also present for care, and this additional workload must be anticipated. As was seen in the Tokyo sarin event, these individuals may rapidly overrun the facility and may indeed pose a threat to continued operations (Matsui, Ohbu, and Yamashina 1996).

*Evacuation.* Released agents may remain airborne for a significant period of time. If the facility is downwind from the site of release, provisions must be established to rapidly decide if evacuation of patients, staff, and visitors is necessary. Transportation assets and receiving facilities must be identified. The establishment of alternate treatment facilities, until such time as environmental surety has been established, should also be included.

*Shelter-in-place.* When sufficient time to evacuate the facility is not available, expedient shelter-in-place provisions must be developed. Policies concerning securing of ventilation systems, internal movement of patients, and provision of PPE to critical facility personnel must be addressed. Sheltering-in-place can be accomplished horizontally (movement along the same level or floor into an area of the facility away from risk) or vertically (movement to higher or lower floors to escape threats where damage has occurred or where height is an issue, such as in flooding, fire, or high winds).

*Detection.* Detection is one of the weak links in the chain of emergency management and response. Most biological agents will not produce immediate symptoms, many chemical agents have delayed presentations, and, short of massive radiation doses, weeks may pass before those exposed may feel ill. Detection may occur through trend analysis if done in a near-real-time fashion through syndromic surveillance. Syndromic surveillance is a public health epidemiological process of collecting and analyzing patient data based on predetermined signs and symptoms, referred to as a syndrome. The goal of this analysis is to identify abnormal changes or trends in the numbers of patients presenting at portals of entry to the healthcare system. However, this must occur prior to the diseases that cause these syndromes progressing to the point of fatalities or severe morbidity, so that preventive and treatment measures may be instituted early in the course of the outbreak. Detection may also occur clinically or through laboratory analysis. The EOP should identify detection methods used and the procedures to be followed should an event be suspected.

*Identification.* Separate from detection, identification of agents that produce similar clinical syndromes or effects but have different treatment and protection regimens is a critical capability. Because most hospital laboratories do not have these sophisticated testing capabilities, methods of linking to CDC's Laboratory Response Network must be included in EOPs.

*Triage.* Triage of victims of a CBRNE event differs from that for other mass-casualty events because many more victims are likely. In the event of a biological-agent attack, two different victims with identical physiological measurements may have significantly different survival probabilities. Specific life-saving procedures, such as the administration of antidotes, may exist that would alter traditional triage algorithms predicated on the ability of the community healthcare network to absorb all casualties in short order—a situation unlikely to occur if the entire community is affected (Burkle 2002).

*Treatment options.* Just as triage of CBRNE victims is different, so are treatment concerns. The nature of traumatic disasters is such that the majority of victims who will eventually die do so at the scene or during the first 24 to 48 hours, and most do not require isolation to protect other patients and staff. Victims of chemical, biological, or radiological events may require sophisticated support (including burn therapy, isolation rooms, invasive monitoring, and mechanical ventilation) and may require these modalities for prolonged periods of time.

*Surge capacity.* The ability to increase facility capacity to accept more victims while facing resource constraints, especially during the initial hours and days after the event, is a huge challenge. Other patients not affected by the disaster may continue to present with emergencies that will require treatment. It is unacceptable to assume that only victims of the disaster will be ministered to during response operations. Early discharges, transfers, and use of home health care services may functionally expand facilities, while cancellation of elective procedures and same-day surgery may free more beds and staff. Extending shift times for staff from 8 hours to 12 hours for a short period (less than one week) effectively increases staff by 50 percent (Schultz, Mothershead, and Field 2002).

Surge capacity also applies to material resources. A facility may elect to increase caches of materials and supplies, but storage capabilities and costs of procurement may be a hindrance. Service-level or backup agreements or even memoranda of understanding with local pharmacies and hospital-supply distributors may provide a functional supply surge capacity at a fraction of the cost. This also obviates the need to dedicate space and personnel to store and maintain these goods.

*Prophylaxis.* Determining who will receive prophylaxis, and at what priority, in the event of a biological release and methods for distributing and dispensing these pharmaceuticals must be included in an EOP. Keep in mind that unprotected staff will most likely not work, nor will staff who are concerned about their families. The facility's role in providing or dispensing prophylactic antibiotics to the community must also be ascertained.

*Fatality management.* A large event may produce a significant number of casualties who die after arrival at a hospital, overwhelming hospital morgues. If surge facilities for temporary interment cannot be identified through traditional services (e.g., city morgues, funeral homes), alternate sites must be established and appropriately equipped, staffed, and secured. It is unwise to presume that other response organizations will assume this responsibility. This issue, as others, should be addressed at the community-planning level, with all providers informed of the plan for mass-fatality management.

*Counseling services.* As seen after the World Trade Center and Murrah Federal Building attacks, responders may suffer both acute and long-term stress reactions, including delayed development of post-traumatic stress disorder (North et al. 2002). It is the responsibility of the healthcare organization to take care of its employees, and the provision of counseling services cannot be ignored. The healthcare system will also most likely be called on to provide these services for victims, victims' families, and the community at large. Depending on the nature of the disaster, counseling requirements may far outstrip other medical needs of survivors and the community.

*Horizontal and vertical integration.* Integrating health services with other local or regional response organizations is essential for successful emergency operations. The prolonged phases of emergency response require that healthcare networks operate together and that various actions by other response organizations be interdependent. Organizations must not plan in a vacuum. Federal law requires the use of an incident-management system in such operations (U.S. Congress 1996). A terrorist event involving CBRNE agents also mandates activation of the Federal Response Plan, which is soon to be replaced with the National Response Plan being developed by the Department of Homeland Security. (See Chapter 7 for more information on organized emergency management systems and the Federal Response Plan.)

*Law enforcement and incident forensics.* Any terrorist event is a criminal act, and law enforcement investigators will be intimately involved throughout all phases of response. Additional requirements for maintaining a legal chain of custody while handling and transporting samples, patient information sharing, and other cooperative ventures will require new approaches to incident management by all response organizations.

### Resource Procurement and Management

Invariably, gaps or deficiencies in resources will be identified in the course of developing EOPs. These deficiencies may be in personnel, material resources, or both. Ways to approach eliminating these deficits include procuring and maintaining those assets required for internal use (which is the most difficult and costly solution) and developing backup agreements or service-level agreements (which are contractual arrangements with other organizations to provide those resources under specific circumstances). For example, personnel requirements could be contracted to temporary-staffing agencies or agreements made with a supply house to provide material resources. Another method of procuring deficient resources is through memoranda of understanding with both traditional and nontraditional organizations. For example, interfacility transport services may provide emergency medical technicians who, with prior agreement and clearances, could serve as patient care technicians in a WME event (state laws allowing).

A program to manage donations and volunteers is imperative. If requested, members of the community who are licensed professionals may donate their services. Most disasters are marked by an outpouring of the surrounding communities to donate goods to use in response and recovery operations. Methods of soliciting donations and handling those goods and services need to be prospectively developed.

It should be noted, however, that in the event of a terrorist attack, unsolicited donations may create additional dangers themselves. Where donations and volunteers pose huge logistical issues for entire communities, they may similarly pose issues for individual hospitals. The hospital level must have preexisting plans to handle donations as well as volunteers who wish to help.

### Education and Training

Staff education and training, both individual and collective, are an employer's responsibility. All staff should be trained in their specific roles in response to a disaster. Depending on responsibilities, this may be education at the awareness level or may include detailed operations or technician training. Training should be competency based, be measurable, and include both initial and ongoing or refresher training. A training assessment based on current and desired competencies should precede any additions to training requirements (U.S. DHHS 2001). Checklist 3.3 provides some suggested training topics that could be adapted to fit your facility needs and staff.

### Exercises

The Federal Emergency Management Agency defines an exercise as "a controlled, scenario-driven, simulated experience designed to demonstrate and evaluate an organization's capability to execute one or more assigned or implicit operational tasks or procedures as outlined in its contingency plan" (FEMA 1997).

Disaster preparedness can be tested through the response to and recovery from an actual event or through drills or exercises. An effective exercise

- includes all staff, on all shifts, for every day of the week;
- reveals existing vulnerabilities; and

- ingrains the emergency plan into the minds of the medical facility's staff.

Although actual disasters cannot be planned, several variations of planned exercises are available. These are described below.

*Orientation or information exercises.* The goal of such exercises or meetings is to provide newly hired staff with an overview of the organization's responsibilities in the event of a disaster, the methods by which these responsibilities will be discharged, and general responsibilities that they will be expected to fulfill.

*Tabletop exercises.* These leadership-level exercises are designed to work through interdepartmental or interorganizational issues. Typically, a scenario is presented and, at various stages, an opportunity is provided for leaders of the various functional or organizational response elements to present their concept of operation. This exercise clears up misunderstandings of responsibilities, capabilities, and methodologies and allows personnel involved to become acquainted and to collaborate prospectively—opportunities that are invaluable if an actual event were to occur.

*Functional exercises.* These operational-level exercises are designed to test specific functional elements of response, such as communications, decontamination procedures, and patient flow. They may involve one or more departments and typically require test actions, as opposed to discussions. Because they may interfere with normal organization operations, they are done less frequently.

*Full-scale exercises.* Although expensive, labor intensive, and likely to interfere with normal operations, full-scale exercises provide leaders an unequaled opportunity to see how all elements function together as well as provide valuable, realistic training for all participants. Interactions between functional elements under real-world conditions can be more easily identified in full-scale deployment than through individual functional exercises.

Exercises should be assessed against measurable information or qualitative and quantitative data gathered during the event. If your exercise reveals nothing wrong, something is wrong with your exercise. Your goal should be to stress your system to identify weaknesses. An exercise that results in no recommendations is a waste of precious time. Identified and documented deficiencies and efficiencies should highlight those plans, policies, or procedures that should be changed and the training required.

JCAHO Environment of Care standards require each accredited healthcare organization to regularly test the plan, either through actual disaster response and plan activation or in planned drills. The plan must be executed at least twice yearly. In most healthcare facilities, drills must be performed at least every four months and no more than eight months apart. This critical element of the emergency preparedness program is more than just an exercise. The more realistic the scenario, the better are the opportunities for learning and improvement.

Sidebar 3.1 shares the value of learning "what went wrong" when implementing large-scale paper and simulated exercises of community and regional emergency management plans.

## ISSUES IN RECOVERY AND RESUMPTION OF SERVICES

The survivability of a business may depend on its ability to quickly recover from a disaster. Statistics show that more than 40 percent of businesses seriously affected by disasters do not reopen, and approximately 30 percent that do reopen close within three years (U.S. DHS 2003). Therefore, planning for recovery is vital to the health of your facility.

Recovery should do more than reinstate the predisaster condition, and mitigation ensures that communities are rebuilt better than they were before disaster struck. Thus, a new recovery philosophy is actively encouraged by the Department of Homeland Security (DHS), FEMA, and the insurance industry to proactively decrease enormous costs of recent disasters in this country. Planning for recovery should be given serious consideration prior to a disaster; such planning can make resuming business and day-to-day living activities possible much sooner.

### Short- and Long-Term Recovery Issues

Most communities and facilities easily recover from a crisis that may tax them for a couple of days before everything returns to normal. Long-term recovery, however, may take weeks, months, or years and poses many critical problems for the community as well as for individual entities and businesses. Examples of issues that must be addressed in both situations are outlined below. (The following two lists are adapted from Anderson, B., J. Dilling, P. Mann, and A. Moore. 1996. *Assisted Living Facility Guide and Model Plan*. Developed by Emergency Training & Consulting, International, Silverdale, WA.)

**Sidebar 3.1. Case Examples: Lessons from Three Large Healthcare Exercises**

*Rhode Island statewide drill*. When unexpected issues and problems arose during a 2003 Rhode Island statewide drill, planners were able to develop alternatives and rewrite existing plans. Trucks delivering supplies were stuck in beach traffic; the ordering system for hospitals to request supplies proved too time consuming; hospital radio and telephone networks were limited, creating a need for the operations center to relay information to field responders; local accidents and emergencies (ruptured gas lines) forced relocations of preplanned gathering sites; and signage in ambulatory care areas proved inadequate. Rhode Island Director of Health Patricia Nolan stressed that "the best way to find out what is working and what is not is to put an emergency response plan through its paces" (Anderson 2003).

*Operation Topoff*. In Operation Topoff (May 2000) three hospitals in metropolitan Denver participated in a bioterrorism exercise with a simulated release of *Yesinia pestis,* leading to more than 2,000 cases of pneumonic plague. Isolation of patients proved impossible, and quarantine of the city's two million inhabitants was unsuccessful. The single, most important lesson learned was that unless controlling the spread of the disease and providing triage and treatment for ill persons in hospitals receive equal effort, the demand for healthcare services will not diminish. By the third day following the release, 500 persons had presented with symptoms, and antibiotic and ventilator shortages were beginning to occur. By exercise conclusion, after one week, an estimated 3,700 cases of plague had been reported, with 950 to 2,000 deaths. In the early stages of the epidemic, hospitals were seeing two to three times their normal patient volume, and later up to ten times normal volumes (U.S. GAO 2003).

*Dark Winter*. The 2001 national exercise entitled Dark Winter, a simulated covert smallpox attack in the United States, taught evaluators shocking and critical lessons of how the medical system as a whole would respond under such a dire situation. It was discovered that following a bioterrorist attack, the key decisions of area and government officials would depend on data and expertise from the medical and public health sectors. However, few systems exist for rapid flow of information in these sectors.

It was difficult to identify the locations of the original attacks, know how many persons were exposed, determine how many were hospitalized and where, or keep track of how many had been vaccinated. There were severe vaccine shortages, and this scarcity led to violence and flight by persons desperate to get vaccinated, which had a great impact on the decisions made by political leaders (O'Toole and Inglesby 2002).

*Short-Term Recovery*

- Obtaining temporary food, water, and housing
- Maintaining medical services
- Restoring power, water, communications, etc.
- Temporarily closing roads and rerouting traffic
- Clearing downed trees
- Repairing public/private buildings and homes
- Restoring order and ensuring law enforcement; establishing safety and security

*Long-Term Recovery*

- Demolishing damaged buildings and homes
- Removing massive amounts of debris
- Restoring lifeline systems (critical infrastructure components)
- Instituting major reconstruction programs
- Revising building and land-use codes
- Solving cash-flow and economic problems
- Dealing with business failures or closures and high unemployment
- Addressing political issues

Recovery planning can be accomplished by envisioning the worst-case scenario in which your facility structure is damaged beyond repair. Healthcare administrators should address the questions outlined in Checklist 3.4 in their planning, training, and education.

Physical restoration of an area may be an arduous process; however, full recovery, including restoration of people, may pose different challenges. The pychological scars of victims and the members of the emergency response community may take much longer to heal. Preplanning for the provision of psychological support must not be ignored. Chapter 1 discusses issues involved in providing psychological care following a large-scale disaster.

## Locating and Accessing Resources

Many sources for assistance with planning as well as the actual recovery processes are available. It is wise to make contacts and to understand how and whom to contact when assistance is needed. Fewer surprises will occur if you know what to expect within the various levels of government and within the private sector. A listing of local, state, federal, and private resources is provided in Table 3.2.

State and federal agencies assist local governments. Their primary functions include supplementing local response/recovery operations with personnel, materials, and other resources from outside the affected area. (Chapter 13 outlines the process for securing FEMA funds to help in disaster relief.) In addition to being familiar with federal provisions, it is also important to identify local businesses and national companies that supply the types of resources and materials you will need. A facility should maintain a list with contact numbers (including phone, fax, cell, and beeper) as well as catalogs of vendors to assist in restoring facility operations.

### Resuming Normal Activities

The healthcare facility will need to return to normal activities as soon as possible to ensure patient safety and care and to prevent the loss of residents to other facilities and valued employees to other jobs. The facility disaster planning committee should be used to move the business forward toward resumption of operations. The recovery issues outlined in Checklist 3.5 should be considered.

## CONTINUOUS QUALITY IMPROVEMENT

No emergency preparedness program is complete without a continuous quality improvement (CQI) program. The optimal way to ensure that programs and plans are updated and effective is through the use of a sound CQI program that evaluates the various parts of the emergency management program, identifies deficiencies and issues for action, and develops and tracks solutions for those identified problems. Plans will need to be changed or modified as resources, requirements, threats, and vulnerabilities fluctuate.

CQI programs should include prospective, concurrent, and retrospective review. *Prospective review* may evaluate resource inventory control and tracking, personnel training, or currency of memoranda of understanding. *Concurrent review* usually occurs as drills, exercises, or response operations are conducted and evaluated. *Retrospective review*

## Table 3.2. Types of Resources Available in Planning and Recovery Efforts

| Local Resources | State and Federal Resources | Private Resources |
|---|---|---|
| • Local EMA: assistance with all aspects of planning is available<br>• Utility companies: contact name and title, phone numbers; how they work and what to expect in restoration of service; priority of your facility for restoration of services<br>• Other healthcare providers/businesses: potential sources for short-term relocation, supplies, other resources, and personnel<br>• Volunteers or families/friends of patients: recruit, educate, and enlist assistance<br>• Realtors: good sources for alternate and potential new locations<br>• Banks: discuss potential for funding requirements; establish lines of credit for postdisaster needs<br>• Insurance company: discuss coverage and pertinent details or requirements to maximize response<br>• Legal counsel: identify and address all potential liability issues<br>• Local vendors: supplies and resources commonly available; time required for resupply | • State EMA and DHS/FEMA provide planning materials and training courses in comprehensive emergency management, including public- and private-sector concerns, roles, and responsibilities<br>• Federal agencies contribute technical expertise, resources, and other forms of assistance<br>• In major disaster declarations, financial disaster relief is available from DHS/FEMA in certain situations established by law and regulation | • Temporary employment and staffing agencies<br>• Carpenters, plumbers, electricians<br>• Medical/surgical suppliers<br>• Business and office suppliers<br>• Suppliers of furniture for patient rooms and common areas<br>• Suppliers of recreational materials<br>• Suppliers of kitchen furnishings, equipment, and materials<br>• Food suppliers<br>• Suppliers of bathroom, shower, and personal hygiene equipment and products<br>• Linens and towels<br>• Computer companies and technical support, data retrieval services, and temporary IT services |

*Note*: DHS = Department of Homeland Security; EMA = emergency management agency; FEMA = Federal Emergency Management Agency; IT = information technology

*Source*: Adapted from Anderson, B., J. Dilling, P. Mann, and A. Moore. 1996. *Assisted Living Facility Guide and Model Plan*. Developed by Emergency Training & Consulting, International, Silverdale, WA. Used with permission.

often involves identifying specific events (such as a motor vehicle accident involving multiple casualties) and performing a retrospective record review to determine areas of difficulty in operations that may translate to further problems in the event of an even larger disaster.

A periodic review of the facility plan is advisable every six months to one year. The plan should also be reviewed after any exercise to accommodate shortfalls or better ways to accomplish certain disaster tasks. However, the best and most critical time to review your facility plan is after a real disaster that tests every part of your plan. A critique of the disaster from impact to recovery should indicate areas of the plan that worked well and areas that did not work as planned.

After objectively reviewing the findings from your disaster critique, the plan is ready for revision, addressing any gaps and shortfalls discovered. Action to be taken should be fully documented, with time frames for completion or implementation. Those you cannot act on at the present time should be noted and carried forward for future action. A substitute or other means of remedying the situation or problem should be found.

After the plan has been revised, approved, and shared with all involved, it must be tested and reviewed once again, implementing suggestions for improvement at each opportunity. A good planning and quality improvement process never ends.

## FUTURE CHALLENGES FOR DISASTER PREPAREDNESS

Preparedness for incidents due to terrorism or the release of CBRNE agents and materials is a daunting task. These events will test the ingenuity and resources of response organizations more than will traditional disasters encountered in the United States. Nonetheless, the same principles apply, and a CBRNE emergency management program should be built on and incorporated into a solid foundation of a preparedness program for all potential disasters.

Especially challenging to healthcare organizations in developing EOPs will be protection of facility and personnel; detection of covert events and identification of causation; and unique procedures of providing prophylaxis, triage and treatment, and surge capacity of all elements of response. Even so, comprehensive plans are not synonymous with preparedness. Preparedness requires threat and vulnerability analyses, capability and capacity assessments, resource procurement, and a CQI program that captures and addresses deficiencies and lessons learned.

## REFERENCES

Anderson, B., J. Dilling, P. Mann, and A. Moore. 1996. *Assisted Living Facility Guide and Model Plan*. Silverdale, WA: Emergency Training & Consulting, International.

Anderson, L. 2003. "Dress Rehearsal for a Nightmare." *Providence (RI) Journal*, August 24, B1, B4.

Burkle, F. M. 2002. "Mass Casualty Management of a Large-Scale Bioterrorist Event: An Epidemiological Approach that Shapes Triage Decisions." *Emergency Medical Clinics of North America* 20 (2): 409–36.

Electronic Industries Association. 1971. "Failure Mode and Effect Analyses." G-41 Committee on Reliability. *Reliability Bulletin* No. 9, November.

Federal Emergency Management Agency (FEMA). 1997. *Capability Assessment for Readiness.* Report to the United States Senate Committee on Appropriations, December 10. [Online report; retrieved 12/1/03.] http://www.fema.gov/pdf/rrr/car.pdf.

Healthcare Association of Hawaii. 2001. *Hospital Capability Assessment for Readiness.* [Online information; retrieved 7/12/03.] http://www.hah-emergency.net/PUBLIC /PUBLIC-library/HAH%20Hosp%20Capability%20Assessment%20Readiness.doc.

Levitin, H. W., and H. J. Siegelson. 1996. "Hazardous Materials. Disaster Medical Planning and Response." *Emergency Medical Clinics of North America* 14 (2): 327–48.

Matsui, Y., S. Ohbu, and A. Yamashina. 1996. "Hospital Deployment in Mass Sarin Poisoning Incident of the Tokyo Subway System—An Experience at St. Luke's International Hospital, Tokyo." *Japan Hospital* 15 (July): 67–71.

North, C. S., L. Tivis, J. C. McMillen, B. Pfefferbaum, E. L. Spitznagel, J. Cox, S. Nixon, K. P. Bunch, and E. M. Smith. 2002. "Psychiatric Disorders in Rescue Workers After the Oklahoma City Bombing." *American Journal of Psychiatry* 159 (5): 857–59.

O'Toole, T., and T. Inglesby. 2002. *Shining Light on Dark Winter.* Baltimore, MD: Johns Hopkins Center for Civilian Biodefense Studies, Johns Hopkins University.

Schultz, C. H., J. L. Mothershead, and M. Field. 2002. "Bioterrorism Preparedness. I: The Emergency Department and Hospital." *Emergency Medical Clinics of North America* 20 (2): 437–55.

U.S. Armed Services. 1984. "Procedures for Performing a Failure Mode Effects and Criticality Analysis." US Mil-Std-1629 (ships) Nov. 1, 1974; US Mil-Std-1629A, Nov. 24, 1980; US Mil-Std-1629A/notice 2, Nov. 28, 1984.

U.S. Congress. House of Representatives. National Security Committee, Judiciary Committee. 1996. *Defense Against Weapons of Mass Destruction Act of 1996.* Public Law 104-201. [Online information; retrieved 7/12/03.] Thomas Legislative Information. http://thomas.loc.gov/bss/d104/d104laws.html.

U.S. Department of Health and Human Services (DHHS). 2001. *Objectives, Content, and Competencies for the Training of Emergency Medical Technicians, Emergency Physicians, and Emergency Nurses to Care for Casualties Resulting from Nuclear, Biological, or Chemical (NBC) Incidents.* Final Report of the DHHS/ACEP Taskforce. Washington, DC: U.S. Department of Health and Human Services.

U.S. Department of Homeland Security (DHS). 2003. "Emergency Preparedness and Response." [Online article; retrieved 10/6/03.] *The National Strategy for Homeland Security.* http://www.whitehouse.gov/homeland/book/sect3-5.pdf.

U.S. General Accounting Office (GAO). 2003. *Hospital Preparedness: Most Urban Hospitals Have Emergency Plans but Lack Certain Capacities for Bioterrorism Response.* Report GAO-03-924, August. Washington, DC: GAO.

# Checklists

## CHECKLIST 3.1. CONDUCTING A FAILURE MODE, EFFECTS, AND CRITICALITY ANALYSIS

❑ Describe the process being evaluated.
❑ Define functions or operations performed in achieving the process.
❑ Identify potential failure modes.
❑ Describe the effects of the failure.
❑ Determine causes by performing a root cause analysis.
❑ List current failure-detection methods and controls.
❑ Calculate risk/cost should a failure occur.
❑ Take action (mitigate).
❑ Assess results.

## CHECKLIST 3.2. TEN STEPS TO DEVELOPING A DISASTER PREPAREDNESS PROGRAM

❑ Assemble key stakeholders for a team approach to planning.
❑ Assess current resources.
❑ Assess the facility's capability to deliver services, or weaknesses that may prevent such.
❑ Develop detailed, comprehensive, written response plans.
❑ Distribute the plan to staff and employees; conduct education on the plan.
❑ Conduct drills and exercises based on the plan.
❑ Review and assess response from exercises or drills.
❑ Assess knowledge, skills, and abilities of staff and employees to respond to the plan.
❑ Modify training as needed from review of the plan.
❑ Continuously repeat the cycle of process, practice, and improvement.

*Source*: Based in part on the unpublished work of Gary Green, M.D., Johns Hopkins University Medical Center, Baltimore, MD, 2003.

## CHECKLIST 3.3. SUGGESTED TRAINING TOPICS

- ❏ Facility emergency operations plan
- ❏ Establishment and functions of the emergency operations or command center
- ❏ Emergency roles and responsibilities
- ❏ Understanding incident management and who is in charge
- ❏ Alert and notification procedures
- ❏ What to report and to whom
- ❏ Warnings—what they mean
- ❏ The role of the media and media relations
- ❏ Primary and alternate communications systems
- ❏ Safeguarding records
- ❏ Securing the facility
- ❏ Securing your department
- ❏ Emergency medical supplies/equipment
- ❏ Principles of triage
- ❏ Mutual-aid agreements—what they are and what they mean
- ❏ Evacuation procedures
- ❏ Emergency transportation of residents
- ❏ Shelter-in-place
- ❏ Preparing the facility for severe storms/winds, etc. (i.e., any natural hazard to your locale)
- ❏ Sandbagging techniques
- ❏ When and how to shut off utilities
- ❏ When and how to close air vents
- ❏ When and how to seal windows and doors
- ❏ Alternate power—what is available and how to request additional sources (e.g., type, size)
- ❏ Emergency food and water provisions
- ❏ Emergency sanitation—short and long term
- ❏ Emergency equipment and supplies—where and how to use them
- ❏ Sweeping a building by assigning specific sections for search/evaluation for damage, with reporting procedures as sections are completed
- ❏ Conducting a quick damage assessment
- ❏ Patient decontamination
- ❏ Facility decontamination
- ❏ Using volunteers in disaster (professionals and lay people)

❏ Mental health aspects of disaster
❏ Special-needs populations in disaster

## CHECKLIST 3.4. ISSUES IN RECOVERY PLANNING

❏ How will we care for our patients outside the existing facility?
❏ What role, if any, will families and friends assume in caring for patients?
❏ Have arrangements been made for at least two alternate sites to accommodate facility patients for a week to ten days or longer?
❏ How does the option of moving to an alternate site affect facility staff members?
❏ How quickly can another building be located, rented/purchased, furnished, equipped, etc., to meet patients' requirements and to continue business? How far from our current location will we have to locate such a structure?
❏ What other types of skills (general labor, professional, specialists, etc.) may be needed to accommodate patients in an alternate facility?
❏ Where will we find human resources if local ones are committed elsewhere?
❏ What type of funding arrangements will be required to make the alternate site suitable for our patients and their specific needs?
❏ If nothing is salvageable from the original facility, have arrangements been made to contract for furnishings, equipment, and supplies? From where will these come, and how long will it take for delivery of these items?
❏ Do we carry insurance coverage for all-hazards disasters?
❏ How will we document and prove losses affecting the facility or business?
❏ What special liability issues may arise during recovery from a disaster event?
❏ What fiscal management procedures will be used during disaster response and recovery?
❏ What accounting documentation processes are in place for response/recovery activities?
❏ How will we address the fears and lack of stability in lives of patients and staff members?

❏ What additional care or support has been arranged to respond to the psychosocial needs of those in our facility?

❏ What others items, specific to our facility or location, must be addressed?

*Source*: Adapted from Anderson, B., J. Dilling, P. Mann, and A. Moore. 1996. *Assisted Living Facility Guide and Model Plan*. Developed by Emergency Training & Consulting, International, Silverdale, WA. Used with permission.

## CHECKLIST 3.5. RESUMING NORMAL OPERATIONS

### Weighing Options and Priorities

❏ Based on evaluation of the damaged facility structure or site, what are the options available for the resumption of services? Repair? Rebuild? Relocate?

❏ What legal issues related to the damaged site, hazard abatement, and cleanup should be addressed?

❏ Will a comparison of costs per option change the determined course of action?

❏ What impact will new or revised building codes have on recovery actions and decisions?

❏ What materials, equipment, or supplies are salvageable?

❏ Are suitable buildings available for interim operation of business?

❏ Have arrangements for temporary housing or care of patients or residents been discussed with like facilities that suffered no damage?

❏ Is contracting with area hotels/motels for short-term use of rooms a viable and appropriate option for your short- or long-term-care population?

### Modifying Service Levels

❏ What services are absolutely vital to resumption of business in a temporary or reoccupied facility?

❏ What impact will fewer services have on patients or a long-term resident population?

❏ What impact will modified services have on the number of employees needed to resume business operations?

❏ If regular employees are unavailable, how will you supplement the workforce? Are positions prioritized to guide fulfillment based on service level to be provided?

### Contracting for Services

❏ What work will be required to make an interim location viable for the facility-specific needs?
❏ Are building materials, contractors, and workforce sufficient to assist you in upgrading an alternate location as well as repairing or rebuilding the permanent location?
❏ How long will it take to acquire needed facility furnishings, equipment, and supplies for business resumption?
❏ Are sufficient numbers of knowledgeable personnel available through agencies or other sources that will supply temporary staff if regulars are unavailable?

### Communications Issues

❏ How do you plan to communicate with medical staff and employees to keep them apprised of plans for resuming normal operations? Phone? Mail? E-mail? Meetings?
❏ Do staff know how, when, and under what conditions they will be contacted?
❏ Have residents and staff been encouraged to maintain communications with the facility, and is there an easy method for them to do so (e.g., a "round-robin" system, e-mail, phone call, etc.)?
❏ Have arrangements been made for announcements of emergency communication of pertinent information via local radio and/or television?

*Source*: Adapted from Anderson, B., J. Dilling, P. Mann, and A. Moore. 1996. *Assisted Living Facility Guide and Model Plan*. Developed by Emergency Training & Consulting, International, Silverdale, WA. Used with permission.

### CHAPTER FOUR

# Understanding and Implementing Standards and Guidelines for Emergency Management

Peter W. Brewster

S everal regulations, guidelines, and standards have improved the management of emergencies and disasters in the United States over the last two decades. Such publications have been developed and released by organizations and government agencies such as ASTM International (formerly the American Society for Testing and Materials), the Occupational Safety and Health Administration (OSHA), the Environmental Protection Agency (EPA), the Joint Commission on Accreditation of Healthcare Organizations (JCAHO), the Department of Veterans Affairs (VA), and the National Fire Protection Association (NFPA).

This chapter explains the principles within these standards and guidelines regarding

- mass-casualty incidents,
- hazardous materials,
- decontamination, and
- emergency management program development.

---

The views expressed in this chapter are those of the author and do not necessarily represent the views of the Department of Veterans Affairs or of the Government of the United States.

Peter W. Brewster is area emergency manager for the Emergency Management Strategic Healthcare Group at the Veterans Health Administration in Indianapolis, Indiana.

## Multiple- and Mass-Casualty Incident Standards

ASTM standard F-1288, Standard Guide for Planning for and Responding to a Multiple Casualty Incident, covers planning, needs assessment, training, interagency coordination, mutual aid, and other important issues as they relate to multiple-casualty incidents. It identifies key terms and activities and explains how the incident management process is organized at the scene (ASTM 1990).

In addition to that standard, George Washington University recently developed a peer-reviewed model for mass-casualty response that integrates the functional requirements of medical, public health, and emergency management agencies in the Medical and Health Incident Management System (MaHIM) (available online at http://www.gwu.edu/~icdrm/). The model was based on the definition of a mass-casualty incident involving 5,000 casualties, 10 percent of which would be considered significant (Barbera and Macintyre 2002). *Casualty* refers to any human accessing health or medical services, including mental health services and fatality care, as a result of a hazard impact. The MaHIM model clarifies the types of activities that may become necessary at the community-health-system level and how they would be organized in a mass-casualty incident.

It is a useful tool for jurisdictional and regional system development, education, and planning. The Department of Health and Human Services (U.S. DHHS 2002) and the Department of Homeland Security (U.S. DHS 2003) promote this type of management-system framework and are considering applying MaHIM to support current public health and hospital bioterrorism preparedness (CDC 2003). MaHIM is entirely consistent with broader efforts to create a national incident-management system (The White House 2003).

## Hazardous-Materials Legislation

A sentinel event occurred in 1985 in Bhopal, India, in which thousands were killed and injured as a result of the release of a toxic gas from a nearby industrial facility. Congress responded to the concerns of such a disaster occurring in the United States by enacting the Superfund Amendments and Reauthorization Act (SARA) of 1986, amending the Comprehensive Environmental Response, Compensation and Liability Act of 1980.

The basic purpose of SARA Title III, also known as the Emergency Planning and Community Right-to-Know Act, was to promote emergency planning to respond to chemical releases and to ensure that information regarding chemicals in the community is available to the public and emergency response agencies. These goals are accomplished by

- establishing state emergency response commissions and local emergency planning committees (LEPCs) with responsibility to develop emergency plans to be followed in the event of a chemical release and
- implementing a series of notification and reporting requirements to state and local emergency planning activities with respect to type and quantities of specific chemicals.

### Occupational Safety and Health Administration

OSHA regulations for compliance with SARA Title III are found in the Code of Federal Regulations (CFR 29 Part 1910). Items of specific interest to hospital leaders are listed in Table 4.1.

Of much concern and debate has been OSHA 1910.120, Hazardous Waste Operations and Emergency Response (HAZWOPER). This regulation applies to hospitals in at least three scenarios, as follows (OSHA 1991):

1. When hospitals have an internal release of a hazardous substance that requires an emergency response
2. When hospitals respond as an integral unit in a communitywide emergency response to a release of a hazardous substance
3. If a hospital is a treatment, storage, or disposal facility under the OSHA Resource Conservation and Recovery Act

OSHA's definition of the term *emergency* is dependent on several factors, including the hazards associated with the substance, the exposure level, the potential for danger, and the ability to contain the substance. OSHA does not require that hospitals receive accident victims, but if a victim is part of an emergency involving hazardous substances

TABLE 4.1. KEY OSHA HAZARDOUS-MATERIALS REGULATIONS

*Subpart H—Hazardous Materials (1910.101–.126)*

1910.120—Hazardous Waste Operations and Emergency Response (and Appendixes A–E)

*Subpart I—Personal Protective Equipment (1910.132–.139 and Appendix B)*

1910.132—General Provisions
1910.133—Eye and Face Protection
1910.134—Respiratory Protection (and Appendixes A–D)
1910.136—Occupational Foot Protection
1910.138—Hand Protection

*Subpart Z—Toxic and Hazardous Substances (1910.1000–.1450 Appendix B)*

1910.1200—Hazard Communication (and Appendixes A–E)

*Source*: OSHA. 2003. "Occupational Safety and Health Standards." *Code of Federal Regulations*, title 29, sec. 1910. Washington, DC: U.S. Government Printing Office.

and hospital personnel are needed to decontaminate, HAZWOPER will apply (OSHA 1992).

### Environmental Protection Agency

As part of SARA Title III, the EPA will not enforce HAZWOPER for environmental consequences stemming from necessary and appropriate actions such as decontamination during the phase of an emergency response where an imminent threat to human health and life is present. However, once this phase passes, every attempt should be made to contain the runoff and dispose of it properly (Makris 1999).

Beyond industrial or transportation accidents involving hazardous materials, recent events have directed major emphasis on preparedness for occurrences involving weapons of mass destruction. Because of this threat, hospitals and health departments have become much more involved in communitywide emergency preparedness efforts.

One question that has been hotly debated is how SARA Title III, or more specifically HAZWOPER, applies to healthcare facility preparedness for these types of hazardous materials. OSHA's position until lately had been that if the contaminating substance was unknown, staff performing decontamination at a hospital who were not in the immediate area of the release were required to wear Level B personal protective equipment (PPE), including a mask supplied by an external air source.

Many experts disputed the necessity of this elevated measure of protection, contending that Level C PPE using a full face mask with powered or nonpowered canister filtration systems was adequate for hospital decontamination (Macintyre et al. 2000). In September 2002, OSHA took the position that as long as the choice of PPE was based on a risk assessment conducted by the employer, the agency would not require any particular level of PPE and respiratory protection (Fairfax 2002). For a complete discussion of PPE issues for hospital staff and personnel, including OSHA requirements for training in PPE use, see Chapter 9.

## Decontamination

Healthcare facilities that do not prepare for the potential arrival of contaminated patients face a dilemma. Refusing to assess and, if necessary, stabilize a contaminated patient is a violation of the Emergency Medical Treatment and Active Labor Act (U.S. GAO 2001). Employees who have not been adequately trained or equipped to deal with the situation can refuse to participate, leaving the facility only one choice: to dial 911 and request support from the local public safety system. These same resources, however, may already be fully involved at the site of the release.

### Department of Veterans Affairs

The VA developed a mass-casualty decontamination program that is based on a site-specific hazards vulnerability and capability analysis of the facility and surrounding community. Permanent or semipermanent showering facilities (in smoking shelters, along an external wall, etc.) are seen as advantageous over temporary tent-type facilities because of the speed of setup and lower expense (VA 2002a). Macintyre et al. (2000) believe that the following aspects are key to an effective decontamination protocol:

1. Event recognition
2. Activation
3. Primary triage

4. Patient registry
5. Collection of clothing and personal property
6. Decontamination
7. Secondary triage
8. Treatment and post-incident activities (e.g., media and family relations, medical surveillance, critique, etc.)

Healthcare-facility-decontamination training programs should follow NFPA standard 473, Standard for Competencies for EMS Personnel Responding to Hazardous Materials Incidents (Beatty 2003). NFPA 473 (this standard may be reviewed at http://www.nfpa.org/PDF/473.pdf? STC=nfpa) identifies the levels of competence required of emergency medical services personnel who respond to hazardous-materials incidents (NFPA 2002a). It specifically covers requirements for basic (Level I) and advanced (Level II) life-support personnel in the prehospital setting. This standard also provides information on training, recommended support resources, medical treatment considerations, patient decontamination, and hazardous-materials characteristics and references.

## Emergency Management Standards

### Joint Commission on Accreditation of Healthcare Organizations

In January 2001, JCAHO updated its emergency preparedness standards (standards EC.1.4, EC.2.4, and EC.2.9.1[1] found in the Environment of Care, or EC, section), adopting the four phases of comprehensive emergency management: mitigation, preparedness, response, and recovery. Other key additions to the emergency management standards were requirements for a hazards vulnerability analysis (HVA), the requirement that healthcare organizations implement an incident command system (ICS) consistent with that used by their community, and the acceptance of tabletop exercises for one of two required annual drills. Specific requirements for drills include the following:

- A facility designated as business occupancy must execute one drill annually.
- Hospitals, long-term-care organizations, ambulatory care facilities, and behavioral health facilities not classified as business occupancy

must conduct drills twice a year at least four months, but not more than eight months, apart.

- Facilities offering emergency services or designated as disaster receiving stations must base one exercise on an external disaster, and it must include volunteer/simulated patients who must be triaged, put on stretchers or in wheelchairs, and transported through the system as if they were actual patients.
- An organization must participate in a community drill that is relevant to its priority emergencies and that will assess communications, coordination, and the effectiveness of the organization's and the community's command structures.

The events of terrorism that took place in the United States in fall 2001 brought several more changes to the overall 2002 standards, including clarification on the process and products of the HVA (in particular, that procedures should be developed for each priority hazard identified), a requirement for cooperative planning with other healthcare facilities in the geographic area, and procedures for emergency credentialing. In 2003, components of the hospital emergency management standards were extended to long-term care, ambulatory care, behavioral health care, and home health care settings (*Environment of Care News* 2002). For 2004, the EC standards have been renumbered and reformatted but have not undergone any substantive changes in requirements.

*National Fire Protection Association*

NFPA emergency management Standard 99, Chapter 12, entitled "Healthcare Facilities," contains very similar requirements to JCAHO (NFPA 2002b). One big difference between the standards is the additional material in the annexes of the NFPA standard: explanatory material, references, and additional planning considerations (NFPA 2002a).

NFPA Standard 1600, Emergency Management and Business Continuity Programs, has gained international recognition and consensus among the public and private sectors. This standard articulates the generic elements of these programs and serves as the basis for an emergency management program evaluation and accreditation system by state, local, and tribal governments (NEMA 2001). Thus, NFPA 1600 represents a standard for communitywide emergency management programs (NFPA 2002c).

## IMPLEMENTATION ISSUES

For help with planning, training, and funding, hospitals should coordinate with the LEPC, which is responsible for planning for emergencies and providing funds to community emergency responders to improve emergency planning, preparedness, mitigation, response, and recovery capabilities (OSHA 1991). In many locations, the local or state emergency management agency (EMA) or public health agencies may be the appropriate first contact for this type of assistance. Several federal grant programs are focused on this need, including the Domestic Preparedness Program, the Metropolitan Medical Response System, the Hospital Bioterrorism Preparedness Program, and the Public Health Preparedness and Response to Bioterrorism Program. See Chapter 3 for more details on these programs.

Implementation of the various emergency management regulations, guidelines, and standards can require considerable time, effort, and expense. By integrating the principles and developing an implementation program, planning and education efforts can be simplified.

There is a difference between planning actions to respond in an emergency and the activities taken during the response to an actual emergency (Quarantelli 1994). An emergency operations plan (EOP) describes how the facility intends to react during the response and initial recovery from a threat or event. As such, it contains information about responsibilities for each group in the organization, how and where coordination will occur, and so forth. Attached to the EOP are standard operating procedures (SOPs). JCAHO requires that procedures reflect mitigation, preparedness, response, and recovery activities, and the SOP format integrates these actions (VA 2002b). The following list illustrates the VA's template for SOPs.

1. Description of the threat or event
2. Impact on mission-critical systems
3. Operating units and key personnel with responsibility
4. Mitigation/preparedness activities
   a. hazard-reduction strategies and resource issues
   b. preparedness strategies and resource issues

5. Response/recovery from the threat/event
    a. hazard-control strategies and resource issues
    b. hazard-monitoring strategies
    c. recovery strategies, priorities, and resource issues
6. Notification procedures
    a. internal
    b. external
7. Specialized staff training
8. References and further assistance
9. Review date

With changes to the 2001 JCAHO standards in place, the VA developed guidelines for its facilities that were largely based on Y2K preparedness activities. In this model, the VA formatted its EOP according to Federal Emergency Management Agency guidelines, incorporating the ICS functions as shown in Table 4.2. By organizing the EOP in this manner, the VA integrated planning for disasters with the process for implementing that plan. This simplified understanding of where the various JCAHO requirements fit. Table 4.3 highlights key requirements of JCAHO standard EC.1.4 as it relates to an EOP that is structured according to the ICS functions.

**Program Development Process**

Figure 4.1 illustrates a process for developing an emergency management program (EMP). In this model, three main components to developing a comprehensive EMP build on each other. Each is discussed below.

*Leadership and Direction Activities*

Leadership and direction activities include assigning responsibilities to an EMP coordinator and emergency management advisory committee. Members of the committee should represent all key functional areas within the entity and should include appropriate external groups (emergency medical services providers, public health department, American Red Cross, etc.), possess expertise and knowledge of their functional area, and have the authority to commit resources.

TABLE 4.2. STRUCTURE OF THE VA EMERGENCY OPERATIONS PLAN

- Basic emergency operations plan
    - –Purpose
    - –Scope
    - –Policies
    - –Situations
    - –Assumptions
    - –A concept of operations
- Functional annexes
    - –Management and planning
    - –Logistics and finance
    - –Operations groups
        - • Business continuity
        - • Equipment, plant, and utilities
        - • Safety and security
        - • Health and medical
- Standard operating procedures
- Job action sheets
- Checklists

*ICS Functions*

*Source*: U.S. Department of Veterans Affairs. 2002b. *Emergency Management Program Guidebook*. St. Louis, MO: VHA Center for Engineering & Occupational Safety and Health, and Washington, DC: VHA Emergency Management Strategic Healthcare Group, Emergency Management Academy.

Laws, authorities, and regulations should be reviewed as necessary to establish the facility's emergency management policy, mission statement, and role in the communitywide program. The existing EMP, including plans, agreements, education and training, and exercise records, should also be reviewed. Program review opportunities include annual life-safety reviews, after-action reviews or critiques from drills or real-world events, interviews with managers and staff, and document reviews.

Developing a strategic administrative plan to guide the multiyear capability development includes establishing goals and objectives, strategies, work plans, and a budget. The plan can also facilitate gaining executive support. Finally, creating regular opportunities for intra- and interorganizational coordination is important, such as inviting community experts as guest speakers or having hospital leaders observe or participate in community exercises.

## Mitigation and Recovery Activities

The recovery phase is linked to mitigation; while a facility is identifying the capabilities it may lose as a result of internal or external hazards, listing

## Table 4.3. Key Requirements of JCAHO Standard EC.1.4 and Their Relationships to ICS Functions

| | ICS Function | JCAHO Emergency Management Element |
|---|---|---|
| *Emergency Operations Plan* | Command and management | • Initiate the response and recovery activities<br>• Notify staff and external authorities<br>• Identify and assign staff<br>• Manage communications with the news media |
| | Planning | • Cooperative planning among healthcare organizations, to include<br> —Names, numbers, and roles of staff in command structure<br> —Resources and assets that could be shared<br> —Names of patients and deceased individuals<br>• Establish procedures for tracking patients |
| | Logistics | • Backup internal and external communications<br>• Staff and family support<br>• Critical supplies<br>• Transportation of patients, staff, and necessities<br>• Alternative means of meeting essential utility requirements<br>• Facilities for isolation and decontamination |
| | Operations | • Patient treatment<br>• Evacuation<br>• Alternative care sites<br>• Security<br>• Reestablishing usual operations after the emergency |
| | Finance/ administration | • Accounting for all incident-related items<br> —Personnel time and attendance<br> —Procurement<br> —Compensation<br> —Claims<br> —Costs |

restoration priorities for those losses should also take place. Start by identifying critical systems, equipment, information, operations, and materials/supplies, and continue by conducting the HVA.

The HVA is a process of hazard identification, risk assessment, and consequence analysis. (See Chapter 3 for more information on conducting an HVA.) The risk assessment subjectively prioritizes identified hazards and threats and is an important educational and preparedness activity for the emergency management advisory committee. The outcome of this process identifies operating systems, infrastructure, and essential resources that the facility can expect to lose or to be affected in each type of hazard studied.

FIGURE 4.1. PROCESS FLOW OF A COMPREHENSIVE EMERGENCY MANAGEMENT PROGRAM

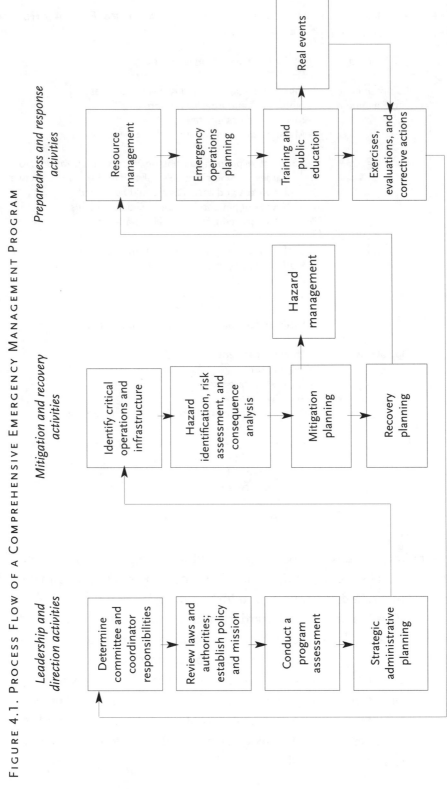

This knowledge is important to developing the facility's recovery plan, which should include short- and long-term restoration priorities, resources needed to achieve restoration, critical time frames, and other procedures. Looking at ways to reduce both structural and nonstructural loss establishes the mitigation program and is the final step in this component.

*Preparedness and Response Activities*

The first preparedness steps build on the output of the HVA: identify and inventory resources within the facility that are critical to response and recovery/restoration efforts. Agreements with suppliers and community partners should be developed and reviewed at least annually. Certain equipment and supplies (such as satellite telephones, communication devices, primary and support vehicles, pharmaceutical caches, etc.) need to be purchased, maintained, and tested in exercises.

Hospital leaders and the emergency management committee should also review the current disaster plan on an annual basis. EOPs can reduce the length of department- or service-based internal and external plans and more clearly illustrate the process of coordination. Transitioning to the EOP format is relatively simple. Figure 4.2 shows how various hospital organizational services and units relate to the ICS functions.

Education, training, and exercises need to be conducted for management, staff, and patients as well as patients' family members. For management, regular tabletop exercises conducted using realistic threats and events can improve decision making, and coordination processes can be challenging and even enjoyable. Whether from exercises or real events, evaluations, critiques, and corrective actions are very important to the overall success of a future response. Ensuring the loop is closed on the identified issues is one important responsibility of the emergency management committee.

An effective EMP, as prescribed by standards and regulations, is based on an ongoing process that involves representatives from the healthcare facility and community. It is important to retain preexisting authority while at the same time linking disaster-relevant groups such as emergency medical services providers, the public health department, the EMA, and the media. Other important activities include encouraging regular interorganizational contact; establishing joint operating facilities; and creating a process for collecting and sharing information, establishing priorities, and assisting in decision making (Dynes 1994).

FIGURE 4.2. RELATIONSHIP OF HOSPITAL SERVICES AND
DEPARTMENTS TO ICS FUNCTIONS

| VA Departments | Management and Planning | Finance and Logistics |
|---|---|---|
| Director's office | LS-M | |
| Canteen | | ● |
| A&MM | | LS-L |
| Ambulatory care | | |
| Chaplain | | |
| Chief of staff | | |
| Dental | | |
| Nutrition and food | | ● |
| Emergency management | LS-P | |
| Engineering | | ● |
| Environmental management | | |
| Fiscal | | LS-F |
| Human resources | | ● |
| IT | ● | ● |
| Pathology/laboratory | | |
| MAS | | |
| Medicine | | |
| Nursing | | |
| Pharmacy | | ● |
| Police and security | | |
| Psychiatry | | |
| Public affairs | ● | |
| Radiology | | |
| Safety | | |
| Social work | | |
| Voluntary | | ● |

*Note:* This table designates the lead service (LS), or hospital department, that takes the lead for coordinating these various functional areas.

## NOTE

1. Standards EC.1.4 (planning) and EC.2.4 (implementation) have been combined and renumbered as EC.4.10 in the 2004 JCAHO standards.

## REFERENCES

ASTM International. 1990. "Standard Guide for Planning for and Response to a Multiple Casualty Incident." ASTM 1288. Committee F30 on Emergency Medical Services. Washington, DC: ASTM International.

FIGURE 4.2. *(continued)*

| Business Continuity | Equipment, Plant, and Utilities | Safety and Security | Health and Medical |
|---|---|---|---|
|  |  |  |  |
|  |  |  |  |
| ● |  |  |  |
|  |  |  | ● |
|  |  |  | ● |
|  |  |  | LS |
|  |  |  | ● |
|  |  |  |  |
|  |  |  |  |
| ● | LS | ● |  |
|  | ● |  |  |
|  |  |  |  |
|  |  |  |  |
| ● | ● |  |  |
|  |  |  | ● |
| ● |  |  | ● |
|  |  |  | ● |
|  |  |  | ● |
|  |  |  | ● |
|  |  | LS |  |
|  |  |  | ● |
|  |  |  | ● |
|  |  | ● |  |
|  |  |  | ● |
|  |  |  |  |

A&MM = acquisition and materiel management; IT = information technology; MAS = medical administrative service; LS = lead service; LS-F = finance; LS-L = logistics; LS-P = planning; LS-M = management

Barbera, J., and A. Macintyre. 2002. *Medical and Health Incident Management System (MaHIM): A Comprehensive Functional System Description for Mass Casualty Medical and Health Incident Management*, 1-1. Washington, DC: George Washington University.

Beatty, J. 2003. Personal communication, Veterans Health Administration, April.

Centers for Disease Control and Prevention (CDC). 2003. "Emergency Preparedness and Response." [Online information; retrieved 12/2/03.] www.bt.cdc.gov/index.asp.

Dynes, R. 1994. "Community Emergency Planning: False Assumptions and Inappropriate Analogies." *International Journal of Mass Emergencies and Disasters* 12 (2): 151–52.

*Environment of Care News*. 2002. "Comparing JCAHO and NFPA 99: Emergency Management Standards Dovetail." *Environment of Care News* March/April: 10–11.

Fairfax, R. 2002. U.S. Occupational Safety and Health Administration (OSHA), Letter concerning OSHA requirement of certain personal protective equipment, September 5.

Macintyre, A. G., G. W. Christopher, E. Eitzen, Jr., R. Gum, S. Weir, C. DeAtley, K. Tonat, and J. A. Barbera. 2000. "Weapons of Mass Destruction Events with Contaminated Casualties: Effective Planning for Health Care Facilities." *Journal of the American Medical Association* 283 (2): 242–49.

Makris, J. 1999. Letter concerning containment of runoff, September 17. Washington, DC: U.S. Environmental Protection Agency.

National Emergency Management Association (NEMA). 2001. "Capability Assessment for Readiness (CAR) and Emergency Management Accreditation Program (EMAP), 1997–2001." Lexington, KY: Council of State Governments.

National Fire Protection Association (NFPA). 2002a. Standard for Competencies for EMS Personnel Responding to Hazardous Materials Incidents. NFPA 473. [Online report; retrieved 10/7/03.] http://www.nfpa.org/PDF/473.pdf?STC=nfpa.

———. 2002b. "Health Care Facility Emergency Management." Standard 99/12. Quincy, MA: NFPA.

———. 2002c. "Emergency Management and Business Continuity Programs." Standard 1600. Quincy, MA: NFPA.

Occupational Safety and Health Administration (OSHA). 1991. "Hospitals and HAZWOPER." Interpretive Letter, June. Washington, DC: OSHA.

———. 1992. "Hospital Preparedness for Receiving Contaminated Victims." Interpretive Letter, October. Washington, DC: OSHA.

———. 2002. "Risk Assessment." Interpretive Letter, October. Washington, DC: OSHA.

———. 2003. "Occupational Safety and Health Standards." *Code of Federal Regulations*, title 2, sec. 1910. Washington, DC: U.S. Government Printing Office.

Quarantelli, E. 1994. "Preparedness and Disasters: A Very Complex Relationship." Conference presentation based on "Disaster Research Center Preliminary Paper 199," University of Delaware, Newark.

U.S. Department of Health and Human Services (DHHS), Office of Emergency Response, Metropolitan Medical Response System. 2002. "Welcome to NDMS." [Online information; retrieved 12/2/03.] www.oep-ndms.dhhs.gov.

U.S. Department of Homeland Security (DHS). 2003. "Emergency Preparedness and Response." [Online article; retrieved 10/6/03.] *The National Strategy for Homeland Security.* http://www.whitehouse.gov/homeland/book/sect3-5.pdf.

U.S. Department of Veterans Affairs (VA). 2002a. "Steps Required to Establish a Practical Medical Center Emergency Mass-Casualty Decontamination Capability." Veterans Health Administration Directive 2002-033, June. Washington, DC: VA.

———. 2002b. *Emergency Management Program Guidebook.* St. Louis, MO: VHA Center for Engineering & Occupational Safety and Health, and Washington, DC: VHA Emergency Management Strategic Healthcare Group, Emergency Management Academy.

U.S. Government Accounting Office (GAO). 2001. *Emergency Care: EMTALA Implementation and Enforcement Issues*, GAO-01-747. Report to Congressional Committees, June. Washington, DC: GAO.

The White House. 2003. Homeland Security Presidential Directive/HSPD-5, Management of Domestic Incidents. [Online policy; retrieved 12/20/03.] http://www.whitehouse.gov/news/releases/2003/02/20030228-9.html.

### CHAPTER FIVE

# Protecting the Healthcare Population and Facility

Barbara Vogt and John H. Sorensen

Healthcare providers must protect themselves to avoid becoming victims of secondary contamination from exposure to a chemical or biological persistent agent. Routes of potential exposure of staff to a hazardous substance include

- direct contact with a hazardous substance,
- liquid (droplets or aerosols),
- inhalation of vapors or aerosols, or
- ingestion (unlikely, but possible).

Staff can avoid exposure by wearing personal protective equipment (PPE) when treating potentially contaminated patients (or through barrier protection options such as vaccination), understanding the appropriate procedures of decontaminating victims, and avoiding secondary contamination. This chapter explores the types of and need for PPE and decontamination to protect healthcare workers and facilities as well as the issues surrounding sheltering-in-place versus evacuation to protect the public and healthcare facilities.

Barbara Vogt, Ph.D., is a sociologist on the research staff of the environmental sciences division at Oak Ridge National Laboratory in Oak Ridge, Tennessee. John H. Sorensen, Ph.D., is a distinguished researcher at Oak Ridge National Laboratory in Oak Ridge, Tennessee.

## PERSONAL PROTECTIVE EQUIPMENT

The major factors in protecting healthcare providers against secondary contamination and protecting the healthcare environment are using proper contamination-control measures and using the appropriate PPE when treating patients exposed to a known or unknown substance. Treating potentially contaminated patients also increases the problem of maintaining a clean environment for healthcare providers.

Medical staff may not know when patients have been exposed to a hazardous substance. Victims may have self-evacuated to the medical facility (as happened in the Tokyo subway when sarin was released) or been sent to the emergency department (ED) by personnel responding to an incident in the field. In the latter case, communications between field and healthcare facility about the contaminant characteristics are essential to preparing ED staff to respond appropriately once the patient(s) arrives.

### Secondary Exposure and Cross-Contamination

Being alert to the potential for secondary contamination is critical to maintaining a clean environment. Secondary contamination, which can occur through direct or indirect exposure to a hazardous substance, most commonly occurs from hazardous vapors from patients' clothing or belongings. "Off-gassing" of toxic vapors can quickly sicken unprotected ED personnel as well as other patients or employees in the immediate vicinity. Patients have reported to the ED with clothing and articles sealed in bags, according to protocols, and then opened the bags in the ED to retrieve personal items such as cell phones and wallets.

In some instances involving unknown contaminants on patients, entire EDs have been closed for several hours while medical personnel were treated or replaced and the equipment, walls, and floors decontaminated (Vogt and Sorensen 2002). There is also the possibility that the entire ED staff would require immediate decontamination and quarantine should the contaminant subsequently be found to be a highly infectious biological agent—or even as a precaution if the unknown substance was determined benign—which are expensive and lengthy procedures.

The problem of cross-contamination from radiologically contaminated patients is not a major issue unless the patient is extremely heavily contaminated. Medical care should always receive priority over decontamination of radiological casualties. Unlike chemicals, radiological contamination does not pose an acute threat, and decontamination does not have to be immediate. In addition, the level of contamination and the effectiveness of decontamination are easier to measure than for chemicals because the appropriate detection equipment for measuring levels of radiation in the body is generally available.

Sidebar 5.1 illustrates the problems medical facilities have when contaminated victims self-evacuate to EDs. Without knowledge of the substances to which patients reporting to the ED have been exposed, it is uncommon for staff to routinely don PPE to treat patients. But the consequences can cause major headaches, as shown in the case example.

### Types of PPE

In the *Code of Federal Regulations* Section 1910, the Occupational Safety and Health Administration (OSHA) defines the types of PPE and the situations in which employees are required to wear PPE. The types of PPE provide different levels of protection and are labeled A, B, C, and D, as shown in Figure 5.1.

*Level A* is a total encapsulating, chemical-resistant ensemble—often called the "moon suit"—with self-contained breathing apparatus (SCBA), gloves, and boots. It provides full protection against liquids and vapors. *Level B* can be used when full respiratory protection is needed but the hazard from vapor is less. It differs from Level A in that the suit is not fully encapsulating and airtight, but it provides splash protection against liquids. *Level C* utilizes a splash suit with a full-face positive or negative pressure filtering mask rather than an SCBA. *Level D* is essentially a work uniform using latex gloves and mouth and eye protection, if necessary.

Butyl rubber gloves (available from industrial supply companies) for medical use come in two thicknesses: 7 and 14 milliliters (mil). Both protect from liquid chemical agents, but the 7-mil glove protects for 6 hours, whereas the 14-mil glove protects up to 24 hours after exposure. These gloves should be issued to workers along with the standard 25-mil gloves. The 7-mil gloves should be issued to personnel requiring extreme tactile ability, such as triage officers, paramedics, or computer operators. The 14-mil gloves should be used by workers who perform duties that require tactile ability but who will subject the gloves to harsher treatment. Regardless of thickness, if the gloves become contaminated, they should be safely removed and treated as hazardous waste.

**Sidebar 5.1. Case Example: Toxic Pesticide Exposure and Resulting Hospital Contamination**

In early September 2000, workers at a lawn and garden treatment product company in upstate New York inadvertently overheated the pesticide chemical dimethoate, which caused the product to emit fumes. An organophosphate pesticide, dimethoate can, if inhaled, quickly result in severe respiratory problems, increased watery nasal discharge, a sensation of chest tightness, and prolonged wheezing. Absorption by the lungs may produce symptoms of cholinesterase inhibition within a few minutes or up to 12 hours after exposure. The manufacturer recommends those exposed to immediately seek medical treatment, which the employees proceeded to do.

Eleven workers who were transported to a hospital in a neighboring community walked into the ED without being decontaminated. Seven hospital employees treating the workers suddenly became ill themselves. When the ED doctor saw his staff becoming ill, he immediately called the assistant fire chief, who was the hazardous-materials (HAZMAT) coordinator for the county, at his home to ask why the staff was getting sick. The chief recognized the symptoms as secondary contamination and told the doctor to immediately move all victims from the ED and to treat everyone who had been in contact with them as contaminated.

Outside in the hospital parking lot the male plant workers were decontaminated in a temporary unit set up by the fire department's HAZMAT team. The ED staff and three female plant workers were decontaminated inside the hospital ED shower area. Some male workers refused at first to be decontaminated, saying they worked with the chemicals every day, but they finally agreed to undergo decontamination. Fire department personnel wore Level B personal protective equipment when decontaminating victims.

It took approximately one hour for 20 people to be processed through the decontamination sequence. To prevent the pesticide from entering the area drain, neoprene pads were placed over the drain. The wastewater was then pumped into 55-gallon drums and given to the hospital for proper disposal.

Hospital housekeeping staff, dressed in scrubs, gloves, and hairnets and wearing air filters, were responsible for cleaning the ED where the exposed had first been taken and for the articles in those rooms. All walls were washed as well. The entire ED was shut down for the two hours it took to decontaminate the area before the decision was made to reopen the ED to patients.

Disposable latex gloves, eye protection, and mouth coverings will not protect healthcare providers from exposure to toxic vapors from chemical warfare nerve agents nor from some hazardous reactant chemicals that affect the mucous membranes, such as sulfuric acid. Normal hospital

## FIGURE 5.1. LEVELS OF PROTECTION

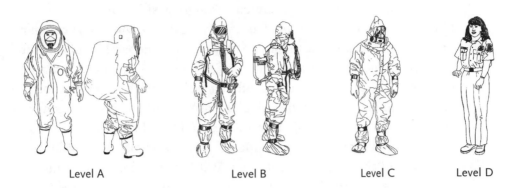

| Level A | Level B | Level C | Level D |

*Source*: Adapted from U.S. Department of Health and Human Services, Public Health Service Agency for Toxic Substances and Disease Registry. 2000a. *Managing Hazardous Material Incidents: Volume II. Hospital Emergency Departments: A Planning Guide for the Management of Contaminated Patients*. Washington, DC: U.S. Department of Health and Human Services, Public Health Service Agency for Toxic Substances and Disease Registry.

barrier protection will provide satisfactory protection for hospital personnel treating patients exposed to radiation.

Although the Joint Commission on Accreditation of Healthcare Organizations (JCAHO) has standards for hospital plans and training for hazardous-material incidents, it does not specify details on level of PPE (NRC 1999). However, a 1996 study by Levitin and Siegelson found that most hospitals are ill prepared to treat contaminated patients (see also Cox 1994). The PPE ensembles used in your facility for treatment of contaminated patients will likely be Level C and include a splash suit, vinyl gloves with cotton inserts, and boots (NRC 1999). The ensemble includes a one-piece chemical-resistant coverall with or without attached boots and hood or a two-piece unit. Further protection may require manual taping of sleeves and cuffs. This is appropriate when decontaminating victims of a known contaminant and its concentration established as not life threatening. If these two criteria are not met, OSHA regulations call for Level B protections (NRC 1999).

### Types of Respirators

There are basically two types of respirators: air-purifying and atmosphere-supplying. *Air-purifying respirators* pass air through a filter element or canister to remove gaseous or particulate contaminants from the outside air. Air flow across the filter may be generated by negative flow or inhalation, or it may be generated through positive pressure from a blower connected to a powered air-purifying device. *Atmosphere-supplying respirators* supply air to the breathing zone independent of the outside toxic atmosphere. For example, SCBAs provide air from a backpack or tank on the user's back using either a closed or open circuit. Another option is to use a common source of compressed air to supply several respirators at once, called an air-line respirator. Table 5.1 highlights the positive and negative characteristics of these two types of respirators.

Powered air-purifying respirators (PAPRs) are often used in healthcare facilities as part of PPE. PAPRs are classified by face piece size (quarter, half, or full), tightness of fit (tight-fitting or loose-fitting full face piece), and type of contaminant removed (particulate, gas and vapor, or gas and particulate). A tight-fitting, full-face PAPR will provide a higher level of protection than the hood type. The PAPR ensemble includes

- a spectacle kit adjusted to the user's needs and protective lenses;
- a belt-mounted turbo unit with a filtration cartridge to supply air to the face piece;
- a battery pack with battery charger (batteries must be kept fully charged when stored);
- a breathing tube assembly; and
- appropriate filter material.

All but the battery charger must be assembled to make the complete respirator.

Negative full-face respirators are used by the military to protect against chemical agent vapors and aerosols. Positive-pressure PAPRs may be used by emergency responders when chemical agent concentrations do not exceed 50 times the allowable acute exposure guideline limits (AEGLs) and the immediately dangerous to life and health (IDLH) values. These devices afford a higher level of protection because the positive pressure means air is leaking out, not in. OSHA recommends emergency responders wear a PAPR with six-cubic-feet-per-minute blower units to afford maximum protection. The challenge is measurement, as a detection monitor to estimate AEGLs or IDLH values is frequently not available in emergency departments. Figure 5.2 describes the three AEGLs.

TABLE 5.1. COMPARISON OF TYPES OF RESPIRATORY PROTECTION

| Type of Respirator | Advantages | Disadvantages |
|---|---|---|
| **Air purifying**<br>Air-purifying respirator (including PAPRs) | • Enhanced mobility<br>• Lighter in weight than SCBA; generally weighs 2 pounds or less (except for PAPRs) | • Cannot be used in IDLH or oxygen-deficient atmospheres (less than 19.5% oxygen at sea level)<br>• Limited duration of protection; may be hard to gauge safe operating time in field conditions<br>• Only protects against specific chemicals and only up to specific concentrations<br>• Can only be used (1) against gas and vapor contaminants with adequate warning properties or (2) for specific gases or vapors, provided that service level is known and a safety factor is applied or if the unit has an ESLI |
| **Atmosphere supplying**<br>SCBA | • Provides the highest available level of protection against airborne contaminants and oxygen deficiency | • Bulky, heavy (up to 35 pounds)<br>• Finite air supply limits work duration<br>• May impair movement in confined spaces |
| Air-line respirator (also called positive-pressure-supplied air respirator [SAR]) | • Enables longer work periods than SCBA<br>• Less bulky and heavy than an SCBA; weighs less than 5 pounds (or around 15 pounds, if escape SCBA protection is included)<br>• Protects against most airborne contaminants | • Not approved for use in IDLH or oxygen-deficient atmospheres (less that 19.5% oxygen at sea level) unless equipped with an emergency egress suit, such as an escape-only SCBA, that can provide immediate emergency respiratory protection in case of air-line failure<br>• Impairs mobility<br>• Mine safety and health administration/NIOSH certification limits hose length to 300 feet<br>• As the length of hose is increased, the minimum approved airflow may not be delivered at the faceplate<br>• Air line is vulnerable to damage, chemical contamination, and degradation<br>• Decontamination of hoses may be difficult<br>• Workers must retrace steps to leave work area<br>• Requires supervision/monitoring of the air supply line |

*Note*: PAPR = powered air-purifying respirator; IDLH = immediately dangerous to life and health; ESLI = end-of-service indicator; SCBA = self-contained breathing apparatus; NIOSH = National Institute for Occupational Safety and Health

*Source*: U.S. Department of Health and Human Services, Public Health Service Agency for Toxic Substances and Disease Registry. 2000. *Managing Hazardous Material Incidents: Volume I. Emergency Medical Services: A Planning Guide for the Management of Contaminated Patients*, Appendix B. Washington, DC: U.S. DHHS, Public Health Service Agency for Toxic Substances and Disease Registry.

FIGURE 5.2. GENERAL DESCRIPTION OF AEGLs*

> AEGL 3
Above AEGL 3, effects become
increasingly severe and possible
death occurs without treatment

> AEGL 2 < AEGL 3
Above AEGL 2, effects become
more significant and may impair
ability to escape, may be long
lasting, or may be permanent

> AEGL 1 < AEGL 2
Above AEGL 1, there may be
some discomfort, odor, irritation;
effects, if any, are not impairing
and only temporary

* AEGLs indicate the concentrations of a chemical in air above which different types of health
effects could begin to occur in an unprotected civilian population. The effects described are general in nature and do not reflect the specific effects associated with any particular chemical.

Source: U.S. Department of Health and Human Services. 2000b. *Managing Hazardous Material
Incidents: Volume I Emergency Medical Services: A Planning Guide for the Management of
Contaminated Patients.* Washington, DC: U.S. Department of Health And Human Services, Public
Health Service Agency for Toxic Substances and Disease Registry.

## Rudimentary Respiratory Protection

Although respirators offer good protection for emergency workers, they are
not designed for use by persons without adequate training. The number
of fatalities in Israel among civilian populations using respirators during Scud missile attacks in January 1991 ranged from 11 from suffoca-
tion to more than 100 from medical complications induced by the use
of masks (Barach et al. 1998). Some nontechnical publications have suggested using expedient measures such as a wet towel or handkerchief
folded over the nose and mouth. This practice is useful for large partic-
ulates such as smoke but offers low protection from aerosols and no protection from most vapors. Difficulties in maintaining a seal around the

face further reduce the protection offered by this option (Sorensen and Vogt 2001).

Disposable masks offer no protection against chemical aerosols or vapors, although they may provide protection against biological aerosols (such as anthrax) and droplets (such as a virus from a cough or sneeze). The level of protection is determined by the type of mask and the quality of the fit. Some disposable masks are approved by the National Institute for Occupational Safety and Health (NIOSH) and are rated as "95" or "100"; these numbers refer to the percentage of particles 0.3 microns in size that would be removed by the mask.

## Training for PPE Use

OSHA prescribes the training that must accompany the wearing of respiratory devices for worker protection. Before training with equipment, workers who may use respiratory protection in their job are also mandated to undergo a health examination for physiological impairments (e.g., asthma) or psychological effects (e.g., feelings of claustrophobia or entrapment) that can impede wearing the equipment and subsequent task handling. In addition, OSHA, in regulation CFR 1910.120, requires workers to be trained in equipment maintenance, work rules, and appropriate wear and rest times.

Many healthcare providers feel uncomfortable wearing any type of PPE that includes respiratory protection when treating patients, citing the effect on communicating with patients and other staff. Other drawbacks cited include the cumbersome and confining nature of the equipment (e.g., vinyl gloves) that affects tactile movements and the rapid buildup of heat within the chemical-resistant suits. This can affect work schedules because using the equipment is fatiguing and OSHA work rules require frequent rest times for all workers in PPE.

It is critical to remember that PPE restricts heat-loss mechanisms because of the garment's high insulation and low permeability to water vapor. The amount of heat accumulation depends on several factors, including the following:

- Amount of physical activity
- Level of hydration
- Clothing worn

- Load carried
- State of heat acclimatization
- Terrain, altitude, and climatic conditions
- Physical fitness and fatigue of the user

It is very important that staff wearing hazardous-materials PPE take appropriate measures to rehydrate and to open the clothing during rest times to prevent the body from overheating.

Many staff do not have the time nor the inclination to maintain the PPE, preferring instead to dispose protective items after use. This is not possible with some PPE because of the expense and disposal options. Because each healthcare provider must be individually fitted for respiratory equipment, the delays in refitting individuals in emergency situations are untenable. Therefore, a PPE program should have procedures for periodic fit testing and equipment maintenance.

## DECONTAMINATION

The National Research Council (NRC 1999) defines *decontamination* as the process of removing or neutralizing a hazard from the environment, property, or life form. However, no consensus nationally or among agencies has been reached on standard operating definitions of decontamination, and existing procedures may contradict best healthcare practices for protecting potentially exposed victims as well as healthcare providers.

For decontamination to be effective, the following three elements must be in place:

1. The contaminants are correctly identified.
2. The procedures and equipment are available and properly employed to neutralize (or remove) the contaminant.
3. The reduction of risk is defensible by scientific or regulatory standards (which is not always possible).

Furthermore, most current decontamination systems are labor intensive and require excessive quantities of water. As Macintyre et al. (2000) note, most decontamination guidelines for treatment of exposed victims were created following military models and are inappropriate in today's civilian healthcare settings.

This discussion is not intended as an all-inclusive treatment on decontamination dos and don'ts but is meant to alert managers to the potential difficulties and pitfalls in planning procedures for decontaminating victims exposed to hazardous substances.

## Types of Decontamination

To protect the healthcare facility, it is important to understand where and how (or if) decontamination is performed outside the medical facility, because the problems associated with decontamination of victims (including secondary contamination) in the ED can often be attributed directly to those factors. The degree to which a patient is decontaminated in the prehospital setting depends on the medical decontamination plan, available resources and medically trained personnel, the weather, and characteristics of the contaminant.

General protocols suggest that patients exposed to a hazardous chemical or biological substance should receive, at a minimum, gross decontamination before transport and treatment. Gross decontamination involves showering clothed patients with copious amounts of water, often conducted by a HAZMAT team with a fire hose or by having victims move through a HAZMAT decon tent or other treatment facility. Patients requiring additional medical attention, antidotes, or other emergency care should receive that care depending on the substance's effects and the ability of staff to protect themselves during treatment. For some situations, such as a patient exposed to a radiological or nonvolatile chemical substance, use of barrier nursing clothing is ample protection. However, if the chemical is highly volatile or persistent, staff should never attempt care or bring potentially contaminated patients into the hospital without appropriate respiratory protection. This includes admitting patients to ED waiting areas where the possibility of secondary contamination could shut down operations.

Hazardous-materials teams traditionally handle decontamination of the environment and persons exposed to hazardous substances, generally relying on a conservative model that advocates precautionary decontamination of potentially exposed victims. The HAZMAT definition of *medical decon* or *patient decon* is what most healthcare providers would consider gross decontamination. The procedures, however, are not much different from those proscribed in hospital settings. The first step is removal and disposal (i.e., bagging and sealing) of patients' clothing and personal belongings. (Cox [1994] estimates that this simple process removes 70 percent to 80 percent of the contaminant, but little scientific data support that assertion.) Victims are then given a quick overall rinse with water.

Secondary decontamination involves washing rapidly with a decontamination solution—usually a diluted bleach or soap and water—and rinsing again. At this point, victims can be dried, given clean clothes, and sent home or transported to a medical facility. The degree of proficiency will vary depending on equipment, resources, and training. One problem is providing privacy to victims, as not all HAZMAT teams are equipped with individual decontamination units or trailers.

Alternatively, mass decontamination processes victims in one or more groups. Chemical warfare agents can cause large numbers of casualties if dispersed in a vapor or aerosol, as manifested in the sarin incident in the Tokyo subway. Such a situation could also occur in a high-profile event at a stadium, a concert, or an airport. The process requires cordoning off several exits where a decontamination corridor can be set up with fire department aerials and/or deluge guns in close proximity. The nozzles are set at low volume so as not to inflict damage but to maximize the amount of water to which each victim is exposed. Ambulatory victims progress through the deluge so that they may be grossly decontaminated. In conjunction with removal of clothing, this will likely suffice to decontaminate those victims not exhibiting signs or symptoms of chemical agent exposure.

A second method is to set up a sprinkler head near the exit point as a rudimentary decontamination shower. In this scenario, water delivered at 500 gallons per minute will produce 8 gallons per second. If the victim remains in the shower for 3 seconds on average, he or she is exposed to 12 gallons, or the amount used in a normal shower.

In either scenario some clothing is left on, which reduces the effectiveness if vapor has penetrated to the skin. Also at issue is the runoff of wastewater with possible contaminants, the disposal of which must comply with local or state environmental regulations. The Environmental Protection Agency (EPA) has published guidelines on this issue, as described in Chapter 4.

Self- and buddy-decontamination techniques can also be employed by first responders, workers in hazardous situations, and groups trained in self-help for emergencies. Such techniques may be needed in situations in which immediate removal of contaminants is essential and no time is available to set up a decontamination operation.

Water temperature is a comfort issue that can affect the time spent showering. Normal fire hydrant water temperature is 55 to 65 degrees Fahrenheit. Discomfort during showering is a particular issue with children and the elderly who may suffer additional distress, especially if the ambient air temperature is much cooler or the weather is windy and cloudy. The outside decontamination process is more traumatic than that conducted in an enclosed environment, especially if victims feel a lack of privacy during the process.

## Need for Decontamination

Patient decontamination is needed in medical settings to prevent further risk to the patient from persistent or penetrating contaminants or secondary contamination of emergency responders and/or healthcare providers. Because little scientific documentation is available for when and how patient decontamination should be performed or how a patient is determined "clean" after decontamination, prehospital and hospital staff are left to decide what they think is right, not what has been scientifically proven to work best (NRC 1999). This has led to multiple decontaminations of the same patient, even for nonpersistent, nonvolatile, or benign substances (Vogt and Sorensen 2002). Conversely, the lack of decontamination of exposed patients has led to temporary closure of EDs when hospital staff were not informed that patients had been exposed to a hazardous substance.

Knowing when and how to decontaminate is especially critical when managing patients exposed to unknown substances. Those patients may self-evacuate or be brought to the ED with or without prior decontamination. The absence of personnel to screen such patients *before* they enter the facility happens as often in small medical clinics as in large, well-staffed hospitals. Although such patients may be quickly isolated and medical staff alerted, the damage of secondary exposure is often completed within minutes of the patient's arrival. One way to partially alleviate the problem is to have ED managers maintain close contact with all emergency medical technicians and paramedics delivering patients. Another method is to train security staff to recognize signs and symptoms of victim exposure to hazards. One problem is that security personnel may have other more pressing priorities during an incident.

## Training for Decontamination

All staff must be equally competent in procedures and protocols of de-contamination because multiple teams are often required to fully decon-taminate victims and to rotate in and out of PPE. Knowledgeable instructors and adequate time are required to train personnel to perform various decontamination tasks in appropriate PPE. Equipment can be expensive and must be available in sufficient quantities, especially when resupply is needed over extended periods to keep the ED fully functional. This is especially important considering respiratory PPE cannot be shared.

In addition, healthcare providers must be trained to decontaminate their own PPE after each use. In HAZMAT terms, *technical decon* is performed in nine sequential steps to clean PPE worn by responders and vehicles. Once completed, equipment can be returned to service. Figure 5.3 illustrates how those steps integrate with maintaining a clean envi-ronment.

Planning and training exercises should also include coordination with other agencies and state and local jurisdictions (as described in Chapter 3).

## Triage and Logistics for Mass Exposures

To healthcare providers, weapons of mass destruction may be thought of as weapons of mass effect or "exposure" with the attendant problems of extremely large numbers of victims seeking treatment at hospitals and clinics. *Triage* is a process developed by the military to cope with large numbers of victims from combat or disaster situations. The purpose of triage is to sort the injured by priority and determine the best use of avail-able resources and personnel. Triage centers on the use of diagnosis-based criteria, involving the evaluation of each patient's respiration, perfusion, and mental status to determine how he or she is classified: ur-gent (or immediate), delayed, or deceased. The patient's eventual desti-nation and treatment priority is indicated on a triage tag or colored ribbon or wristband. This may change as more resources and personnel become available.

Not all victims may live through such an event, so attention should also be given to events with contaminated mass fatalities. This topic is

FIGURE 5.3. NINE-STEP PERSONAL DECONTAMINATION PLAN DIAGRAM

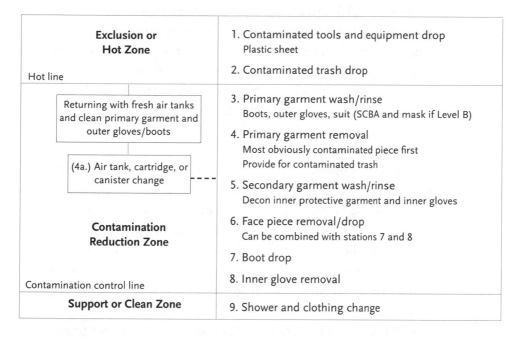

| | |
|---|---|
| **Exclusion or Hot Zone**<br><br>Hot line | 1. Contaminated tools and equipment drop<br>    Plastic sheet<br>2. Contaminated trash drop |
| Returning with fresh air tanks and clean primary garment and outer gloves/boots<br><br>(4a.) Air tank, cartridge, or canister change<br><br>**Contamination Reduction Zone**<br><br>Contamination control line | 3. Primary garment wash/rinse<br>    Boots, outer gloves, suit (SCBA and mask if Level B)<br>4. Primary garment removal<br>    Most obviously contaminated piece first<br>    Provide for contaminated trash<br>5. Secondary garment wash/rinse<br>    Decon inner protective garment and inner gloves<br>6. Face piece removal/drop<br>    Can be combined with stations 7 and 8<br>7. Boot drop<br>8. Inner glove removal |
| **Support or Clean Zone** | 9. Shower and clothing change |

*Source*: Adapted from U.S. Department of Health and Human Services, Public Health Service Agency for Toxic Substances and Disease Registry. 2000a. *Managing Hazardous Material Incidents: Volume II. Hospital Emergency Departments: A Planning Guide for the Management of Contaminated Patients.* Washington, DC: U.S. Department of Health and Human Services, Public Health Service Agency for Toxic Substances and Disease Registry.

beyond the scope of this book, but your state health department can provide further information on obtaining assistance from federal sources to handle large numbers of contaminated fatalities.

Multiple casualties frequently present major logistics issues. A site location and layout for mass decontamination of victims proximate to the facility should be predetermined and well known to emergency care operators. Securing immediate perimeter control and maintaining clean work areas (i.e., a cold zone) away from contaminated areas (i.e., hot zones) or areas where victims will arrive can present problems if not everyone is aware of the potential danger for cross- or secondary contamination. All personnel should know how to proceed through decontamination stations. An ideal location for a decontamination station is in a parking lot adjacent to the ED entrance. This helps to ensure that the ED stays free of contaminants. Such coordination requires planning and field exercises for staff.

The increasing number of EDs that have had to temporarily cease operations because of contamination is a growing concern among healthcare providers. In a mass casualty situation, the effects could create a domino effect, exacerbating the damage throughout the healthcare system as reliance on external mutual resources is often an important part of a hospital administration's emergency plans. The Greater New York Hospital Association (GNYHA 2002) interprets JCAHO recommendations for mass-decontamination situations to suggest the following steps:

1. Set up the decontamination area outdoors at the main facility to protect staff, equipment, and other patients from being contaminated. In cold weather, use tents or other temporary structures.
2. Address in the emergency management plan how the facility would respond to loss of part of the facility from contamination.
3. Use a dedicated decontamination room only when victims are few and will not involve transport through EDs or other common areas.
4. Coordinate decontamination efforts with HAZMAT response teams from communities that have the potential to send victims to the hospital.
5. Review heating, ventilation, and air conditioning (HVAC) systems to determine how to prevent a contaminant from spreading through the building.

Figure 5.4 provides a conceptual layout for mass decontamination and triage operations from the field to the hospital. Entry control, which consists of physical security and patient screening, is critical to prevent secondary contamination.

## Disposal Issues

Disposal of decontamination solutions and wastes from chemical or biological agents is an issue that should be discussed with local and state health departments. Although the EPA has issued guidelines recommending that "Good Samaritan" laws be applied in emergency situations, coordination is still required if other agencies or regulations are involved. (See Chapter 4 for further discussion on disposal regulations.)

FIGURE 5.4. TRIAGE AND ENTRY CONTROL

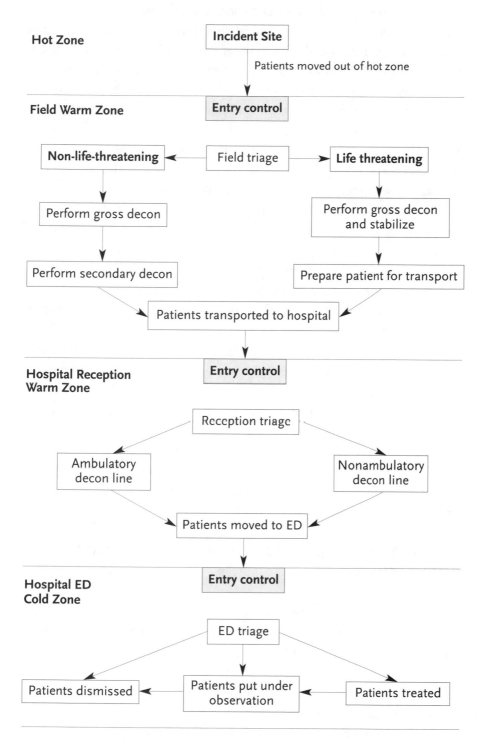

Some facilities have found that waiting until the contaminant in the wastewater was positively identified saves thousands of dollars in disposal fees. This approach has been used when the contaminant was unknown, decontamination was undertaken, and the substance was later found benign. Because the wastewater was not hazardous, no special means of disposal was required, which saves time and resources.

Several surveys have been conducted in the past several years on hospital preparedness for hazardous-materials accidents. A key focus of the surveys is capabilities for performing decontamination of patients. When Ghilarducci, Pirrallo, and Hegmann (2000) surveyed 256 Level I trauma centers in the United States, only 6 percent had all the necessary equipment and facilities to perform safe decontamination.

Wetter, Daniell, and Treser (2001) studied 224 hospitals with emergency rooms in Federal Region X (Pacific Northwest states); only 21 percent had an indoor, integrated decontamination space with showers and water containment. Another 24 percent reported having an outdoor decontamination capability, and an additional 27 percent had access to conventional showers. A total of 25 percent had no decontamination capabilities at all.

Treat, Williams, and Furbee (2001) performed a similar study in Federal Region III (Mid-Atlantic states), where they found that only 13 percent of the hospitals surveyed had a mobile decontamination unit. Most would use an ad hoc room to perform the decontamination if it was needed. Furthermore, 13 percent had no plans or capabilities for decontamination.

Overall, the surveys indicate that the majority of U.S. hospitals have little capability for conducting safe decontamination operations and would be unprepared for a mass casualty situation.


## PROTECTIVE ACTIONS FOR HOSPITAL AND HEALTHCARE POPULATIONS

When faced with possible exposure to chemical, biological, or radiological hazards in the outdoor atmosphere—that is, a primary exposure—a hospital has only three basic options to choose from:

1. shelter patients in place in the facility,
2. evacuate the hospital, or
3. shelter some of the occupants and evacuate others.

To choose in-place sheltering, there should be a reasonable assurance that the movement of patients and staff beyond the facility will endanger their health and safety more so than allowing them to remain in place. The decision to evacuate the public should be based on the reasonable assurance that the movement of people to an area outside of that which is affected is in the best interest of their health and safety and is of minimal risk to them.

Conceptually, the evacuation/in-place protection decision is simple and revolves around the following two questions (Glickman and Ujihara 1989):

1. Will shelter-in-place provide adequate protection?
2. Is there enough time to evacuate?

The answers to these questions indicate the appropriate response. Obviously, if the answer to only one is "yes," the appropriate response has been determined. If the answer to both questions is "yes," either option is satisfactory. The issue then should be decided on the basis of other considerations (e.g., patient disruption or cost). However, if the answer to both questions is "no," emergency planners and officials face a serious problem and must consider exceptional measures.

Table 5.2 lists some factors to consider in the decision to shelter versus evacuate. The feasibility of evacuation or length of time it takes to evacuate can be estimated in evacuation drills and exercises. Estimating the level of protection from sheltering may require engineering expertise and testing.

Another possible hazard hospitals face is a deliberate release of a hazardous substance into the ventilation system of the building. As the recent hostage situation in a Moscow theater illustrates, little protection currently exists for this scenario. Checklist 5.1 at the end of this chapter offers some questions to consider regarding physical facilities. NIOSH (2002) developed this checklist to help building managers determine the protective capability of a building.

## SHELTERING CONSIDERATIONS

Positive-pressure filtration systems draw contaminated air into the building through special filters that remove the contaminants. This creates a slight positive pressure in the building, which in turn prevents the

## TABLE 5.2. FACTORS TO CONSIDER IN PLANNING PROTECTIVE ACTIONS: SHELTERING VERSUS EVACUATION

| Attribute | Shelter-in-Place | Evacuation |
|---|---|---|
| Infiltration rate | Tight building | Leaky building |
| HVAC | Easy to shut down | Cannot shut down |
| Staff/patient ratio | Low | High |
| Plume duration | Short | Long |
| Time of day | Night | Day |
| Population density of area | High | Low |
| Availability of transportation | Poor | Good |
| Road geometry | Closed | Open |
| Road conditions | Poor | Good |
| Patient mobility | Immobile | Mobile |
| Traffic flow | Constrained | Unconstrained |
| Memorandum of understanding for relocation | No | Yes |
| Toxic load of hazardous material (threat of risk) | High | Low |

nonfiltered, contaminated air from leaking into the building. Experience suggests that such systems, however, are expensive and difficult to properly engineer. A less expensive but less protective measure is to engineer the building controls so that the HVAC system could be completely shut down. Little outside air would be drawn into the structure if all doors and windows were closed.

The ability of an action to adequately protect people in a healthcare facility depends on the characteristics of the toxic agent(s) involved, the size and nature of the release, meteorological conditions, the characteristics of the population affected, and the ability of the threatened structures to provide protection from outdoor agent concentrations. Deciding to shelter-in-place requires a prediction of the outdoor plume concentration of the toxic agent that will occur in the risk area, an estimation of the concentration that will occur inside the buildings at risk, and a calculation of the indoor estimated level of exposure. Deciding to evacuate requires an estimation of how long it will take to move patients and staff out of the building and when they will reach a safe distance compared to the outside concentration that people will experience while evacuating; that is, calculating exposures to those who evacuate in the plume will be considered against exposures to those who have not left (Sorensen, Shumpert, and Vogt 2002).

The indoor concentration of a contaminant is determined by infiltration rates into a building and the inside circulation of air. The inside environment will have a lower peak concentration of a contaminant than the outside air. The lower the air exchange, the lower the peak concentration. Infiltration is measured by air changes per hour (acph) between the outside and the inside or the number of times each hour that an enclosure's total volume of air is exchanged with outside air. An average air exchange rate for office buildings is estimated to be 0.66 acph and an industrial building to be 0.31 acph with the HVAC system(s) off and doors and windows closed (Engelmann 1990). Little is known about the movement of contaminants inside buildings, especially large and complex structures such as hospitals.

Overall exposure to contaminants in a closed indoor environment will be similar to the overall outdoor exposure because contaminants remain in the building after the plume has passed. If reducing total exposure is the goal, as opposed to reducing peak concentration, then the facility needs to be evacuated or ventilated after the plume has passed or the outdoor concentration is less than the indoor concentration (Rogers et al. 1990).

Sheltering for a biological hazard is slightly different from that for a chemical vapor in that hospital HVAC systems are designed to filter out most aerosols in the size range of biological agents (0.5 to 10 microns) (Weik and Weik 2001). Thus, leaving the HVAC system on would be warranted if the hospital is not under positive pressure.

Sheltering for a radiological hazard is somewhat different from that for chemical hazards in that a building will provide some protection against radiation from inhalation exposure as well as exposure from atmospheric clouds and ground deposition. The amount of protection against radiation is determined by the type of structure and location in the structure. Interior rooms and basements in buildings such as hospitals would typically reduce exposure from a cloud source by 70 percent to 90 percent and from a ground source by 98 percent to 99 percent (Schleien 1983).

## EVACUATION CONSIDERATIONS

Evacuations of hospitals and other healthcare facilities can be lengthy and complex events. A 1990 study examined the evacuation of 34 hospitals and 46 nursing homes (Vogt 1990). In the 34 hospital evacuations at facilities that ranged from 99 to 310 beds, the largest facility took 5 hours to evacuate 127 patients, whereas the smallest hospital took 2 hours to evacuate 27 patients. The most rapid evacuation involved the movement of 57 patients in 1.5 hours (Vogt 1990). In addition to results of nursing home evacuations, it was found that the time to evacuate was not related to the number of patients evacuating. The strongest predictors of evacuation time were the nature of the threat (weather versus nonweather events), the ratio of staff to patients, and whether the facility was in an urban area (Vogt 1991). A more recent study documents the evacuation of 575 patients from a hospital prior to a hurricane (Cocanour et al. 2002). In this case, completing the evacuation took almost 28 hours. Of the 575 patients, 169 were discharged and 406 were taken to 29 other facilities.

Both Vogt (1990) and McGlown (2001) examine factors influencing the evacuation process in healthcare facilities. Although Vogt focuses on the implementation of an evacuation at an organizational level whereas McGlown focuses on individual decision making, the two studies have similar findings. Processes are shaped by factors such as threat, risk, time, resources, infrastructure impediments, internal and external environment, organizational characteristics, social linkages, and social climate— all factors that were outlined in Table 5.2. Sidebar 5.2 describes the evacuation of a hospital in Arkansas following an incident at a local plant.

In terrorist events, both patients and workers in healthcare facilities are vulnerable groups. Patients are at risk because they lack the ability to protect themselves. Workers are at risk because of the nature of their roles as caregivers and because of the extra burden that an emergency creates. Despite such difficulties, responding to an emergency can be successful with careful planning, training, and exercising.

## REFERENCES

Barach, P., A. Rivkind, A. Israeli, M. Berdugo, and E. D. Richter. 1998. "Emergency Preparedness and Response in Israel During the Gulf War." *Annals of Emergency Medicine* 32 (2): 224–33.

Cocanour, C. S., S. J. Allen, J. Mazabob, J. W. Sparks, C. P. Fischer, J. Romans, and K. P. Lally. 2002. "Lessons Learned from the Evacuation of an Urban Teaching Hospital." *Archives of Surgery* 137 (10): 1141–45.

Cox, R. D. 1994. "Decontamination and Management of Hazardous Materials Exposure Victims in the Emergency Department." *Annals of Emergency Medicine* 23 (4): 761–70.

Engelmann, R. 1990. *Effectiveness of Sheltering in Buildings and Vehicles for Plutonium.* Department of Energy Report DOE/EH-0159T. Washington, DC: U.S. Department of Energy.

**Sidebar 5.2. Case Example: Hospital Evacuations in Arkansas**

Shortly after 1:00 p.m. on Thursday, May 8, 1997, clouds of foul-smelling smoke began pouring from a herbicide and pesticide packaging plant in West Helena, Arkansas. The incident began when smoke was emitted from a 1,500-pound bulk container of azinphos-methyl, a commercial brand of parathion, which is a chemical with toxicity levels similar to sarin (Vogt and Sorensen 1999). An alert was sounded, employees were evacuated, and the West Helena fire department was called. As the smoky, malodorous cloud drifted away from the plant, authorities ordered residents in a two-mile area downwind of the plant to evacuate and those in the two- to three-mile zone downwind to shelter-in-place.

Phillips County Regional Medical Center was the one medical facility evacuated following the release. Located across the highway from the fields surrounding the industrial park, the complete service hospital, providing care for residents in a 50-mile radius, employs about 330 people and has 155 beds.

The evacuation of the medical center was facilitated by efforts taken six months earlier to update the hospital's evacuation plan and reconfirm support agreements for relocation sites and supplies. When the plan was updated, the entire staff had also participated in a mock drill. At the time of the incident, the safety officer observed the buildings across the highway being evacuated and questioned officials on the possibility of also being evacuated. When the director of nursing gave the "code white" alert (the signal that an evacuation to an off-site facility would follow), an evacuation plan that was familiar to staff was in place and had been practiced, and staff were amply prepared to move patients.

All patients who could be discharged were sent home with a physician's nurse. Another four or five patients (the most seriously ill) were transferred to a hospital about one-half hour away. Approximately 17 patients in the rehabilitation unit were transferred to a vacant wing of the Crestpark Nursing Home accompanied by hospital support staff. One maternity patient evacuated to the nearby Phillips Community College, where the hospital staff had evacuated and opened emergency room services.

The evacuation of patients began at 1:40 p.m., and all but three patients (two on ventilators and one being stabilized in the emergency room) were out 55 minutes later. The remaining three patients were evacuated 15 minutes later. As per the evacuation plan, a variety of vehicles transported patients—vans, school buses, ambulances, private cars, and mortuary services vehicles. As a precaution, National Guard personnel provided security at the evacuated hospital.

Until the hospital could be reopened, hospital personnel operated a triage area, an emergency room, and a laboratory at the recently completed fine arts building at the community college. The space provided by the college suited the hospital's needs. In addition to the space, dressing rooms with showers and toilets were readily available. The college also has an emergency medical technician program

*(continued on following page)*

and a school of nursing. One of the rooms used for training nurses was used to house maternity patients until stabilized, but no other patients were kept overnight. Ambulance operators rerouted patients to other medical facilities as needed. Staff maintained records using a notebook computer. The college also provided a separate extension phone line for hospital staff use.

Although monitors indicated no contamination in the facility, the state health department required a thorough cleanup of the hospital before patients could be admitted. This meant that all hard services had to be scrubbed and all soft materials (drapes, etc.) had to be removed. The health department also required that all filters in the building be replaced before the interior cleanup was started. Staff were unable to locate the filters because of the special design and the fact the company making them did not operate on weekends. Recognizing the urgency of having the regional hospital operational, state officials exerted pressure to convince the company to alter its policy to aid in the recovery from this incident. The filter company extended its hours and worked through the night, delivering the replacement filters to the hospital on the following Saturday. The hospital staff began cleaning on Sunday in shifts, starting with the rooms where filters were replaced. The emergency room was considered the highest priority and cleaned first. The hospital was reopened on May 13, six days after the initial evacuation.

*Source*: Vogt, B. M., and J. H. Sorensen. 1999. *Description of Survey Data Regarding the Chemical Repackaging Plant Accident, West Helena, Arkansas*. ORNL/TM-13722. Oak Ridge, TN: Oak Ridge National Laboratory.

Ghilarducci, D., R. Pirrallo, and K. Hegmann. 2000. "Hazardous Materials Readiness of United States Level 1 Trauma Centers." *Journal of Occupational and Environmental Medicine* 42 (7): 683–92.

Glickman, T. S., and A. M. Ujihara, eds. 1989. *Proceedings of the Conference on In-Place Protection During Chemical Emergencies*, November 30–December 1, 1988. Washington, DC: Resources for the Future, Center for Risk Management.

Greater New York Hospital Association (GNYHA). 2002. "Summary of 'Nuclear, Biological, and Chemical Decontamination,'" from *Joint Commission Perspectives*, 2001, pages 20–21. [Online article; retrieved 12/3/02.] www.gnyha.org/eprc/general/templates/JCAHO_Summary_NBC_Decon.pdf.

Levitin, H. W., and H. J. Siegelson. 1996. "Hazardous Materials. Disaster Medical Planning and Response." *Emergency Medical Clinics of North America* 14 (2): 327–48.

McGlown, K. J. 2001. "Evacuation of Health Care Facilities: A New Twist to a Classic Model." *Natural Hazards Review* 2 (2): 90–99.

Macintyre, A. G., G. W. Christopher, E. Eitzen, R. Gum, S. Weir, C. DeAtley, K. Tonat, and J. A. Barbera. 2000. "Weapons of Mass Destruction Events with Contaminated Casualties: Effective Planning for Health Care Facilities." *Journal of the American Medical Association* 283 (2): 242–49.

National Research Council (NRC). 1999. *Strategies to Protect the Health of Deployed U.S. Forces.* Washington, DC: National Academy Press.

National Institute for Occupational Safety and Health (NIOSH). 2002. *Guidance for Protecting Building Environments from Airborne Chemical, Biological, or Radiological Attacks.* Washington, DC: NIOSH.

Rogers, G. O., A. P. Watson, J. H. Sorensen, R. D. Sharp, and S. A. Carnes. 1990. *Evaluating Protective Actions for Chemical Agent Emergencies.* ORNL-6615. Oak Ridge, TN: Oak Ridge National Laboratory.

Schleien, B. 1983. *Preparedness and Response in Radiation Accidents.* Washington, DC: U.S. Department of Health and Human Services.

Sorensen, J., and B. Vogt. 2001. *Expedient Respiratory and Physical Protection: Does a Wet Towel Work to Prevent Chemical Warfare Vapor Infiltration?* ORNL/TM-2001/153. Oak Ridge, TN: Oak Ridge National Laboratory.

Sorensen, J., B. Shumpert, and B. Vogt. 2002. *Planning Protective Action Decision-Making: Evacuate or Shelter-In-Place?* ORNL/TM-2000/144. Oak Ridge, TN: Oak Ridge National Laboratory.

Treat, K., J. M. Williams, and P. Furbee. 2001. "Hospital Preparedness for Weapons of Mass Destruction Incidents: An Initial Assessment." *Annals of Emergency Medicine* 38 (5): 562–65.

U.S. Department of Health and Human Services (DHHS), Public Health Service Agency for Toxic Substances and Disease Registry. 2000a. *Managing Hazardous Material Incidents: Volume II. Hospital Emergency Departments: A Planning Guide for the Management of Contaminated Patients.* Washington, DC: U.S. Department of Health and Human Services, Public Health Service Agency for Toxic Substances and Disease Registry.

————. 2000b. *Managing Hazardous Material Incidents: Volume I. Emergency Medical Services: A Planning Guide for the Management of Contaminated Patients.* Washington, DC: U.S. Department of Health and Human Services, Public Health Service Agency for Toxic Substances and Disease Registry.

Vogt, B. 1990. *Evacuation of Institutionalized and Specialized Populations.* ORNL/Sub-7685/1. Oak Ridge, TN: Oak Ridge National Laboratory.

————. 1991. "Issues in Nursing Home Evacuations." *International Journal of Mass Emergencies and Disasters* 9 (2): 247–65.

Vogt, B. M., and J. H. Sorensen. 1999. *Description of Survey Data Regarding the Chemical Repackaging Plant Accident, West Helena, Arkansas.* ORNL/TM-13722. Oak Ridge, TN: Oak Ridge National Laboratory.

————. 2002. *How Clean Is Safe? Improving the Effectiveness of Decontamination of Structures and People Following Chemical and Biological Incidents.* ORNL/TM-2002/178. Oak Ridge, TN: Oak Ridge National Laboratory.

Weik, R., and S. Weik. 2001. *How to Protect Your Home Against Bioterrorism.* Mechanicsville, VA: Oakwood Scientific Laboratory.

Wetter, D. C., W. E. Daniell, and C. D. Treser. 2001. "Hospital Preparedness for Victims of Chemical or Biological Terrorism." *American Journal of Public Health* 91 (5): 710–16.

# Checklist

## CHECKLIST 5.1. BUILDING PROTECTION

❏ What is the mechanical condition of the equipment?

❏ What filtration systems are in place? What are their efficiencies?

❏ Is all equipment appropriately connected and controlled? Are equipment access doors and panels in place and appropriately sealed?

❏ Are all dampers (outdoor air, return air, bypass, fire, and smoke) functioning? Check to see how well they seal when closed.

❏ How does the HVAC system respond to manual fire alarm, fire detection, or fire-suppression device activation?

❏ Are all supply and return ducts completely connected to their grilles and registers?

❏ Are the variable air volume boxes functioning?

❏ How is the HVAC system controlled? How quickly does it respond?

❏ How is the building zoned? Where are the air handlers for each zone? Is the system designed for smoke control?

❏ How does air flow through the building? What are the pressure relationships between zones?

❏ Which building entryways are positively or negatively pressurized? Is the building connected to other buildings by tunnels or passageways?

❏ Are utility chases and penetrations, elevator shafts, and fire stairs significant airflow pathways?

❏ Is there obvious air infiltration? Is it localized?

❏ Does the system provide adequate ventilation given the building's current occupancy and functions?

❏ Where are the outdoor air louvers? Are they easily observable? Are they or other mechanical equipment accessible to the public?

❏ Do adjacent structures or landscaping allow access to the building roof?

*Source:* National Institute for Occupational Safety and Health (NIOSH). 2002. *Guidance for Protecting Building Environments from Airborne Chemical, Biological, or Radiological Attacks.* Washington, DC: NIOSH.

CHAPTER SIX

# Preparedness Issues for Populations with Special Needs

Avagene Moore

Within the various services provided today, many facilities accommodate the specific needs of the so-called "special populations." The Health Resources and Services Administration (HRSA 2003) National Bioterrorism Preparedness Program and its counterpart program at the Centers for Disease Control and Prevention are likewise concerned about these populations, which include people with disabilities, people with serious mental illnesses, minority groups, non-English-speaking people, the elderly, and children.

These individuals have physical, emotional, cognitive, and/or medical conditions that prohibit them from living independently because they need assistance with some degree of their activities of daily living. Facilities that provide assisted living, hospice services, home health care, 24-hour behavioral health and long-term care, rehabilitation, and any other specialty care may be considered as special environments. By location, special populations may be grouped into three categories: in the home, in a healthcare facility, or at a residential facility (on a campus or in a freestanding building). There are differences among the three, especially in resources required, care and assistance needed, equipment

Avagene Moore, CEM, is president and coordinator of the Emergency Information Infrastructure Project in Lawrenceburg, Tennessee.

A major portion of this chapter is based on a planning and training document, *Assisted Living Facility Guide and Model Plan*, developed by Emergency Training & Consulting, International, Silverdale, Washington. The authors of the original text, which was adapted by the present author, include Bev Anderson, Janet Dilling, Phyllis Mann, and Avagene Moore.

required to assist patients, and their ability to assist themselves or others. Table 6.1 outlines the differences between these population environments. Each type of special-population environment serves the community with varying degrees of attention or treatment that meets the individual needs of its residents or clients. Because these environments provide specialized care to their residents, they in turn require special preparedness attention.

In an emergency situation, people with special needs may require help with medical or personal care during evacuation and sheltering because of physical or mental challenges. If they require caregivers on a daily basis, attendants need to accompany them to either temporary or long-term alternate shelters and be responsible for or assist with the persons' care during disaster evacuation and sheltering. The basic living situation and first-aid care available in a general public shelter would not be adequate to care for these special populations.

## THE NEW THREAT FACING SPECIAL-POPULATION FACILITIES

Emergency management professionals regard the threat of terrorism as just one of many considerations in overall planning for preparedness, response, recovery, and mitigation. Preparing for potential terrorism events adds to the planning effort and to the overall preparedness stature of these professionals as well; yet disasters and emergencies of all types and magnitudes have the potential to affect our communities and facilities.

Whether carried out using the most common terrorist tool—an explosive device—or a chemical, biological, or radiological material or industrial agent release, terrorism is a threat for which your facility must prepare. The issue is critical. Response to a bioterrorism event will require rapid deployment of scarce resources. In addition, America's medical care delivery system and public health infrastructure are not adequately prepared to detect, respond to, or recover from a large-scale bioterrorism event.

Special populations are unusually vulnerable to the potential use of chemical, biological, radiological, nuclear, or high-yield explosive agents or weapons of mass effect of any type. An incident affecting a region would also affect these populations with the possibility of a higher-than-average morbidity or mortality rate. Depending on the type of agent and the amount of exposure, handling the medical problems, plus the potential

## Table 6.1. Concerns for Special Populations in Disaster Response

| Location of Special Populations | Types of Care Delivery | Unique Aspects of Caring for this Population in Disaster |
|---|---|---|
| Home | Hospice<br>Home health care<br>Chronic disease care<br>  (COPD, emphysema,<br>  dialysis) | 1. Keep list of agency or hospital-based home care and hospice patients on a call roster. Identify contact of their primary caregiver and care provider service, types of care required, equipment being used in home, dependency on equipment, provision of alternative power sources. List should include special needs in alerting or warning patients (visually impaired may need audible tones, while hearing impaired may need visual clues).<br>2. Add home health care patients to call list.<br>3. Meet with area EMS or fire service managers concerning evacuation planning. If evacuation of area is required, ensure that their needs are covered and that service providers are aware of their limitations, needs, special equipment, etc. Check on patient and family after any disaster event.<br>4. Visit home health care and hospice patients as soon as possible after a disaster event to assess home safety and security; operation of all critical equipment; availability of all required medications, supplies, and care.<br>5. Ensure chronic care patients have required online power or backup services to operate necessary equipment.<br>6. Ensure psychological needs are met in the aftermath of a disaster or crisis event.<br>7. Identify expectations of primary physician for patient care and coverage, and include them in disaster planning for facility. |
| Healthcare facility | Long-term care<br>Assisted living | 1. Maintain contact records of family or alternate caregiver for each resident.<br>2. Ensure all ambulatory patients know the facility disaster plan and are able to locate the "safe rooms" in the facility.<br>3. Engage competent residents in the disaster planning process; assign the more able to assist staff in moving and caring for those less mobile.<br>4. Provide emergency signage in alternate languages or Braille—all formats to meet current patient and family notification needs.<br>5. Provide multiple methods of warning or alerting residents of danger. Warning technologies should address needs of all impaired patients. |

*(continued on following page)*

*Preparedness Issues for Populations with Special Needs* 127

TABLE 6.1. *(continued)*

| Location of Special Populations | Types of Care Delivery | Unique Aspects of Caring for this Population in Disaster |
|---|---|---|
| | | 6. Provide system for emergency identification of patients during and in aftermath of a disaster (armband, photo-ID card with necklace-type holder). |
| | | 7. List most important personal items that should accompany the patient if evacuation is required. |
| | | 8. Identify pets that should accompany patients in evacuation if possible. Have pet wear identification tag or badge at all times stating name of animal, human owner, facility where animal resides, special pet needs. |
| | | 9. Include all capable patients in writing the disaster plan and procedures. Assign responsibility to those who desire it and are capable of caring for others or performing a critical task to augment staff actions in a disaster. |
| | | 10. Include all patients and families/caregivers in continuing education regarding the disaster plans, evacuation plans, locations, and procedures. |
| On campus or in a free-standing building | Residential care: mentally challenged, specialty rehabilitation, halfway houses, blind, physically restricted | 1. Maintain contact records of family or alternate caregiver for each resident. |
| | | 2. Ensure all ambulatory patients know the facility disaster plan and are able to locate the "safe rooms" in the facility. |
| | | 3. Provide emergency signage in alternate languages or Braille—all formats to meet current patient and family notification needs. |
| | | 4. Provide multiple methods of warning or alerting residents of danger. Warning technologies should address needs of all impaired patients. |
| | | 5. Engage competent residents in the disaster planning process, having them write the disaster plan and procedures. |
| | | 6. Assign responsibility to those who desire it and are capable of caring for others or performing a critical task to augment staff actions in a disaster. Assign the more able to assist staff in moving and caring for those less mobile. |
| | | 7. Provide system for emergency identification of patients during and in aftermath of a disaster (armband, photo-ID card with necklace-type holder). |
| | | 8. Assist residents with important personal items that should accompany them, if evacuation is required. |

TABLE 6.1. *(continued)*

| *Location of Special Populations* | *Types of Care Delivery* | *Unique Aspects of Caring for this Population in Disaster* |
| --- | --- | --- |
| | | 9. Identify pets that should accompany residents in evacuation. Have pet wear identification tag or badge at all times stating name of animal, human owner, facility where animal resides, special pet needs.
10. Identify a meeting place for all staff and residents should evacuation be necessary.
11. Include all patients and families/caregivers in continuing education regarding the disaster plans, evacuation plans, locations, and procedures.
12. Meet with community emergency responders to review the facility's emergency and evacuation plans. Ensure they are aware of locations where special assistance may be required. Provide the service with current information rosters on special needs of residents. |

*Note:* COPD = chronic destructive pulmonary disease; EMS = emergency medical services

of terminal care for special populations, is a daunting scenario that would play out over several days, weeks, or months. Checklist 6.1 at the end of this chapter will help to prepare your special-population facility for a bioterrorism threat.

## MITIGATION ISSUES

An all-hazards approach for the domestic and international emergency management framework applies to the threat of terrorism. Better plans, more training, and greater awareness enhance capabilities to manage natural and technological disasters, day-to-day emergencies that may occur, as well as terrorist incidents. A course recently developed for the Federal Emergency Management Agency's Higher Education Project, "Social Vulnerability Approach to Disasters," is an excellent tool to help in understanding our vulnerability while suggesting strategies and actions (Enarson et al. 2003).

The course describes structural and nonstructural mitigation strategies. Both provide security measures that may be taken to prevent or reduce loss of life and property from terrorist events and acts of violence.

The distinction between structural mitigation techiques and nonstructural mitigation techniques is often made in terms of reducing potential loss (nonstructural) rather than in terms of reducing hazards (structural).

It is relatively easy to provide physical or *structural mitigation* measures to secure a facility or person by providing guards, iron bars, electrified fences, surveillance cameras, and other physical security measures. But these measures are often consuming and are most effective in controlled-access areas; they may be less effective in areas where large numbers of people have access (Enarson et al. 2003).

*Nonstructural mitigation* measures include training to reduce vulnerability and implementing measures into response plans to reduce the likelihood of losses and to speed recovery. These measures may be easier for public agencies to fund and implement than are physical or structural changes to a building (Enarson et al. 2003). For example, facility staff members who are keenly aware and trained to alert their supervisor or shift leader to anything out of the ordinary—a suspicious package or vehicle, someone in the building without a visitor's badge—enhance your facility's safety factor.

Staff skilled in the tools necessary to handle emergency and disaster situations are valuable assets and increase your chances of responding to and recovering from any disaster in a more expedient and timely manner. Training reduces your vulnerability while building capacity and confidence among your facility team players. If residents are competent and willing to help with disaster management and facility security, they can be trained as well. This type of cooperative effort and vested interest in the mutual safety and security of your facility is wise and cost effective. Its benefits are immeasurable in terms of your facility's greatest asset— human resources—and personal self-sufficiency and pride.

In keeping with all-hazards, or "dual purpose," emergency management planning, it is significant to note that terrorism is not the only form of violence common to institutions, workplaces, and all aspects of American society. The primary justification for preparedness is to ensure the readiness of your facility for the potential unknown that may be faced at any time. In addition to terrorism, Americans daily face threats of criminal (physical and sexual), domestic (spouse, family, or other intimates), and other common types of violence (Enarson et al. 2003).

These same threats of violence are present in healthcare facilities and patient care environments. The size and nature of the facility, number of residents and staff, physical location, population and demographics of the area, and many other factors may determine the amount of security measures implemented. Many mitigation actions that reduce vulnerability to all types of violence can be accomplished at little or no cost. Checklist 6.2 provides security guidelines for healthcare facility planning.

## DISASTER-RESPONSE ISSUES

Your facility disaster-response plan is vital to the safety and well-being of special-needs residents and staff during and following any emergency or disaster. (See Chapter 3 for more information on disaster planning for terrorism.) How you organize and assign responsibility for these functions depends on your staffing pattern, the number of residents under your care, their level of physical mobility, and the size of your facility.

Be sure to address and assign responsibility for each function in terms of a staffing schedule. Adapt procedures to fit your needs—daytime, evening, and nighttime coverage or by alternative shift schedules, according to your facility. When a disaster response is activated, each shift should plan at least six hours ahead so the next shift will be able to continue the work already underway and have the benefit of the information posted on the walls to provide a picture of the most current situation (e.g., number of residents injured, locations of damage, availability of drinking water, etc.). It is important to remember that the situation will be changing, and planning must be flexible to adjust to and reflect these changes.

### Command Center

The command center should be located in a secure area and have sufficient space to accommodate necessary staff. An alternate site should also be selected as a backup. Communications equipment should include telephones, fax machines, cellular phones, and two-way or ham radios, if available. A status board—white board, flip chart, bulletin board—must be available to track response actions, decisions made, staff schedules, status of facility/resident needs, and other disaster- and facility-specific information. Laptop computers and printers are helpful tools, as long as power is available to operate them. A conference room can easily be converted into a command center with the equipment and supplies prepositioned and stored until needed.

## Staffing Priorities

If adequate staff are available, disaster-response activities should be undertaken simultaneously, as appropriate depending on the incident, with staff preassigned their primary responsibility. You may wish to establish a preparedness committee of residents, if their physical condition allows, and include members of this committee in both preparedness and response planning for the facility. Involving interested and capable residents and assigning them responsibilities in planning efforts and organized response functions can greatly enhance your overall capability.

If adequate staff members are not available to undertake response functions simultaneously, those functions should be carried out in the following order:

1. *Direction and control.* Determine who is in charge of the emergency response at the time of the disaster. Evaluate the situation and activate response staff as needed. Activate the command center to coordinate emergency activities.
2. *Site security.* Check and turn off gas and/or electricity. Make sure the emergency generator is functioning and emergency power is on. Turn off the water supply if pipes are broken or leaking.
3. *Fire suppression.* Check for fires and suppress small fires. Notify the fire department.
4. *Search and rescue.* Quickly search the facility for people who may be trapped or injured. Assist if possible. Note and record the situation for other responders, including name and location of those trapped.
5. *First aid.* Administer first aid to injured persons. Note and record injury for assistance from other responders, including name and location.
6. *Damage assessment.* Inspect facility. Record damage and report to the command center. Request barricades, off-limits signs, and additional support from security or law enforcement as needed.

Community resources will be overwhelmed in a major disaster, and you could be on your own for a long time. Self-sufficiency is required. Sidebar 6.1 provides the lessons learned by a hospital with a large elderly population during activation of its emergency management plan in response to a hurricane.

**Sidebar 6.1. Considerations for Handling Special Populations During a Catastrophic Event**

Regardless of the size and type of facility, a catastrophic event that requires an evacuation of clients will challenge facility staff in many ways. By thinking of the worst-case scenarios, safeguards and redundancies can be included in your planning that will make the experience much easier for you, your staff, your clients, and the receiving facility. The following are provided for consideration as you plan to manage clients and provide necessary resources and supplies when evacuating from special-care environments.

*Planning should ensure*
- proper identification and monitoring of patients or clients once they are relocated;
- mechanisms for patient data transfer to continue regularly scheduled treatments and medications after relocation;
- sufficient number of caregivers to ensure proper care of relocated patients/clients at the receiving facility; and
- sufficient support of staff in stressful conditions with time off for proper rest and time with families. Remember: staff at both the receiving and sending facility may be victims of the disaster, too.

*Be aware and plan for lack of services and other problems, such as*
- water, sewer, gas, and electrical services;
- supplies such as linens, food, medicine, and water for days;
- creative planning for proper nutrition in lieu of hot meals for several days;
- delivery of meals and provision of services in multistory facilities if elevator not operational;
- assistance for patients who need help with activities of daily living;
- fluid loss in patients and staff due to lack of power, air conditioning and/or heating; and
- communication within the facility and to the outside if phones lines or cell connections are down.

*Source*: Created by A. Moore for use in this book.

### Needs of Pediatric Patients

HRSA reiterates that a host of special anatomical, physiological, and psychological considerations leave children more susceptible to the effects of disasters and acts of terrorism. Planning must consider, but not be limited to, special treatment areas for mass pediatric casualties in hospitals, triage areas, and health centers; development of pediatric response protocols, paying special attention to appropriate medications and dosages; pediatric-specific training and exercise procedures; and provision of psychological support to children and families, including methods to ensure reunification of children with family members, as needed (HRSA 2003).

## SHELTERING ISSUES

In some incidents, it may be wiser and safer to remain inside. To "shelter-in-place" means to make a shelter out of the place you are in. It is a way to make the building, or a portion of it, as safe as possible to protect your residents and your staff (CDC 2003). The decision to shelter-in-place or evacuate may be mandated or may be determined by the nature of the threat and the amount of time predicted before disaster strikes. See Chapter 5 for a detailed discussion of shelter-in-place issues.

### Public Shelters

It is unlikely that patients with special needs can be adequately cared for and monitored in hastily prepared shelters, randomly located and with untrained personnel, in the aftermath of a natural disaster. The best care for the frail elderly during such a crisis would be provided by a facility such as a long-term-care facility that already has in place the resources necessary for all aspects of proper care.

For the frail elderly to be sheltered successfully, their logistical, dietary, communications, staffing, and patient physical and psychiatric care needs must be addressed. None of these areas can be dismissed as trivial or unimportant. Whether concerned with the capacity to maintain climate control, nutritional requirements, adequate hydration, or communications in-house and outside, appropriate staffing is crucial in all areas when the safety and health status of the facility's residents are at stake.

This can be applied to other special populations when planning for any large-scale disaster situation.

To ensure adequate staffing to handle the regular population in addition to an influx of new patients, facilities must provide a host of services and benefits for employees as well as for families; everything from food and bedding to legal assistance should be available (Silverman et al. 1995). During crises that overwhelm resources, staffing will fall below desirable levels. To prepare for these contingencies, train all employees and equip them to aid in the basic care (such as feeding) of individuals who require assistance in their activities of daily living (Silverman et al. 1995).

## Shelter-in-Place

Sheltering-in-place may be the only choice when there is little or no time to warn or evacuate residents and staff. Furthermore, it is the only proper protective action in situations such as a hazardous-materials spill or a tornado warning. Sheltering-in-place can have many advantages, including the following:

- *Immediate protection.* Sheltering-in-place involves little time required after the warning, and it is less disruptive to residents.
- *Ideal life-support systems.* The facility has food, water, sanitation, medicines, bedding, clean air, communications, and medically prepared surroundings.
- *Less staff burden.* Sheltering-in-place requires considerably less emergency staff support than evacuation, without the transportation problems or need for additional security personnel.

## Evacuation

You never know when you may be required to evacuate your facility. Regardless of the reason, it is imperative to have a comprehensive evacuation plan to guide you during the crisis. All facilities are required to have a fire evacuation plan. Your evacuation plan can follow the same basic procedures.

Planning and carrying out an effective evacuation for special populations includes awareness of adaptive physical devices used by residents, necessary medications, patients' mental ability to grasp what is happening, and equipment availability for those residents who have special medical needs such as oxygen or intermittent positive-pressure machines. Checklist 6.3 can be adapted and revised to fit your facility and resident needs.

Threat-specific checklists should be developed for sheltering-in-place and evacuation. In any evacuation, keep the following in mind:

- If you have time, activate your mutual-aid agreements (MAAs) and inform your mutual-aid partner that you will be bringing patients to its facility (see Figure 6.1 for a sample MAA).
- Activate your MAA with your transport company or agency.
- Activate your family-notification roster (see Figure 6.2).
- Provide assistance to the impaired as needed.
- Be sure residents bring their personal preparedness kits (see Checklist 6.4 for a list of recommended items).

The professionals who ordered the evacuation may provide an estimate of how long you could be away from the facility, but you should always be prepared for a longer stay.

### MAAs for Evacuation

Establishing mutual-aid agreements, or informal arrangements when appropriate, for the staffing, equipment, and other resources you may need in a disaster will expedite facility response and recovery when disaster strikes.

If you are in a small community, an informal agreement to use a building as a temporary shelter for your facility residents may be sufficient. However, once moved, it is imperative that the residents are not disrupted unnecessarily or forced to encounter multiple moves. Transportation of residents during an evacuation may also be an informal arrangement with staff members, family or friends of residents, or other persons willing to help. It is a good idea to recruit more people and vehicles than you will actually need to ensure a sufficient number when the circumstances require evacuation of residents.

Formal agreements for the deployment or utilization of another jurisdiction's or political subdivision's staffing or equipment in an emergency or disaster situation, or MAAs, are shown in Figure 6.1.

FIGURE 6.1. SAMPLE MUTUAL-AID AGREEMENT*

This agreement made and entered into this day _____, by and between _____ and _____;

WHEREAS, it is desirable that the resources and facilities of _____ be made available to assist in the sheltering of _____ during a major emergency that impacts the _____ caused by an impending disaster and/or incident that causes _____-_____ to evacuate its facility;

WHEREAS, it is desirable the resources and facilities of _____ be made available to _____ during times of emergencies and disasters that affect _____ (community name);

WHEREAS, an agreement of this nature is authorized under the State of _____;

WHEREAS, it is necessary and desirable that an appropriate agreement be executed for the inter-change of such mutual aid;

NOW, THEREFORE, it is hereby agreed by and between each and all of the parties hereto as follows:

1. Each party to this agreement shall develop a plan known as a Mutual-Aid Operational Plan pro-viding for the effective mobilization and utilization of its resources to manage with agreed-to types of emergencies or disasters. Such a plan shall list the resources and services that can be made available by the parties to this agreement and shall indicate the method and manner by which such resources and services can be utilized by the other parties. Such plan shall also give the amount and manner of payment and/or compensation for the utilization of such resources and services.
2. Each party to this agreement agrees to furnish those resources and services to each other party hereto as necessary to assist in the prevention and combating of emergencies or disaster in accordance with the adopted Mutual-Aid Operational Plan.
3. It is hereby understood that unless an adopted Mutual-Aid Operational Plan dictates otherwise all services and/or resources provided under the terms of this Mutual-Aid Agreement are furnished and/or supplied voluntarily and at the discretion of the furnishing agency. The furnishing agency shall have the primary interest of protecting the welfare of its own resources and properties and does not assume any responsibilities or liabilities in not providing resources and/or services to other parties of this agreement.
4. It is hereby understood that the agreements entered into hereunder and the corresponding Mutual-Aid Operational Plan adopted shall not supplant preexisting mutual-aid agreements nor deny the right of any party hereto to negotiate supplemental mutual-aid agreements.
5. Mutual aid extended pursuant to this agreement shall be furnished in accordance with the provi-sions of (insert state statute), as well as other provisions of law.
6. This agreement shall be effective as to each party when the administrative body of each such party has approved this agreement. Said agreement shall be operative and binding until termi-nated by said participants.
7. This agreement shall remain in effect in perpetuity. However, any party to this agreement may withdraw from the same at any time by giving thirty (30) day written notice to the other party(s).

Dated this _____ day of _____, 20\_\_\_\_.

OWNERS:                      OWNERS:

_____       _____

* All mutual-aid agreements should be reviewed by legal counsel prior to signing.

*Source*: Anderson, B., J. Dilling, P. Mann, and A. Moore. 1996. *Assisted Living Facility and Model Plan*. Training document. Silverdale, WA: Emergency Training & Consulting, International. Used with permission.

Figure 6.2. Family-Notification Template

| Resident's Name* | Family Member | Address | Phone Number In/Out of State |
|---|---|---|---|
|  |  |  |  |
|  |  |  |  |
|  |  |  |  |
|  |  |  |  |

\* List residents in alphabetical order.

To be effective, MAAs should

- be in writing,
- be reviewed by legal counsel,
- be signed by responsible parties from all agencies involved,
- define liability, and
- detail the cost involved.

### Other Contractual Agreements

Contracts and agreements can be used to ensure the provision of re-sources or services that go beyond immediate disaster-relief provisions. Contracted agreements should include the costs, estimated time to provide the service, and duration of the service contract. Examples of contracted services include emergency generators, cleanup and debris removal, food and water services, pharmaceutical supplies, medical and surgical supplies, and oxygen and special gases.

A projection of potential disaster resources should include a roster of specific resource providers or vendors, with current telephone numbers and multiple methods of emergency communication with suppliers. To expedite requests, the roster should also include the business name; location; contact name and title; phone, fax, and cell or beeper numbers; order number or item number of supplies most likely to be requested; and other pertinent information.

## TRAINING ISSUES

The purpose of an active training program designed around your disaster plan is to ensure every staff person and your resident population will react automatically and appropriately in an emergency or disaster situation. The staff must be familiar with the plan, understand their responsibilities within it, and be comfortable in carrying them out.

The best way to ensure staff and resident familiarity with the plan is to include them in its development. During a disaster, critical staff may become victims themselves. Overall understanding and cross-training is a good insurance policy against possible confusion and chaos. Turnover in staff also creates an ongoing need to constantly train staff and residents in disaster planning. Chapter 3 discusses staff training in detail and provides suggested training topics that could be adapted to fit your facility needs and staff.

One of the best ways to fine-tune staff training is through the use of in-house emergency drills and exercises and through participation in all community disaster drills and exercises. Emergency drills and exercises are an integral part of the preparedness phase of your crisis management program. They provide a mechanism to reveal planning strengths and weaknesses; identify resource shortfalls; improve internal and external coordination, collaboration, and communication; and clarify the roles and responsibilities of your staff during an emergency or disaster. They also provide an excellent opportunity to develop or improve your relationship with your local emergency organizations. Chapter 3 presents a full discussion of exercises.

## INCIDENT-MANAGEMENT ISSUES

Establishing who is responsible for direction and control of the facility provides a basis for decision making in an emergency. The facility owner or administrator has the responsibility for directing and controlling emergency response or delegating these responsibilities to the appropriate staff. Your plan must reflect procedures that ensure timely activation and staffing of the facility for emergency functions.

The Incident Command System (ICS) is a widely accepted method for managing emergencies and is used by emergency responders throughout the United States. The system organizes a response to meet the demands of large incidents and disasters in a rapid and efficient manner by dividing labor and responsibilities. (See Chapter 7 for more information on ICS.)

ICS is flexible and allows for the use of people present at the time of an incident. For planning and training purposes, it is preferable to assign people to perform each function so they develop an understanding of what will be required in responding to an actual emergency situation. Within your facility, each employee assigned as either a section chief or support person within ICS sections should be resourceful and calm during emergencies or under duress, well organized, a "team" player, and free of disabilities that might interfere with his or her functioning. Designate backup people for each assigned person in case injuries or absence prevent the assigned persons from assuming their responsibilities. Staff with the best and most current skills, regardless of rank, should perform medical care.

## RECOVERY ISSUES

Chapter 3 describes issues related to recovery and resumption of healthcare services in detail. In addition, there are some special circumstances that facilities with special populations must plan for. Your facility recovery plan should address, at a minimum, the considerations shown in the following list:

- Facility operation
- Facility structure
- Residents and employees (numbers and types)
- Special needs of facility residents
- Role of residents' families
- Notification and warning systems for all-hazards disasters
- Notification of evacuation and options
- Tracking of residents after the disaster
- Options for alternate facility location
- Maintenance of facility/resident records (with backup offsite)
- Actions for restoration and business continuity

Planning for all hazards, including the threat of terrorism, in environments with special populations requires sensitivity and extra care to provide the level of preparedness that special-population residents deserve and require and that their families expect. Diligence in all aspects of the planning process demonstrates a high level of concern for the facility residents and staff. Planning is a team effort. Understanding why planning for all types of disasters and emergencies is important to safeguard lives and property, and that every effort will be made to resume business as soon as possible after a disaster, will make everyone feel that they are part of the team.

## REFERENCES

Anderson, B., J. Dilling, P. Mann, and A. Moore. 1996. *Assisted Living Facility and Model Plan*. Training document. Silverdale, WA: Emergency Training & Consulting, International.

Centers for Disease Control and Prevention (CDC). 2003. "Chemical Agents: Facts About Sheltering in Place." [Online information; retrieved 10/13/03.] http://www.bt.cdc.gov/planning/shelteringfacts.asp.

Enarson, E., C. Childers, B. Morrow, D. Thomas, and B. Wisner. 2003. "Social Vulnerability Approach to Disasters." Course developed for the Federal Emergency Management Agency (FEMA) EMI Higher Education Project. Washington, DC: FEMA.

Health Resources and Services Administration (HRSA). 2003. "National Bioterrorism Hospital Preparedness Program." [Online information; retrieved 8/03.] http://www.hrsa.gov/bioterrorism/bhppguidance.htm.

# Checklists

## CHECKLIST 6.1. BIOTERRORISM PREPAREDNESS IN A SPECIAL-POPULATION FACILITY

❏ Learn facts about anthrax, botulism, pneumonic plague, and small-pox.

❏ Assess preparedness and response capabilities, internally and com-munitywide.

❏ Stay abreast of literature and publications for similar special-popu-lation facilities.

❏ Prepare for personal response and staff protection.

❏ Build relationships with the county emergency manager and others in the local emergency management agency and emergency med-ical services to ensure your inclusion in area planning, and coordi-nate planning with all county and local providers.

❏ Evaluate security needs with backup support identified.

❏ Assess employee/personnel identification program to ensure only authorized individuals are in your facility.

❏ Train staff to be aware of suspicious activity and what to do if it is observed.

❏ Review your disaster plan, and revise it accordingly.

❏ Drill or exercise the newly revised plan frequently.

❏ Be alert for disease or illness patterns that may indicate contact with biological or chemical agents; notify appropriate officials immedi-ately if unusual clusters of illness are found.

❏ If faced with a potential terrorist threat or event, remain calm, exer-cise common sense, and use the resources available within your local government to assist you.

*Source*: Anderson, B., J. Dilling, P. Mann, and A. Moore. 1996. *Assisted Living Facility and Model Plan*. Silverdale, WA: Emergency Training & Consulting, International. Used with permission.

## CHECKLIST 6.2. SECURITY MEASURES BASIC TO ALL DISASTER PLANNING

❏ Involve all staff in upgraded planning and security measures; es-tablish a plan-development committee if you do not have one.

- ❏ Require staff badges with photo ID or other clear identification tag at all times.
- ❏ Increase the number of security personnel, and vary their routines and positioning.
- ❏ Evaluate entrances/exits to control access and visibility and to manage the traffic flow within your facility.
- ❏ If possible, secure all entry doors but one (your main entrance, clearly designated) to visitors or anyone coming in from the outside. Exits should be open to all in case of an emergency.
- ❏ Require sign-in for visitors and know the purpose of the visit. Consider having all visitors escorted when outside the lobby or reception areas.
- ❏ Arrange furnishings in reception area to control access to inner offices and residents' hallways, rooms, and dining and social-gathering areas.
- ❏ Designate areas and procedures for chemical or hazardous-materials storage.
- ❏ Evaluate facility heating, ventilation, and air conditioning system and components with respect to vulnerability to the introduction of dangerous airborne agents.
- ❏ Train facility staff to respond to bomb threats, and develop a bomb-threat reporting form.
- ❏ Encourage staff to be alert and to report anything perceived as a threat or of a suspicious nature.
- ❏ Use the "buddy" system for staff when investigating or responding to suspicious activities or events. Provide checklists to expedite this function.
- ❏ Revisit/revise facility plans and procedures for all hazards, including terrorism.
- ❏ Rehearse/exercise your plans and remedy shortfalls in planning, procedures, and training.
- ❏ Work with local emergency management and emergency services providers, and participate in joint exercises.
- ❏ Consider parking lots and facility grounds for enhanced security measures; that is, cut back or remove overgrown shrubbery, increase lighting, identify or remove suspicious vehicles, provide random security patrols by facility guards or law enforcement.
- ❏ Validate companies, orders, and dates/times for delivery of goods and services to the facility.
- ❏ Make preparedness, safety, and security a team effort.

## CHECKLIST 6.3. EVACUATION OF SPECIAL POPULATIONS

❏ If going to a predetermined private shelter (of similar type to your facility), notify the shelter of your evacuation plans and projected time and mode of arrival.

❏ Notify facility management if they are not on duty.

❏ Notify transport company of the need to evacuate.

❏ Notify the emergency management agency (EMA) and local law enforcement of the need to evacuate and plans to be implemented. Request special assistance if needed. Do not expect to receive outside assistance if your facility has not been involved in area planning and the local EMA is not aware of the need for assistance or special resources that may be requested.

❏ Review the evacuation route with drivers.

❏ Activate family-notification roster.

❏ Notify residents and staff of the need to evacuate and the plans to be followed.

❏ Request residents to bring their emergency supply kits. If kits are not available, remind residents to bring a change of clothes, medication, and any special supplies needed.

❏ Prepare two copies of the current facility resident list: one for the commander of evacuation activities and one for the receiving facility.

❏ Gather all resident medications and documentation of care if those items are under facility control.

❏ Pets should be transported with their owners when possible. If pets are not allowed by the receiving facility, you must activate your plan for an alternative care site and staff to ensure the pets' safety and well-being while out of the original facility.

❏ Lock the facility. You may wish to make sure the police or fire chief has a key for emergency access.

❏ Before returning to the facility, assign staff members to assess it for damage.

## CHECKLIST 6.4. ITEMS IN A 72-HOUR PERSONAL SUPPY KIT*

❏ Medication

❏ Personal hygiene needs (toothpaste, toothbrush, comb, soap, protective undergarments, etc.)

❏ Clothing (one or two changes)
❏ Blanket (take pillow when you evacuate)
❏ Pet reminder (pets should go with owners when possible)
❏ Optional: family picture or other comfort item

* These supply kits should be kept in residents' rooms to assist in providing 72 hours of personal care.

# PART III

*Integrating Healthcare and Emergency Management*

### CHAPTER SEVEN

# Understanding the Government's Role in Emergency Management

Donna F. Barbisch and Connie J. Boatright

ealthcare systems face significant challenges as roles evolve in emergency management. Public health leaders are stepping into new roles as incident managers, and nongovernmental healthcare organizations are developing processes to integrate into publicly managed and funded emergency management systems. Emergency management now has application across the spectrum of healthcare activities.

How does America's healthcare system integrate into the national emergency management process? This chapter reviews the primary initiatives that drive our emergency management system, federal programs that support the process, and existing prehospital emergency medical services (EMS). It also describes how to engage healthcare systems at the state and local level.

Several initiatives were underway to protect U.S. citizens from terrorism long before 9/11. The legislation and resulting programs, discussed

---

The views expressed in this chapter are those of the authors and do not necessarily represent the views of the Department of Veterans Affairs or of the Government of the United States.

Donna F. Barbisch, D.H.A., M.P.H., CRNA, is chief executive officer of Global Deterrence Alternatives in Washington, DC, and a major general in the United States Army Reserve. Connie J. Boatright, M.S.N., R.N., is director of education and research and deputy director of the Emergency Management Strategic Healthcare Group in the Department of Veterans Affairs, Washington, DC, and a colonel in the United States Army Reserve.

in Chapter 12 and highlighted in Sidebar 7.1, focused on preparing personnel, upgrading facilities, and enhancing existing capability. Many of the initiatives, including the Metropolitan Medical Response System (MMRS) and the Strategic National Stockpile (SNS; formerly the National Pharmaceutical Stockpile), directly influence the overall readiness of healthcare facilities.

## BIOTERRORISM PREPAREDNESS FUNDING

Two primary funding efforts by the federal government have been instituted since 9/11 that have significantly shifted the focus of planning and preparedness in healthcare facilities to ensure improved response to bioterrorism or other disease-based mass-casualty events. These programs are described below.

### National Bioterrorism Hospital-Preparedness Program

The Department of Health and Human Services (DHHS) Health Resources and Services Administration (HRSA) began in early 2002 to provide monies for public health departments to develop programs to upgrade the preparedness of the nation's hospitals and for collaborating entities to respond to bioterrorism and deal with nonterrorist epidemics of rare diseases. The program focuses on identifying and implementing bioterrorism preparedness plans and protocols for hospitals and other participating healthcare entities (HRSA 2003). Grant awards were designed for the development and implementation of regional plans to improve the capacity of hospitals and their emergency departments, outpatient centers, EMS systems, and other collaborating healthcare entities to respond to incidents requiring mass immunization, treatment, isolation, and quarantine in the aftermath of bioterrorism or other outbreaks of infectious disease.

### CDC Bioterrorism Cooperative Agreement

The Centers for Disease Control and Prevention (CDC) Bioterrorism Cooperative Agreement is a grant program designed to upgrade state and

**Sidebar 7.1. Federal Guidelines and Legislation for Disaster Relief**

*Stafford Act*. The 1993 Robert T. Stafford Disaster Relief and Emergency Assistance Act, as amended (Public Law 93-288), provides federal assistance to states to manage the consequences of domestic disasters by expediting the rendering of aid, assistance, and emergency services and the reconstruction and rehabilitation of devastated areas.

*Weapons of Mass Destruction (WMD) Act of 1996*. Title XIV of the Defense Against Weapons of Mass Destruction (Public Law 104-201), which became known as the WMD Act of 1996, provided funding for equipment and training for local first responders for the effective management of incidents involving WMD. The Department of Defense was charged with initiating the Domestic Preparedness Program in the nation's 120 largest cities for training first responders, including healthcare facility personnel.

*Bioterrorism Act.* The Public Health Security and Bioterrorism Preparedness and Response Act of 2002, commonly called the Bioterrorism Act (Public Law 107-108), was designed to improve the ability of the United States to prevent, prepare for, and respond to bioterrorism and other public health emergencies. This law established the Office of Public Health Preparedness under the Department of Health and Human Services.

*Homeland Security Act of 2002*. The Department of Homeland Security (DHS) was created under the Homeland Security Act (Public Law 107-296). Many of the functions of different federal agencies were consolidated under a single department. The bill
- transferred the National Pharmaceutical Stockpile, later renamed the Strategic National Stockpile, to DHS, requiring DHS to consult with the Centers for Disease Control and Prevention (CDC) on administration of the program;
- transferred the Office of Emergency Response, which oversees the National Disaster Medical System, from the Department of Health and Human Services to DHS; and
- required CDC to establish the Bioterrorism Preparedness and Response Division.

*Homeland Security Presidential Directives (HSPDs)*. Presidential directives designed to promulgate presidential decisions on homeland security matters are designated Homeland Security Presidential Directives.
- HSPD-5: Management of Domestic Incidents
- HSPD-6: Integration and Use of Screening Information
- HSPD-7: Critical Infrastructure Identification, Prioritization, and Protection
- HSPD-8: National Preparedness

local public health jurisdictions' preparedness for and response to bioterrorism, other outbreaks of infectious disease, and other public health threats and emergencies (CDC 2003). DHHS requires each state that receives funds to develop a statewide plan identifying how it will respond to a bioterrorism event and other outbreaks of infectious disease and also how it will strengthen core public health capacities in all relevant areas. The program initially identified the following six focus areas for improvement:

1. Planning and readiness
2. Surveillance and epidemiology
3. Biological-laboratory capacity
4. Communications and information technology
5. Health information dissemination
6. Education and training

CDC funding, through the state public health departments to the local community, is projected to continue for a number of years to ensure continuity of programs in public health. The regional or local coordinator is responsible for working with healthcare organizations to improve preparedness and response capability in each of the focus areas described in Sidebar 7.2.

## OVERVIEW OF EMERGENCY MANAGEMENT SYSTEMS

The public health community is charged with organizing the preparedness and response of the health and medical services in the United States. After years of decay, public health is evolving in its leadership role for domestic disaster organizational response. For healthcare executives to engage in domestic preparedness, it is essential to develop solid relationships with local and regional public health officials, local and area emergency management agencies (EMAs), and local responder organizations.

Before establishing the Department of Homeland Security (DHS), the approach to disaster management for terrorist events was divided into two discrete functions: crisis management and consequence management. *Crisis management* is a security/law enforcement function focused on identifying the perpetrators of an event, collecting and protecting evidence and the chain of custody, and ensuring justice for those involved. At the federal level, crisis management currently falls under the jurisdiction of the Federal Bureau of Investigation. *Consequence management* refers to addressing the consequences of a disaster and is currently under the jurisdiction of the Federal Emergency Management Agency (FEMA). Under DHS, federal guidelines will merge the elements of crisis and consequence management into a unified command structure.

The Department of Homeland Security, with embedded elements of DHHS, provides a federal structure and system for coordination and oversight of resources that are essential for assisting areas affected by disaster. FEMA's ten geographical regions work closely with state and local EMAs, ensuring consistency of services to all areas and citizens.

At the state level, EMAs assume a multitude of different organizational structures. The emergency management community consists of professional emergency managers, emergency operations center personnel, 911 telecommunicators, and first responders—that is, fire departments, emergency medical services, medical transport, and law enforcement. When activated for disasters, the EMA expands to coordinate all primary agencies with designated roles in response to a declared disaster. These may vary in number and are dependent on the size and extent of the disaster. However, once a governor has declared a state of emergency, the EMA becomes the coordinating hub for activation of the local and/or state emergency operations plan. Mirroring the Federal Response Plan, representatives from each of the emergency support functions coordinate services from the EMA.

Emergency management uses an "all hazards" framework based on the premise that most incidents will draw on similar resources and will apply a similar structure in managing the response to an incident, as opposed to identifying a different structural response for different types of emergencies. In developing an all-hazards plan, unique aspects of incidents are addressed in annexes to existing plans rather than in a separate plan produced for each event.

## Incident Command System

The Incident Command System (ICS) provides a total-systems approach for response in emergency situations that require assistance above that available from a one-organization response. ICS provides an on-scene structure of management-level positions, dividing functions into four primary areas: planning, operations, logistics, and finance (Figure 7.1). The functional ICS components given in the list that follows provide the keys

FIGURE 7.1. THE INCIDENT COMMAND SYSTEM

**Command**
- Sets objectives and priorities
- Has overall responsibility at the incident or event

| Planning | Operations | Logistics | Finance |
|---|---|---|---|
| • Develops the action plan to accomplish the objectives<br>• Collects and evaluates information<br>• Maintains resource status | • Conducts tactical operations to carry out the plan<br>• Develops the tactical objectives<br>• Organizes and directs all resources | • Provides support to meet incident needs<br>• Provides resources and all other services needed to support the incident | • Monitors costs related to incident<br>• Provides accounting<br>• Records procurement time<br>• Provides cost analyses |

to effectively planning the management of any incident:

- Common terminology
- Integrated communications
- Modular organization
- Unified command structure
- Manageable span of control
- Consolidated action plans
- Comprehensive resource management

Within ICS, roles are defined and the chain of command is established, which incorporates four sections—planning, operations, logistics, and finance—under the overall leadership of an incident commander. Each of the four sections operates under its own section chief and has its own tasks or job descriptions. These tasks identify priorities that arise during a disaster event and provide for a uniformly structured response and recovery efforts. The four section chiefs are described below.

1. The *plans chief* provides current information on the facility situation and projects short- and long-term needs for recovery and return to normal operation.
2. The *operations chief* directs the execution of initial response functions and the reporting of results and situation status to the incident commander and other section chiefs.

3. The *logistics chief* coordinates the use of existing resources and the procurement of needed resources to ensure the health and safety of residents, staff, and volunteers.
4. The *finance chief* is responsible for overseeing the processing and documentation of all costs associated with the disaster and response efforts.

Appendix D at the end of this book provides a template for ICS section chief assignments as well as job action sheets for each position.

The Hospital Emergency Incident Command System (HEICS), described below, is one example of how ICS can be applied to healthcare facilities. Where community responder agencies are organized based on ICS, hospitals benefit from this unique system designed specifically to meet the needs of healthcare institutions.

## Hospital Emergency Incident Command System

The first initiative to organize healthcare facilities along the lines of ICS was HEICS, designed by the San Mateo County Health Services Agency and the California Emergency Medical Services Authority in 1992 (San Mateo County 1998). Like ICS, HEICS organizes the functional components of hospital management and operations in the four major areas of planning, operations, logistics, and finance. HEICS uses a defined-management structure and responsibilities to unify hospitals with other emergency responders. The system also provides for improved documentation for accountability and cost recovery, prioritized response checklists, and cost-effective emergency planning within healthcare organizations. Figure 7.2 presents the organizational schematic for the HEICS system, and Sidebar 7.3 describes HEICS in greater detail.

## Medical and Health Incident Management System

The Medical and Health Incident Management System (MaHIM), developed in 2002, connects multiple healthcare systems in disasters (Barbera and Macintyre 2002). As incidents increase in magnitude, the number of organizations and agencies that respond increases and relationships become more complex. The system uses the principles of public health

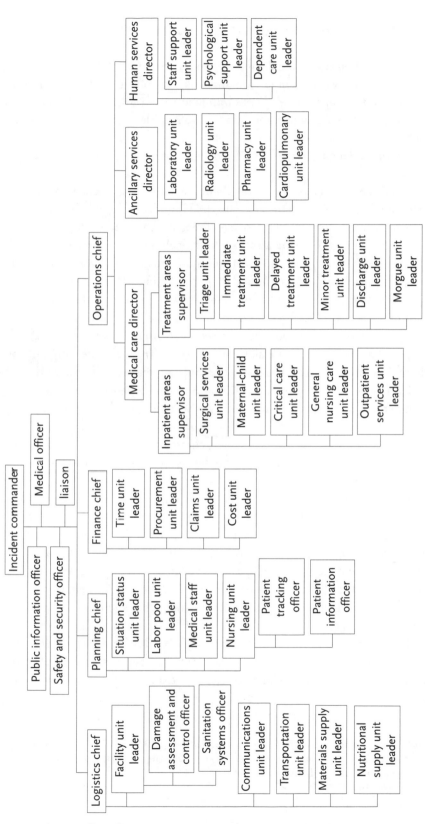

**Sidebar 7.3. The Hospital Emergency Incident Command System**

"The Hospital Emergency Incident Command System (HEICS) is a nationally recognized emergency management tool that has been utilized in California for over 10 years. Modeled after the Incident Command System (ICS) used by public emergency services agencies and responders, HEICS employs a logical management structure, defined responsibilities and job action sheets, clear reporting channels, and a common language to help unify hospitals with emergency responders in the community.

"HEICS is a tool that is incorporated into the emergency management plan, providing job actions that parallel day-to-day job functions and a flexible structure that expands and contracts to the size and magnitude of the incident. The system assists in patient tracking and locating (response) and in tracking incident costs and expenses (recovery). HEICS meets the standards for emergency preparedness planning set by the Joint Commission on Accreditation of Healthcare Organizations (JCAHO). The JCAHO emergency preparedness standard, Environment of Care (EC) 1.4, mandates that hospitals identify specific procedures to mitigate, prepare for, respond to, and recover from the priority emergencies (EC 1.4 c.), and define a common ("all-hazards") command structure within the organization for responding to and recovering from emergencies that links with the command structure in the community (EC 1.4 e.). The emergency plan must define alternate roles and responsibilities of personnel during emergencies, including who they report to within the organization's command structure, and, when activated, within the command structure of the local community. HEICS provides these important elements and is a tool that can be incorporated into the facility's emergency management plan.

"Implementing HEICS into the hospital is an ongoing process reinforced by education, training and exercising and those are the primary costs to the hospital. The cost of HEICS equipment (HEICS vests at approximately $1000/set), supplies (storage bins, office supplies, white boards/status boards at less than $500) and forms for documentation (patient tracking charts at $400 per set of 200 charts) are relatively inexpensive and easily stored. The benefits of HEICS become evident when training and exercises are conducted and the system is integrated into all aspects of facility emergency management.

"More information about HEICS can be found on the California Emergency Medical Services Authority website at www.emsa.ca.gov/dms2/heics3.htm. The complete HEICS manual can be downloaded and includes training and education materials, and sample policies and procedures. An introductory CD outlining HEICS is available free of charge by emailing HEICS@emsa.ca.gov."

*Source*: California Emergency Medical Services Authority. 1998. *HEICS III: Hospital Emergency Incident Command System Update Project.* [Online report; retrieved 1/7/04.] http://www.emsa.ca.gov/Dms2/heics3.htm.

incident management and is one of the first efforts to define operational roles in that framework.

**Comprehensive Emergency Management**

Comprehensive emergency management (CEM) addresses disasters and other catastrophic events by arranging them across the four phases of mitigation, preparedness, response, and recovery. The process is circuitous, with activities often overlapping across phases. The process typically begins with identifying hazards and threats and taking action to identify new threats and reduce risks from future events (mitigation). The process moves to managing resources, planning, training, and conducting exercises (preparedness); establishing priorities and directing, controlling, and coordinating activity (response); and taking action to return to a state of pre-event normalcy (recovery). Through the methodical process of implementing CEM, a healthcare facility CEO can identify and assign existing staff roles and responsibilities to the four phases.

## EMERGENCY MANAGEMENT SYSTEM: HOW IT WORKS

The primary objectives of an emergency management system are to

- improve the outcome of disasters,
- save lives,
- reduce injuries, and
- return a chaotic and compromised environment to normalcy.

Emergency management principles reinforce the premise that all disasters are local; thus, local needs drive national planning initiatives. As a disaster unfolds and the capacity of the local healthcare system is overwhelmed, response organizations provide support to the community. When the local capability is committed or exhausted, the local government requests support from the state government through the governor. The state EMA can provide support through its own resources and those available under mutual-aid agreements with other states. If state assets are overwhelmed or committed, the state may request support from the federal government through a direct request of the governor to the president.

## FIGURE 7.3. PROCESS FOR REQUESTS FOR ASSISTANCE IN DISASTER

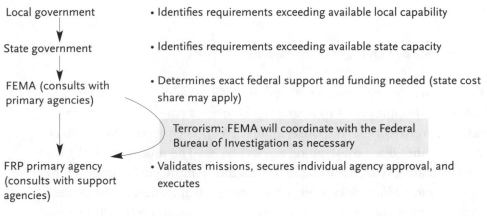

Local government • Identifies requirements exceeding available local capability

State government • Identifies requirements exceeding available state capacity

FEMA (consults with primary agencies) • Determines exact federal support and funding needed (state cost share may apply)

Terrorism: FEMA will coordinate with the Federal Bureau of Investigation as necessary

FRP primary agency (consults with support agencies) • Validates missions, secures individual agency approval, and executes

*Note*: FEMA = Federal Emergency Management Agency; FRP = Federal Response Plan

DHS has the responsibility of providing support to state and local governments and for coordinating the national response. Figure 7.3 illustrates the flow for requests for assistance from the local to the federal level.

At every level, legal guidelines identify the fiduciary responsibility of municipalities. Proclamation of a state or federal disaster affects the reimbursement of services at all levels. A formal declaration releases federal funds to ameliorate the loss due to the disaster. Without a federal declaration, healthcare facilities have only traditional billing and reimbursement guidelines to recover financial losses, which generally fall short of complete restitution. Documentation is crucial in identifying and proving resource allocation and use in disaster response; submitting the required paperwork is known to maximize reimbursement for disaster-response efforts. It is imperative that healthcare administrators proactively and preemptively communicate with their local EMA director to make sure appropriate processes are in place.

### Coordinating Federal Assistance to State and Local Resources

To define roles and determine relationships among agencies, 26 federal agencies and the American Red Cross developed an operational plan to coordinate federal assistance to supplement state and local efforts and capabilities when authorized by the president. The resulting Federal Response Plan (FRP) provides a basis for all federal assistance to states in response to managing the consequences of domestic disasters. FEMA is currently involved in consolidating all existing federal government emergency response plans into a single, coordinated National Response Plan (NRP), which will follow the principles of the FRP.

*FEMA and the Current Federal Response Plan*

The FRP assigns responsibility for 12 categories of support to different federal agencies (illustrated in Figure 7.4), with FEMA acting as the lead federal agency. Although the original plan focused on natural disasters, a terrorism annex was added to the FRP in 1998 to manage the complex issues surrounding terrorism and the use of weapons of mass destruction (FEMA 1992).

The most applicable and relevant of the 12 federal support categories to healthcare executives is Emergency Support Function (ESF) #8, Health and Human Services. The lead agency for ESF #8 is the DHHS Public Health Service, which utilizes National Disaster Medical System (NDMS) assets as required for FRP support. Figure 7.4 highlights ESF #8 and the role for health and medical services, indicating the other tasks in which DHHS has a secondary or support role in the federal response.

Although no direct federal assistance is authorized prior to a presidential disaster declaration, FEMA can authorize limited predeclaration assistance in situations such as imminent hurricane or flood damage to provide critical supplies and equipment such as food, water, generators, or emergency medical teams.

*VA Medical Centers: Federal Healthcare in Local Communities*

Although the Department of Veterans Affairs' (VA) primary mission is to care for veterans, it is also the largest healthcare system in the country and is the "federal presence" in virtually every local community in the country. Like all healthcare facilities, the VA must ensure that its facilities are sufficiently shielded to protect staff and patients and to maintain the ability to serve veterans. The VA also provides training to clinical and nonclinical personnel focused on emergency management.

At the federal level, the VA is a primary support agency. Through activation of the FRP or in other homeland security initiatives, VA medical

FIGURE 7.4. ROLE OF DHHS IN THE FEDERAL RESPONSE PLAN

**The Federal Response Plan:
An Interagency Template**

| # | 1 | 2 | 3 |
|---|---|---|---|
| Emergency Support Function | Transportation | Communications | Public Works and Engineering |
| Lead Federal Agency | DOT | NCS | DOD, Corp of Engineers |
| Supporting Agencies | USDA, DOD, DOE, DOS, GSA, ICC, TVA, USPS | USDA, DOC, DOD, DOI, DOT, FCC, FEMA, GSA | USDA, DOC, DOE, DHHS, DOI, DOL, DOT, DVA, EPA, GSA, TVA |

| # | 7 | 8 | 9 |
|---|---|---|---|
| Function | Resource Support | Health and Human Services | Urban Search and Rescue |
| Responsible Agency | GSA | DHHS: Public Health Service | FEMA |
| Supporting Agencies | USDA, DOC, DOD, DOE, DHHS, DOL, DOT, DVA, FEMA, NCS, OPM | USDA, DOD, DOJ, DOT, DVA,, AID, ARC, EPA, FEMA, GSA, NCS, USPS | USDA, DOD, DHHS, DOL, DOT, AID, EPA, GSA |

| | | | |
|---|---|---|---|
| AID | Agency for International Development | DOI | Department of the Interior |
| | | DOJ | Department of Justice |
| ARC | American Red Cross | DOL | Department of Labor |
| DHHS | Department of Health and | DOS | Department of State |
| | Human Services | DOT | Department of Transportation |
| DHUD | Department of Housing and | DVA | Department of Veterans Affairs |
| | Urban Development | EPA | Environmental Protection |
| DOC | Department of Commerce | | Agency |
| DOD | Department of Defense | FCC | Federal Communications |
| DOE | Department of Energy | | Commission |

centers are national assets that train to maintain their own operations as well as to support other federal departments or agencies as needed. Chapter 10 provides greater detail on the integration of military medical resources.

Among the variety of programs and tools developed by the agency is the VA's *Emergency Management Program Guidebook* (available at http://www.va.gov/emshg/apps/emp/emp.htm). Developed for use by the VA's 163 medical centers, the guidebook contains a checklist of nine steps to establish a successful emergency management plan, standard operating procedures, and checklists and templates that can assist in building and

FIGURE 7.4. (continued)

**The Federal Response Plan:
An Interagency Template**

| 4 | 5 | 6 |
|---|---|---|
| **Firefighting** | **Information and Planning** | **Mass Care** |
| USDA: Forest Service | FEMA | ARC |
| DOC, DOD, DOI, EPA, FEMA | USDA, DOC, DOD, DOE, DHHS, DOI, DOJ, DOT, TREAS, ARC, EPA, GSA, NASA, NCS, NRC, SBA | USDA, DOC, DOD, DHHS, DHUD, DOT, DVA, FEMA, GSA, USPS |
| **10** | **11** | **12** |
| **Hazardous Material** | **Food** | **Energy** |
| EPA | USDA: Food and Nutrition Service | DOE |
| USDA, DOC, DOD, DOE, DHHS, DOI, DOJ, DOL, DOS, DOT, FEMA, GSA, NRC | DOD, DHHS, DOT, ARC, EPA, FEMA | USDA, DOD, DOS, DOT, GSA, NCS, NRC, TVA |

| | | | | |
|---|---|---|---|---|
| FEMA | Federal Emergency Management Agency | OPM | Office of Personnel Management |
| GSA | General Services Administration | SBA | Small Business Administration |
| ICC | Interstate Commerce Commission | | |
| NASA | National Aeronautics and Space Administration | TREAS | Department of Treasury |
| | | TVA | Tennessee Valley Authority |
| NCS | National Communications System | USDA | US Department of Agriculture |
| NRC | Nuclear Regulatory Commission | USPS | US Postal Service |

*Note:* DHS/FEMA is the lead federal agency.

evaluating the emergency management program. The VA's nine-step plan is presented below (VHA EMSHG 2002):

1. Designate an emergency management committee (EMC), identify operating roles, and assign responsibilities.
2. Conduct a hazards vulnerability analysis (HVA), and complete templates.
3. Review the HVA, and determine priorities for developing standard operating procedures.

4. Implement mitigation and preparedness strategies.
5. Report results to the EMC.
6. Develop, publish, and distribute the emergency operations plan (EOP).
7. Train staff in the EOP.
8. Test and evaluate the EOP in response to a drill or actual event.
9. Conduct an annual review of effectiveness of the emergency management program.

## Implementing a Federal Response

The federal government supports a number of systems to aid state and local governments in an effective response. Emergency medical teams may be activated from NDMS, a top-down federal support structure, or MMRS, a bottom-up capability initiated by DHHS and supported by local public health. These medical support programs can be used as elements of the larger national response during complex emergencies that extend beyond medical needs, or they can be used independently in the event of an emergency confined within the medical community. In addition to NDMS, the top-down approach also includes Federal Coordinating Centers (FCCs) and SNS. Each approach is described in the following sections.

### National Disaster Medical System

A nationwide medical response system, NDMS is a section within the U.S. Department of Homeland Security, Federal Emergency Management Agency, Response Division, Operations Branch. It is responsible for managing and coordinating the federal medical response to regional emergencies and federally declared disasters. NDMS serves as the lead federal agency for medical response under the National Response Plan.

NDMS was established in 1984 by President Reagan and is a partnership between DHHS Public Health Service, VA, the Department of Defense (DoD), FEMA, and private hospitals (Brandt et al. 1985). Not until 2002 was NDMS stated in public law as part of the Public Health Security and Bioterrorism Preparedness and Response Act of 2002 (see Sidebar 7.1).

The mission of NDMS is to provide field medical response, patient transport, and definitive care. Some facts about NDMS are shown in Table 7.1. Although the original focus of NDMS was to evacuate stable patients

TABLE 7.1. FACTS ABOUT THE NATIONAL DISASTER MEDICAL SYSTEM

- More than 7,000 participating health professionals
- 24,000 to 52,000 hospital beds available within 24 hours
- 95,000 hospital beds available within 30 days
- Governance structure
  - Assistant Secretary for Health (Domestic Emergencies)
  - Assistant Secretary of Defense for Health Affairs (Military Contingency)
- Participating agencies
  - DHS provides primary and specialized care (including four rapid-response, WMD-trained) teams
  - DoD provides victim transportation
  - DoD and VA provide access to private-sector hospital care remote from the disaster site

*Note:* DoD = Department of Defense; DHS = Department of Homeland Security; VA = Department of Veterans Affairs; WMD = weapons of mass destruction

*Source:* VHA Emergency Management Strategic Healthcare Group (EMSHG). 2002. *Emergency Management Program Guidebook.* Section 3. [Online information; retrieved 10/03.] http://www.appc1.va.gov/emshg/apps/emp/emp.htm.

who were occupying hospital beds in a disaster area to provide definitive care for disaster victims, a field medical response was added in 1990 to provide medical and mental health services (VA 1995). NDMS cares for patients in five categories: medical/surgical, critical care, pediatrics, burn, and psychiatric.

*Field medical response.* NDMS field medical response includes numerous teams made up of individuals who train for and agree to respond during disasters. Response teams consist of paid federal staff and a significant number of volunteer staff who become "federalized" staff when deployed in an NDMS full or partial activation. Deployed staff are paid and receive legal coverage for personal practice liability under the Federal Tort Claims Act. Compensation is provided in the form of travel, lodging, daily expenses, and salary while providing emergency services as an NDMS team member.

Six types of specialty NDMS teams are described in Table 7.2. These teams are composed of members with appropriately validated credentials and licenses who have submitted applications and received extensive training. Most team members are medical specialists who practice professionally in their respective communities.

When employed members of NDMS teams are activated, "permission" will be sought for temporary leave from their usual work setting. Their activation can present a challenge to healthcare CEOs during

## TABLE 7.2. TYPES OF NDMS TEAMS

| Category | Composition | Capability |
|---|---|---|
| Disaster Medical Assistance Team | Physicians, nurses, and other medical and support staff | Provide acute medical care |
| Disaster Mortuary Operational Response Team | Funeral directors, medical examiners, forensics experts, etc. | Provide fatality management |
| Specialized Disaster Medical Assistance Teams (e.g., burn, surgical, mental health) | Physicians, nurses, and other medical and support staff in specialization area | Provide care specific to the disaster needs |
| National Medical Response Team | Physicians, nurses, epidemiologists, chemists, and other medical and support staff | Specially trained for response to events involving agents defined as weapons of mass destruction |
| Management Support Team | Leadership and administrative support staff | Provide management support to deployed teams and interface with local medical disaster system |
| Veterinary Medical Assistance Team | Veterinarians and support staff | Provide emergency support to rescue pets and other animals affected by disaster |
| National Nursing Response Team | Nurses | Activated for situations specifically requiring nurses and not full DMATs |
| National Pharmacy Response Team | Pharmacists | Activated for situations specifically requiring pharmacists and not full DMATs |

*Source*: National Disaster Medical System (NDMS) Office of Emergency Response. 2003. *Federal Coordinating Center Guide*. Rockville, MD: NDMS.

times of staffing shortages. In facilities where a large number of nursing or medical staff—especially from critical care or specialty units—are NDMS volunteers, preplanning for their activation is a wise move and will afford additional time to identify alternative ways of providing patient care.

*Patient transport.* Although systemwide patient transport has never been fully deployed, NDMS provides for patient regulation (managing the flow of patients to ensure appropriate distribution of casualties), transport, and tracking of victims from the disaster area to lesser-affected areas. DoD has primary responsibility for oversight of patient transport and may provide it through U.S. Air Force aircraft; commercial air, rail, or bus; or other means. A systematic transport process is established through a memorandum of understanding (MOU; see Figure 7.5, discussed later in the chapter) with airports, local emergency medical service, and healthcare facilities to provide reception and treatment of victims.

*Definitive care.* NDMS provides a process to expand hospital bed capacity by identifying hospitals or other healthcare facilities (e.g., convalescent centers) willing to provide staffed beds for victims of the disaster. Formal MOUs identify specific resources and reimbursement arrangements.

The bed-reporting system requires a physical count of the available staffed beds across the nation and is tested regularly in exercises. The bed-reporting system has been "activated" during heightened alert conditions, providing senior leadership with a snapshot of available bed capacity within the NDMS system. The "staffed bed" numbers are usually projected in terms of those available immediately or at intervals such as 24, 48, or 72 hours. Although the exercises identify actual available beds, if an event occurs or is anticipated (as in an impending hurricane or terrorist attack), the NDMS-enrolled healthcare facilities need to expand capacity by discharging or transferring stable patients and canceling or reducing elective surgeries to support projected needs.

FCCs report the categorized bed numbers to the Global Patient Medical Regulating Center of the Air Force, providing them with a national overview of available beds on any given day. These reported numbers, combined with the minimum/maximum beds committed by the healthcare facility, are necessary for deliberately planned definitive care. Other factors in critical patient care capacity include fluctuation of bed space due to influenza or other epidemics that affect admissions; nursing or other staffing shortages; or temporary staff shortages due to, among other things, mobilization of military reservists or the National Guard.

Although elements of NDMS have been activated individually, DHHS's assistant secretary of health has never fully activated the entire system for domestic emergencies. Most commonly, the field medical response components of NDMS mobilize in support of a presidentially declared disaster, mass-casualty or fatality incidents, or high-visibility national security events such as economic summits, large sporting events, or presidential inaugurations. During the devastating 9/11 terrorist

## Table 7.3. Federal Coordinating Center Sites

| VA Managed | Also Responsible for |
|---|---|
| VAMC Birmingham, AL | Birmingham/Montgomery |
| VAMC Tucson, AZ | Tucson |
| VAMC N. Little Rock, AK | Little Rock |
| VAMC Long Beach, CA | Long Beach/Greater Los Angeles |
| VA Mare Island OPC | Oakland/San Francisco |
| VAMC Bay Pines, FL | Bay Pines, St. Petersburg, Tampa |
| VAMC Decatur, GA | Atlanta |
| VAMC Indianapolis, IN | Indianapolis |
| VAMC Kansas, MO | Wichita, KS |
| VAMC Lexington, KY | Louisville/Lexington |
| VAMC New Orleans, LA | New Orleans/Baton Rouge |
| VAMC Jackson, MS | Shreveport, LA |
| VAMC Leeds, MA | Boston/eastern MA/Northampton |
| VAMC Detroit, MI | Detroit/Flint/Ann Arbor/Grand Rapids |
| VAMC Minneapolis, MN | Minneapolis/St. Paul |
| VAMC Lyons, NJ | Newark/northern and central NJ |
| New Mexico VA Health Care System, Albuquerque, NM | Albuquerque/Santa Fe |
| New York Harbor Health Care System, New York, NY | Nassau/ Suffolk/Brooklyn/Queens/ Manhattan/Staten Island |
| VAMC Albany, NY | Rochester/Buffalo/western NY/ Syracuse |
| VA Hudson Valley Health Care System, Castle Point, NY | Southern tier/mid-Hudson/NY northern metro/Bronx |
| VAMC Salisbury, NC | Entire state NC |
| VAMC Brecksville, OH | Cleveland/Akron |
| VAMC Oklahoma City, OK | Oklahoma City/Tulsa |
| VAMC Portland, OR | Portland, OR/Vancouver, WA |
| VAMC Philadelphia, PA | Philadelphia/southern NJ |
| VAMC Pittsburgh, PA | Pittsburgh/northern WV |
| VAMC San Juan, PR | Puerto Rico/Virgin Islands |
| VAMC Nashville, TN | Nashville/Knoxville |
| VAMC Dallas, TX | Dallas/Ft. Worth |
| VAMC Houston, TX | Houston |
| VAMC San Antonio, TX | San Antonio |
| VAMC Denver, CO | Salt Lake City, Utah |
| VAMC Richmond, VA | Richmond/central/western VA |
| VAMC Hines, IL | Milwaukee, WI |
| Keesler Air Force Base, MS | Mobile, AL |
| Luke Air Force Base, AZ | Phoenix |
| Naval Hospital, Camp Pendleton, CA | Orange County |
| Travis Air Force Base, CA | Sacramento/Travis |
| Naval Medical Center, San Diego, CA | San Diego |
| E. Army Co Hospital, Ft. Carson, CO | Denver/Boulder |
| Naval Ambulatory Care Center, Groton, CT | New Haven/Hartford |
| Dover Air Force Base, DE | Wilmington/Dover |
| Jacksonville Naval Hospital, FL | Jacksonville/Orange Park |
| Fort Gordon, GA | Augusta |
| Tripler Army Medical Command, HI | Honolulu |
| POMI, Naval Hospital, Great Lakes, IL | Chicago/Gary, IN/Hammond, IN |

TABLE 7.3. *(continued)*

| VA Managed | Also Responsible for |
|---|---|
| Walter Reed Army Medical Center, Washington, DC | Baltimore, MD |
| National Naval Medical Center, Bethesda, MD | DC/Maryland |
| Scott Air Force Base, O'Fallon, IL | St. Louis, MO |
| Offutt Air Force Base, NE | Omaha/Lincoln |
| Newport Naval Ambulatory Care Clinic, Newport, RI | Providence |
| Charleston Naval Hospital, Charleston, SC | Charleston |
| Moncrief Army Command Hospital, Ft. Jackson, SC | Columbia/Greenville/Spartanburg |
| Wm. Beaumont Army Medical Center, El Paso, TX | El Paso/Las Cruces |
| Mar Naval Medical Center, Portsmouth, VA | Norfolk/Virginia Beach |
| Andrews Air Force Base, MD | Northern Virginia suburbs |
| Madigan Army Medical Center, Tacoma, WA | Seattle/Everett/Tacoma |
| Wright-Patterson Air Force Base, White Plains, OH | Cincinnati/Columbus/Dayton/Toledo |

*Source:* VHA Emergency Management Strategic Healthcare Group (EMSHG). 2002. *Emergency Management Program Guidebook.* Section 3. [Online information; retrieved 10/03.] http://www.appc1.va.gov/emshg/apps /emp/emp.htm.

attacks, the system was on alert and teams were deployed. However, the number of live victims requiring inpatient care did not exceed health and medical care capabilities of local resources and mutual-aid agreements.

### Federal Coordinating Centers

Federal Coordinating Centers are the healthcare facility's link to federal support; they oversee and coordinate NDMS bed availability at VA medical centers or DoD medical centers in 70 locations throughout the United States (Table 7.3). The VA manages 37 sites, and DoD manages 33 sites within the Air Force, Army, and Navy.

FCCs prepare to receive casualties from other locations that are overwhelmed and unable to provide care for their population (NDMS Office of Emergency Response 2003) and coordinate the reception of patients from overseas military conflicts. Each site has an area emergency manager who is the primary coordinator for his or her area.

FCCs plan and facilitate regional assets to ensure the following:

- A minimum of 2,500 acute care beds in the region with an array of available services (e.g., medical, surgical, psychiatry services)
- Coordination of local healthcare facilities, transportation and communication resources, and patient administration services

- An airport that can accommodate aeromedical aircraft within a 50-mile radius of the FCC

The CEO in local healthcare facilities is critical to the success and viability of FCCs and, ultimately, to the health and medical care component of a national disaster response. Success of the system relies on the willingness of community healthcare facilities to dedicate available staffed beds.

*NDMS civilian facilities.* There are approximately 1,800 civilian NDMS-enrolled facilities throughout the United States. Enrolled facilities agree to make staffed beds available for definitive care of patients who are victims of disaster, war, or other catastrophic events or who are "displaced" from their usual care settings for similar reasons. The mechanism for dedicating staffed beds as needed includes establishing an MOU signed by the facility CEO and FCC director. The MOU specifies

- the minimum and maximum number of beds dedicated and available to NDMS on request;
- the expectation that the NDMS-enrolled healthcare facility will participate in exercises coordinated by the FCC; and
- the process for patient care and bed reporting, as well as reimbursement of healthcare facilities, in the event that definitive-care beds are used.

A sample MOU is provided in Figure 7.5. Hospitals that wish to become NDMS enrolled may obtain information from the nearest FCC facility or by contacting the VA area emergency manager for enrollment assistance.

As with all viable emergency-service-oriented programs, preparedness and planning are crucial to successful implementation. Continuous planning initiatives include meetings and exercises between FCCs and NDMS-enrolled healthcare facilities. The exercises require essential players from the healthcare facilities, transport entities, and airport reception teams to train, rehearse, and evaluate existing NDMS plans.

## Metropolitan Medical Response System

The Metropolitan Medical Response System was established in 1996 to develop or enhance existing locally based emergency preparedness systems

## FIGURE 7.5. MEMORANDUM OF UNDERSTANDING BETWEEN HOSPITALS AND NDMS

Memorandum of Understanding Between
National Disaster Medical System
and

_____

To ensure that our Nation is prepared to respond medically to all types of mass casualty emergency situations, whether from a natural or man-made disaster in this country or from the United States military casualties being returned from an overseas conventional conflict, a coordinated response of both the federal and civilian health care facilities is required. We acknowledge the willingness of the various medical communities within the United States to respond to a catastrophic medical emergency, and the need for unusually rapid and complex response, transportation, treatment, and hospitalization. A rapid response requires the development of a comprehensive emergency medical plan whereby some casualties would receive definite treatment in private sector hospital located throughout the United States. In response to this need, the National Disaster Medical System (NDMS) has been created to care for victims of any incident that exceeds the medical care capability of the affected state, region, of federal medical care systems.

The _____ agrees that upon activation of the National Disaster Medical System it will make available to the U.S. Government agencies participating in the National Disaster Medical System, a minimum of _____ to a maximum of _____ beds with all necessary treatment and
$\qquad$ *number* $\qquad$ *number*
administrative processing as may be required for the patients hospitalized therein. Subject to the availability of appropriations, payment for this care will be as follows:

(a) For patients eligible for TRICARE/CHAMPUS, payment will be pursuant to otherwise applicable TRICARE/CHAMPUS payment rates and procedures (as set forth in 32 CFR Part 199).
(b) For patients who do not have health insurance coverage, NDMS WILL PAY 110% of the Medicare payment amount that would be applicable to the services provided. NDMS payment is limited to medically necessary care for disaster-related diagnoses.
(c) For patients with health insurance coverage (other than TRICARE/CHAMPUS or Medicaid), the health insurance will be primary payer and NDMS will pay the difference, if any, between the amount paid by the health insurance coverage and the amount payable under paragraph
(b), but not including the deductible amount under the health insurance coverage.
(d) For patients whose only health coverage is Medicaid, NDMS will pay under paragraph (b).

NDMS will not compensate for pre-existing conditions except as they directly impact medically necessary care authorized by NDMS. This care will be compensated at 110% of what Medicare would pay (at the time of the disaster). Benefits through NDMS will be secondary to any other existing medical coverage (other than Medicaid). NOTE—BY LAW MEDICAID IS PAYER OF LAST RESORT.

By this Memorandum of Understanding, the U.S. Government and the aforementioned hospital mutually agree to jointly plan for the admission, treatment, hospitalization and discharge of all patients transferred to the facility under the National Disaster Medical System. The hospital will assume the responsibility for coordination of benefits so that benefits through NDMS will be secondary to any other existing medical coverage except Medicaid. In addition, the hospital agrees to participate in joint annual exercise of the NDMS which will meet external disaster standards established by the Joint Commission on Accreditation of Healthcare Organizations (JCAHO) or by the American Osteopathic Hospital Association.

For the National Disaster Medical System          For the _____

_____          _____

_____          _____

Date:_____             Date:_____

*Source:* VHA Emergency Management Strategic Healthcare Group (EMSHG). 2002. *Emergency Management Program Guidebook.* Section 3. [Online information; retrieved 10/03.] http://www.appc1.va.gov/emshg/apps /emp/emp.htm.

to effectively respond to public health crises—especially events involving weapons of mass destruction—until federal resources arrive (typically 24 to 48 hours) (NDMS Public Health Service 1998). By year-end 2002, the federal government (through the DHHS Office of Public Health Emergency Preparedness) provided funds to 122 local jurisdictions to facilitate the preparation and coordination of public health, medical and mental health, local law enforcement, emergency management, and first-responder personnel to more effectively respond in the first 48 to 72 hours of a public health crisis.

The Metropolitan Medical Response System is the only federal program that directly links all the local elements essential to managing a mass-casualty event. MMRS supports initiatives in major metropolitan areas for

- chemical, biological, or nuclear agent identification;
- medical-intelligence gathering and distribution;
- patient triage and treatment capability and support;
- mass prophylaxis of affected populations;
- mass-fatality management;
- enhanced emergency transport capabilities;
- integration with federal resources (such as NDMS, SNS);
- patient-decontamination capability and support; and
- coordination of patient transportation to receiving facilities.

The MMRS component plan for local hospital and healthcare systems includes procedures for notification, facility protection, triage, and treatment. Figure 7.6 identifies the locations of MMRS teams by the year each was activated. As of 2002, 25 new cities were added to the roster, which means that 80 percent of the U.S. population will be covered by an MMRS response capability.

### Emergency Medical Services

There is no national standardized program for how healthcare facilities formally integrate and coordinate with local emergency management plans and programs, nor is there a predesignated plan for the flow of disaster casualties into the EMS system (Auf der Heide 1989). However,

FIGURE 7.6. METROPOLITAN MEDICAL RESPONSE SYSTEM CITIES, BY YEAR

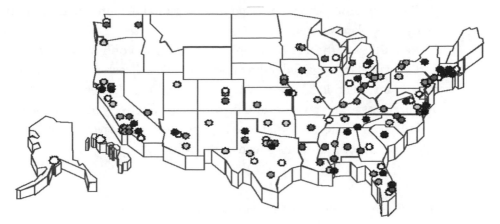

○ Original MMRS (27)
Anchorage, Atlanta, Baltimore, Boston, Chicago, Columbus, Dallas, Denver, Detroit, Honolulu, Houston, Indianapolis, Jacksonville, Kansas City, Los Angeles, Memphis, Miami, Milwaukee, New York, Philadelphia, Phoenix, San Antonio, San Diego, San Francisco, San Jose, Seattle, Washington DC

◉ MMRS 1999 (20)
Albuquerque, Austin, Charlotte, Cleveland, El Paso, Fort Worth, Hampton Roads (Virginia Beach), Long Beach, Nashville, New Orleans, Oakland, Oklahoma City, Pittsburgh, Portland (OR), Sacramento, Salt Lake City, St. Louis, Tucson, Tulsa, Twin Cities (Minneapolis)

◉ MMRS 2000 (25)
Akron, Anaheim, Aurora, Birmingham, Buffalo, Cincinnati, Corpus Christi, Fresno, Jersey City, Twin Cities (St. Paul), Hampton Roads (Norfolk), Las Vegas, Lexington–Fayette, Louisville, Mesa, Newark, Omaha, Riverside, Rochester (NY), Santa Ana, St. Petersburg, Tampa, Toledo, Wichita

● MMRS 2001 (25)
Baton Rouge, Colorado Springs, Columbus (GA), Des Moines, Dayton, Garland, Glendale (CA), Grand Rapids, Greensboro, Hialeah, Huntington Beach, Jackson, Lincoln, Little Rock, Lubbock, Madison, Mobile, Montgomery, Raleigh, Richmond (VA), Shreveport, Spokane, Stockton, Tacoma, Yonkers

● MMRS 2002 (25)
Amarillo, Arlington, Bakersfield, Chattanooga, Columbia, Fremont, Ft. Lauderdale, Ft. Wayne, Glendale, Hampton Roads (Newport News, Chesapeake), Hartford, Huntsville, Irving, Jefferson Parish, Kansas City, Knoxville, Modesto, Orlando, Providence, San Bernardino, Springfield, Syracuse, Warren, Worcester

*Source:* VHA Emergency Management Strategic Healthcare Group (EMSHG). 2002. *Emergency Management Program Guidebook.* Section 3. [Online information; retrieved 10/03.] http://www.appc1.va.gov/emshg/apps /emp/emp.htm.

ample guidance of the roles and responsibilities of the healthcare community in a comprehensive community response is clearly stated in the NRP—an outline that is replicated in all regional response plans and in many state plans as well.

Regardless of the size or complexity of the event or how vast the support provided through federal response assets, a disaster or terrorist incident starts as a local event. The onus is on local leadership to drive preparations for responders and providers to effectively manage the situation. Even if external assistance is requested and arrives, the local incident manager maintains a leadership role.

### Local Emergency Planning Committee

A potential springboard for local coordination is the local emergency planning committee (LEPC). In 1986, as emergency management leaders became concerned about a growing "disconnect" between private industry and the public in the area of hazardous materials production, the Emergency Planning and Community Right to Know Act (Title III of the Superfund Amendment and Reauthorization Act, commonly known as SARA Title III) was passed to address public right-to-know issues and to direct industry to begin disclosing information on manufactured hazardous materials. It also mandated the creation of LEPCs to address issues relevant to hazardous materials. The LEPC focus in many areas is expanding from hazardous materials to more comprehensive emergency management issues to include terrorism (Tierney, Lendell, and Perry 2001).

Public health and the healthcare community in general have essential roles in the evolving process of domestic comprehensive emergency management. Because all events are local, coordinating healthcare initiatives with local public health agencies promotes the development of critical relationships in the multijurisdictional environment of homeland security. Federal support is available to state and local governments, agencies, and organizations to improve readiness. As public health and healthcare assume their position in critical infrastructure protection and comprehensive emergency management, CEOs, staff, and the population they support will become an integral part of planning, training, conducting exercises, and preparedness.

# REFERENCES

Auf der Heide, E. 1989. *Disaster Response: Principles of Preparation and Coordination*, 175. St. Louis, MO: Mosby.

Barbera, J., and A. Macintyre. 2002. *Medical and Health Incident Management System (MaHIM): A Comprehensive Functional System Description for Mass Casualty Medical and Health Incident Management*. Washington, DC: George Washington University.

Brandt, E. N., Jr., W. N. Mayer, J. O. Mason, D. E. Brown, Jr., and L. E. Mahoney. 1985. "Designing a National Disaster Medical System." *Public Health Reports* 100 (5): 455–61.

California Emergency Medical Services Authority. 1998. *HEICS III: Hospital Emergency Incident Command System Update Project*. [Online report; retrieved 1/7/04.] http://www .emsa.ca.gov/Dms2/heics3.htm.

Centers for Disease Control and Prevention (CDC). 2003. "Continuation Guidance for Cooperative Agreement on Public Health Preparedness and Response for Bioterrorism—Budget Year Four." [Online article; retrieved 8/03.] http://www.bt.cdc.gov /planning/continuationguidance/pdf/guidance_intro.pdf.

Federal Emergency Management Agency (FEMA). 1992. *Federal Response Plan*. Washington, DC: FEMA.

Health Resources and Services Administration (HRSA). 2003. "National Bioterrorism Hospital Preparedness Program Cooperative Agreement Guidance." [Online information; retrieved 8/03.] http://www.hrsa.gov/bioterrorism/bhppguidance.htm.

National Disaster Medical System (NDMS) Office of Emergency Response. 2003. *Federal Coordinating Center Guide*. Rockville, MD: NDMS.

National Disaster Medical System, U.S. Public Health Service. 1998. *Field Operations Guide for Metropolitan Medical Response Team*. Rockville, MD: NDMS.

Tierney, K. J., M. K. Lindell, and R. W. Perry. 2001. *Facing the Unexpected: Disaster Preparedness and Response in the United States*, 62–63. Washington, DC: John Henry Press.

U.S. Department of Veterans Affairs (VA), Training and Development, Emergency Medical Preparedness Office. 1995. *Response '95 Training Module, NDMS Purpose*. Indianapolis, IN: VA.

VHA Emergency Management Strategic Healthcare Group (EMSHG). 2002. *Emergency Management Program Guidebook*, Section 3. [Online information; retrieved 10/03.] http://www.appc1.va.gov/emshg/apps/emp/emp.htm.

### CHAPTER EIGHT

# Public Health Aspects of Weapons of Mass Destruction

Eric K. Noji

A s with emerging infectious diseases, early detection and control of biological or chemical attacks depend on a strong and flexible public health system at the local, state, and federal levels. In addition, primary healthcare providers throughout the United States must be vigilant, for they will probably be the first to observe and report unusual illnesses or injuries. The federal Department of Health and Human Services (DHHS) has been taking steps since 1999 to prepare for these challenges, and the anthrax attacks of 2001 constituted a sudden and unanticipated test of these initial steps. Although the response benefited from this initial preparedness, the attacks also demonstrated significant gaps and underscored the need to move much more quickly in building a national public health network and strengthening emergency response capabilities.

This chapter outlines steps for strengthening public health and healthcare capability to protect the population against these dangers. The healthcare industry and traditional healthcare organizations must join with public health departments, law enforcement and intelligence, and emergency management and defense agencies to address potential national security threats.

Eric K. Noji, M.D., M.P.H., is special assistant to the U.S. Surgeon General for Homeland Security and Emergency Preparedness and Response in the U.S. Public Health Service in Washington, DC.

## OVERT VERSUS COVERT TERRORIST ATTACKS

Terrorist incidents in the United States and elsewhere involving bacterial pathogens (Török et al. 1997), nerve gas (Okumura et al. 1998), and a lethal plant toxin (i.e., ricin) (Tucker 1996) have demonstrated that the United States is vulnerable to biological and chemical threats as well as traditional explosive weapons. Recipes for preparing "homemade" agents are readily available (Fester 1997), and reports of arsenals of military bioweapons (Davis 1999) raise the possibility that terrorists might have access to highly dangerous agents that have been engineered for mass dissemination as small-particle aerosols. Agents such as the variola virus, the causative agent of smallpox, are highly contagious and often fatal. Responding to large-scale outbreaks caused by these agents will require the rapid mobilization of public health workers, emergency responders, and private healthcare providers. Large-scale outbreaks will also require rapid procurement and distribution of large quantities of drugs and vaccines, which must be immediately available.

In the past, most planning for emergency response to terrorism has been concerned with overt attacks, such as bombings. Chemical terrorism acts are also likely to be overt because the effects of chemical agents absorbed through inhalation or through the skin or mucous membranes are usually immediate and obvious. Such attacks elicit immediate response from police, fire, and emergency medical services (EMS) personnel.

In contrast, attacks with biological agents are more likely to be covert. They present different challenges and require an additional dimension of emergency planning that involves the public health infrastructure. Because the initial detection of and response to a covert biological or chemical attack will probably occur at the local level, disease surveillance systems at local hospitals and state and local health agencies must be capable of detecting unusual patterns of disease or injury, including those caused by unusual or unknown threat agents. Epidemiologists at state and local health agencies must have expertise and resources for responding to reports of clusters of rare, unusual, or unexplained illnesses.

Covert dissemination of a biological agent in a public place will not have an immediate impact because of the delay between exposure and onset of illness (i.e., the incubation period). Consequently, the first casualties of a covert attack will most likely be identified by physicians or other primary healthcare providers. For example, in the event of a covert release of the contagious variola virus, patients will appear in doctors' offices, clinics, and emergency rooms during the first or second week after release, complaining of fever, back pain, headache, nausea, and other symptoms of what initially might appear to be an ordinary viral infection. As the disease progresses, these persons will develop the papular rash characteristic of early-stage smallpox, a rash that physicians might not recognize immediately. By the time the rash becomes pustular and patients begin to die, the terrorists would be far away and the disease disseminated through the population by person-to-person contact.

Only a short window of opportunity will exist between the time the first cases are identified and a second wave of the population becomes ill. During that brief period, public health officials will need to determine that an attack has occurred, identify the organism, and avoid more casualties through prevention strategies (e.g., mass vaccination in the case of smallpox or prophylactic treatment in the case of anthrax). In the case of smallpox, as person-to-person contact continues, successive waves of transmission could carry infection to other worldwide localities, similar to what occurred in the SARS (severe acute respiratory syndrome) outbreak in spring 2003. These issues might also be relevant for other person-to-person transmissible etiologic agents (e.g., plague or certain viral hemorrhagic fevers).

Certain chemical agents can also be delivered covertly through contaminated food or water. In 1999, the vulnerability of the food supply was illustrated in Belgium, when chickens were unintentionally exposed to dioxin-contaminated fat used to make animal feed (Ashraf 1999). Dioxin, a cancer-causing chemical that does not result in immediate symptoms in humans, was probably present in chicken meat and eggs sold in Europe as early as 1999, because the contamination was not discovered for months. This incident underscores the need for prompt diagnoses of unusual or suspicious health problems in animals as well as humans, a lesson that was also demonstrated in New York City by the winter 1999 outbreak of mosquito-borne West Nile virus first diagnosed in birds and humans. The dioxin episode also demonstrates how a covert act of food-borne biological or chemical terrorism could affect commerce and human or animal health.

## FOCUSING PREPAREDNESS ACTIVITIES

Preparedness for terrorist-caused outbreaks and injuries is an essential component of the U.S. public health system, which is designed to protect the population against any unusual public health event (e.g., influenza pandemics; contaminated municipal water supplies; intentional dissemination of *Yersinia pestis*, the causative agent of plague) (Janofsky 1995).

Early detection of and response to biological or chemical terrorism are just as crucial for state and local organizations. Without special preparation at these levels, a large-scale attack with variola virus, aerosolized anthrax spores, a nerve gas, or a food-borne biological or chemical agent could overwhelm the local, and then perhaps the national, public health infrastructure. Large numbers of patients, including both infected persons and the "worried well," would seek medical attention, with a corresponding need for medical supplies, diagnostic tests, and hospital beds. Emergency responders, healthcare workers, and public health officials could be at special risk.

## Prepare for Unique Attacks

The epidemiologic skills, surveillance methods, diagnostic techniques, and physical resources required to detect and investigate unusual or unknown diseases, as well as syndromes or injuries caused by chemical accidents, are similar to those needed to identify and respond to an attack with a biological or chemical agent. However, public health agencies must also prepare for the special features a terrorist attack probably would have, including mass casualties or the use of rare agents.

Terrorists might use combinations of chemical and biological agents, attack in more than one location simultaneously, use new agents, or use organisms that are not on the critical list (e.g., common, drug-resistant, or genetically engineered pathogens). Lists of critical chemical agents are provided in Chapter 2, Tables 2.1 and 2.2, and their symptoms and antidotes are listed in Table 2.3. Table 2.4 presents the current priority biological agents in three categories and describes the unique characteristics of each category that make them critical elements. These lists will need to be modified as new information becomes available. In addition, each state and locality will need to adapt the lists to local conditions and preparedness needs. Chemical and other agents can be readily found in the United States, and some have been developed for use as weapons. All such agents may cause severe public health risks and require multiagency planning and preparation for an appropriate response. Other agents, listed by category, are provided in Table 2.5.

## Focus on Agents of Greatest Impact

Potential biological and chemical agents are numerous, and the public health, hospital, and healthcare organization infrastructure must be equipped to quickly resolve crises that would arise from a biological or chemical attack. Because of the hundreds of new chemicals introduced internationally each month, treating exposed persons by clinical syndrome rather than by specific agent is more useful for public health planning and emergency medical response purposes. Public health agencies and first responders might render the most aggressive, timely, and clinically relevant treatment possible by using treatment modalities based on syndromic categories (e.g., burns and trauma, cardiorespiratory failure, neurologic damage, and shock). These activities must be linked with authorities responsible for environmental sampling and decontamination.

To best protect the public, preparedness efforts must be focused on agents that might have the greatest impact on U.S. health and security, especially agents that are highly contagious or that can be engineered for widespread dissemination via small-particle aerosols (as we are planning now for mass smallpox vaccination of the U.S. population). Preparing the nation to address these dangers is a major challenge to U.S. public health systems and healthcare providers.

## Focus on Early Detection

Early detection requires increased biological and chemical terrorism awareness among frontline healthcare providers because they are in the best position to report suspicious illnesses and injuries. Also, early detection will require improved communications systems between those providers and public health officials. State and local healthcare agencies must have enhanced capability to investigate unusual events and unexplained illnesses, and diagnostic laboratories must be equipped to identify biological and chemical agents that are rarely seen in the United States.

Fundamental to these efforts is comprehensive, integrated training designed to ensure core competency in public health preparedness and the highest levels of scientific expertise among local, state, and federal partners. Checklists 8.1 and 8.2 at the end of this chapter provide guidance in preparing for chemical and biological exposures from a public health point of view.

## CDC AND FEDERAL PREPAREDNESS

The Centers for Disease Control and Prevention (CDC), located in Atlanta, Georgia, is the lead federal agency to protect the health and safety of U.S. residents at home and abroad, provide credible information to enhance health decisions, and promote health through vital partnerships with other health and community organizations. CDC employs approximately 8,500 employees (representing 170 occupations) in the public health service arena. More than 2,000 of those CDC employees work at locations other than the Atlanta headquarters, including 47 state health departments and offices in 45 countries overseas. CDC includes 12 centers, institutes, and offices that respond individually in their areas of expertise and pool their resources and expertise on cross-cutting issues and specific health threats (CDC 2001).

CDC has been responding to public health emergencies for decades and has been preparing for bioterrorism since 1998 (CDC 1998). CDC's bioterrorism plans were activated in fall 2001, with the first biological attack in the United States. Outbreaks of anthrax proved that the first line of defense is rapid identification. This is essential for ensuring a prompt response to a biological or chemical attack so that exposure can be limited and those affected can be treated. To accomplish rapid identification, regional and state laboratories have strengthened their capability to detect different biological and chemical agents and to communicate the results to CDC and others. Along the same lines, CDC's Health Alert Network (HAN) has upgraded the capability of state and local health agencies to detect and communicate different health threats—including not only bioterrorism but also emerging infectious diseases, chronic diseases, and environmental hazards. These investments will prove useful in an all-hazards disaster situation such as a bioterrorist attack.

To further enhance treatment of victims of a bioterrorist attack, CDC has worked with pharmaceutical companies and other partners to create regional stockpiles of the drugs and supplies that would be needed quickly to treat major outbreaks of anthrax, plague, tularemia, or other diseases in the Strategic National Stockpile (SNS; formerly the National Pharmaceutical Stockpile). This resource was essential in responding to the anthrax outbreak in October 2001. Collectively, these measures strengthen the existing public health system while preparing for bioterrorism, infectious disease outbreaks, and other public health threats and emergencies.

The CDC strategic plan is based on the following five focus areas:

1. Preparedness and prevention
2. Detection and surveillance
3. Diagnosis and characterization of biological and chemical agents
4. Response
5. Communication

Each area integrates training and research. The role of public health in each of these areas is described in the following sections and summarized in Table 8.1.


## Preparedness and Prevention

Detection, diagnosis, and mitigation of illness and injury caused by biological and chemical terrorism are complex processes that involve numerous partners and activities. All cities and states need to be involved in special emergency preparedness activities to meet this challenge.

CDC provides public health guidelines, support, and technical assistance to local and state public health agencies as they develop coordinated preparedness plans and response protocols. CDC also provides self-assessment tools for terrorism preparedness, including performance standards, attack simulations, and other exercises. In addition, CDC encourages and supports applied research to develop innovative tools and strategies to prevent or mitigate illness and injury caused by biological and chemical terrorism.

The Metropolitan Medical Response System (MMRS; formerly Metropolitan Medical Strike Team), created in 1996 and managed by the DHHS Office of Emergency Preparedness, exists to develop new or to enhance existing emergency preparedness systems to effectively manage a weapon of mass destruction (WMD) incident. The goal is to coordinate the efforts of local law enforcement, fire, hazardous-materials response, EMS, hospital, public health, and other personnel to improve local response capabilities in the event of a terrorist attack (see Figure 8.1). DHHS has focused, through the development of the local MMRS, on enhancing the local public health and medical capability and capacity to respond to WMD terrorist incidents by

**Table 8.1. CDC Focus Areas and Implementation Priorities Through 2004**

**Preparedness and Prevention**
- Maintain a public health preparedness and response cooperative agreement that provides support to state health agencies that are working with local agencies to develop coordinated bioterrorism plans and protocols.
- Establish a national public health distance-learning system that provides biological and chemical terrorism preparedness training to healthcare workers and to state and local public health workers.
- Disseminate public health guidelines and performance standards on biological and chemical terrorism preparedness planning for use by state and local health agencies.

**Detection and Surveillance**
- Strengthen state and local surveillance systems for illness and injury resulting from pathogens and chemical substances that are on the bioterrorism critical-agents list.
- Develop new algorithms and statistical methods for searching medical databases on a real-time basis for evidence of suspicious events.
- Establish criteria for investigating and evaluating suspicious clusters of human or animal disease or injury and triggers for notifying law enforcement of suspected acts of biological or chemical terrorism.

**Diagnosis and Characterization of Biological and Chemical Agents**
- Establish a multilevel laboratory response network for bioterrorism that links public health agencies to advanced-capacity facilities to identify and report critical biological agents.
- Establish regional chemical terrorism laboratories that will provide diagnostic capacity during terrorist attacks involving chemical agents.
- Establish a rapid-response and advanced-technology laboratory within CDC and National Institutes of Health to provide around-the-clock diagnostic support to bioterrorism response teams and expedite molecular characterization of critical biological agents.

**Response**
- Assist state and local health agencies in organizing response capacities to rapidly deploy in the event of an overt attack or a suspicious outbreak that might be the result of a covert attack.
- Ensure that procedures are in place for rapid mobilization of federal terrorism response teams (e.g., NDMS, DMATs) that will provide on-site assistance to local health workers, security agents, and law enforcement officers.
- Establish a national pharmaceutical stockpile to provide medical supplies in the event of a terrorist attack that involves biological or chemical agents.

**Communications**
- Establish a national electronic infrastructure to improve exchange of emergency health information among local, state, and federal health agencies.
- Implement an emergency communications plan that ensures rapid dissemination of health information to the public during actual, threatened, or suspected acts of biological or chemical terrorism.
- Create a web site that disseminates bioterrorism preparedness and training information, as well as other bioterrorism-related emergency information, to public health and healthcare workers and the public.

*Note*: DMAT = disaster medical assistance team; NDMS = National Disaster Medical System

*Source*: Centers for Disease Control and Prevention (CDC). 1998. *Preventing Emerging Infectious Diseases: A Strategy for the 21st Century*. Atlanta, GA: CDC.

FIGURE 8.1. LINKING RESPONSE SYSTEMS

Defense agencies

Healthcare industry, health
and first responders (fire/EMS)

Public health

Law enforcement and
intelligence

Emergency
management

*Note:* EMS = emergency medical services

- developing drop-in surveillance capabilities for special events,
- providing guidance to develop active community-surveillance programs, and
- improving communications between local, state, and federal public health agencies (including CDC) and the national security community.

More information on MMRS is provided in Chapter 7.

## Detection and Surveillance

Early detection is essential for ensuring a prompt and effective response to a biological or chemical attack, including the provision of prophylactic medicines, chemical antidotes, or vaccines. CDC integrates surveillance for illness and injury resulting from biological and chemical terrorism into the U.S. disease-surveillance systems while developing new mechanisms for detecting, evaluating, and reporting suspicious events that might represent covert terrorist acts. As part of this effort, CDC and state and local health agencies are forming partnerships with frontline medical personnel in hospital emergency departments, healthcare facilities, poison-control centers, and other offices to enhance detection and reporting of unexplained injuries and illnesses as part of routine surveillance mechanisms for biological and chemical terrorism.

## Diagnosis and Characterization of Biological and Chemical Agents

CDC and its partners plan to create a multilevel laboratory response network for bioterrorism. That network will link clinical laboratories to public health agencies in all states, districts, and territories and selected cities and counties to state-of-the-art facilities that can analyze biological agents. As part of this effort, CDC will transfer diagnostic technology to state health laboratories and others who will perform initial testing. CDC will also create an in-house rapid-response and advanced-technology laboratory. This laboratory will provide around-the-clock diagnostic confirmatory and reference support for terrorism response teams. The lab response network will include the regional chemical laboratories for diagnosing human exposure to chemical agents and provide links with other related departments such as the U.S. Environmental Protection Agency, which is responsible for environmental sampling.

## Response

In a confirmed terrorist attack, the Office of the Assistant DHHS Secretary for Public Health Emergency Preparedness will coordinate with other federal agencies in accordance with Presidential Decision Directive (PDD) 39, which designates the Federal Bureau of Investigation as the lead agency for the crisis plan and charges the Federal Emergency Management Agency (FEMA) with ensuring that the federal response is adequate to address the consequences of terrorism (FEMA 2002).

In addition, PDD 62 states that the DHHS Public Health System (PHS) "is the lead federal agency in planning and preparing for response to WMD-related medical emergencies" (FEMA 2002). PHS supports state and local governments in developing MMRS; maintaining NDMS; and, in conjunction with the Department of Veterans Affairs (VA), stockpiling antidotes and pharmaceuticals in the event of a WMD incident in the SNS.

If requested by a state health agency, DHHS will deploy response teams to investigate unexplained or suspicious illnesses or unusual etiologic agents and provide on-site consultation regarding medical management and disease control. DHHS, with the support of other federal agencies,

- provides enhanced local response capabilities through the development of MMRS;
- develops and maintains NDMS, including National Medical Response Teams;
- works with the Department of Defense (DoD) to ensure NDMS response teams, supplies, and equipment can be rapidly deployed; and
- works with the VA to ensure adequate stockpiles of antidotes and other necessary pharmaceuticals nationwide and to ensure the training of medical personnel in NDMS hospitals.

*Strategic National Stockpile*

To ensure the availability, procurement, and delivery of medical supplies, devices, and equipment that might be needed to respond to terrorist-caused illness or injury, CDC maintains a national pharmaceutical stockpile through SNS. The mission of the SNS program is to ensure the availability of life-saving pharmaceuticals, vaccines, antidotes, and other medical supplies and equipment necessary to counter the effects of nerve agents, biological pathogens, and chemical agents and augment depleted state and local resources for responding to terrorist attacks and other emergencies.

The SNS program stands ready for immediate deployment to any U.S. location in the event of a terrorist attack using a biological, toxin, or chemical agent directed against a civilian population. Both 12-hour push packages and vendor-managed inventory are stored in strategic locations around the United States to ensure rapid delivery anywhere in the country. Table 8.2 summarizes the contents of SNS push packages, and Table 8.3 compares the immediate and rapid response services of the SNS program.

In addition to a pharmaceutical stockpile, a comprehensive medical and public health response to a biological or chemical terrorist event involves epidemiologic investigation, medical treatment, and prophylaxis for affected persons and the initiation of disease prevention or environmental-decontamination measures. CDC will assist state and local health agencies in developing resources and expertise for investigating unusual events and unexplained illnesses.

## TABLE 8.2. CONTENTS OF STRATEGIC NATIONAL STOCKPILE PUSH PACKAGES

**Pharmaceuticals**
- Antibiotics
- Mark I kits (antidote for nerve agents)
- Diazepam
- Atropine
- Pralidoxime

**Intravenous supplies**
- Catheters
- Syringes
- Fluids
- Heparin locks
- Aministration sets

**Airway Supplies**
- Ventilators
- Ambu bags
- Laryngoscopes
- Suction devices
- Oxygen masks
- Nasogastric tubes

**Other emergency medications**
- For hypotension
- For anaphylaxis
- For sedation
- For pain management

**Bandages and dressings**
**Vaccines**

---

### Federal Medical Response

The National Disaster Medical System is a federally coordinated initiative designed to augment the country's emergency medical response capability in the event of a catastrophic disaster (see the discussion in Chapter 7 for a full description of NDMS). This system is a cooperative program of four federal government agencies: DoD, Department of Homeland Security, FEMA, and VA.

NDMS provides an interstate medical mutual-aid system linking the federal government, state and local agencies, and private-sector institutions to address the medical care needs that result from catastrophic disasters. The program was designed to supplement the activities of state or local government in a massive civil disaster or to back up the military medical care system in the event of an overseas conventional conflict. NDMS contains a medical response element to bring organized aid to a disaster-affected area, an evacuation system, and a network of precommitted hospital beds throughout the United States. Its medical response element includes dozens of volunteer, civilian, disaster medical-assistance teams (DMATs) that operate supplemental casualty clearing facilities for triage,

## TABLE 8.3. THE STRATEGIC NATIONAL STOCKPILE PROGRAM

| Immediate Response 12-Hour Push Packages | Rapid Response VMI Packages |
|---|---|
| • Ready for deployment to reach designated airfield within 12 hours of federal activation<br>• Eight packages stored in environmentally controlled and secured facilities<br>• Packaged for rapid identification and ease of content distribution | • To be shipped for arrival within 24 to 36 hours following request<br>• Packages of pharmaceuticals and supplies delivered from one or more VMI sources<br>• Tailored to provide specific material depending on suspected or confirmed agent |

*Note*: VMI = vendor-managed inventory

stabilization, and holding care for disaster victims and evacuation facilities for patients in excess of local hospital capacity.

Specialized National Medical Response Teams–Weapons of Mass Destruction (NMRTs-WMD) are designed to provide medical care following nuclear, biological, and/or chemical incidents. These teams are capable of providing mass-casualty decontamination, medical triage, and primary and secondary medical care to stabilize victims for transportation to tertiary-care facilities in a hazardous-material environment. The four NMRTs-WMD are geographically dispersed throughout the United States.

**Communications**

Preparedness to mitigate the medical and public health consequences of biological and chemical terrorism depends on the coordinated activities of well-trained healthcare and public health personnel throughout the United States who have access to up-to-the-minute emergency information. Effective communication with the public through the news media will also be essential to limit terrorists' ability to induce public panic and disrupt daily life.

During the next five years, DHHS will work with state and local health agencies to

- develop a state-of-the-art communications system that will support disease surveillance,
- initiate rapid notification and information exchange regarding disease outbreaks that are possibly related to bioterrorism,

- disseminate diagnostic results and emergency health information, and
- coordinate emergency response activities.

The Internet-based HAN links state and local public health agencies to public health and private partners, provides for rapid dissemination of public health advisories, and ensures secure electronic data exchange. Through this network and similar mechanisms, DHHS will provide terrorism-related training to epidemiologists and laboratory personnel, emergency responders, emergency department personnel and other frontline healthcare providers, and health and safety personnel.

## FUTURE OF PUBLIC HEALTH PREPAREDNESS

On January 10, 2002, President George W. Bush signed appropriations legislation providing $2.9 billion for DHHS, a tenfold increase in the department's funding for bioterrorism preparedness. The funds have been used to develop comprehensive bioterrorism preparedness plans; upgrade infectious-disease surveillance and investigation through HAN; enhance the readiness of hospital systems to deal with large numbers of casualties; expand public health laboratory and communications capacity; and improve connectivity between hospitals and city, regional, and state health departments to enhance disease reporting. As the lead federal agency in preparing for the threat of bioterrorism, DHHS works closely with states, local government, and the private sector in building the needed, new public health infrastructure and accelerating research into likely bioterrorism-related diseases.

Reflecting the need for broad-based public health involvement in terrorism preparedness and planning, staff from different agencies in DHHS participated in developing a strategic WMD plan. These agencies include CDC, the Health Resources and Services Administration (HRSA), and the Office of Emergency Preparedness. CDC will target state and local programs supporting statewide preparedness activities for bioterrorism, infectious diseases, and public health emergency. HRSA will provide funding, which will be used by states to create regional hospital plans to respond in the event of a bioterrorism attack.

Future goals of federal public health preparedness efforts include the following:

- Having at least one epidemiologist in each metropolitan area with a population greater than 500,000
- Developing an education and training plan that will reach health professionals, emergency department physicians and nurses, local public health officials, and the public with information relating to bioterrorism, new and emerging diseases, and other infectious agents
- Targeting bioterrorism research to new vaccines, antiviral drugs, and new diagnostic tools to better protect against biologics

Implementation of the objectives outlined in DHHS's strategic plan will be coordinated through the DHHS Office of the Assistant Secretary for Emergency Preparedness and Response. DHHS program personnel are charged with helping build local and state preparedness, developing U.S. medical expertise regarding potential threat agents, and coordinating medical response activities during actual bioterrorist events. Program staff have established priorities for fiscal year 2004 regarding these focus areas (see Table 8.1). Checklist 8.3 presents the critical benchmarks for hospitals in planning for bioterrorism preparedness.

Successful implementation of these priorities will require state and local public health agencies to collaborate and partner with a number of other persons and groups, including the following:

- Medical research centers
- Healthcare providers and their networks
- Professional societies
- Medical examiners
- Emergency response units and responder organizations
- Safety- and medical-equipment manufacturers
- Federal agencies
- International organizations

Recent threats and use of biological and chemical agents against civilians have exposed the United States's vulnerability and highlighted the need to enhance our capacity to detect and control terrorist acts. The United States must be protected from an extensive range of critical biological and chemical agents, including some that have been developed and stockpiled for military use. Even without threat of war, investment in national defense ensures preparedness and serves as a deterrent against hostile acts. Similarly, investment in the public health and healthcare systems provides the best civil defense against bioterrorism.

Tools developed in response to terrorist threats serve a dual purpose. They help detect rare or unusual disease outbreaks and respond to medical emergencies, including naturally occurring outbreaks or industrial injuries that might resemble terrorist events in their unpredictability and ability to cause mass casualties (e.g., a pandemic influenza outbreak or a large-scale chemical spill). Federal WMD terrorism-preparedness activities, including the development of a public health communication infrastructure, a multilevel network of diagnostic laboratories, an integrated disease surveillance system, and an MMRS will improve our ability to investigate rapidly and control public health threats that emerge in the twenty-first century (U.S. DHS 2003a, 2003b).

## REFERENCES

Ashraf, H. 1999. "European Dioxin-Contaminated Food Crisis Grows and Grows." *Lancet* 353 (9169): 2049.

Centers for Disease Control and Prevention (CDC). 1998. *Preventing Emerging Infectious Diseases: A Strategy for the 21st Century.* Atlanta, GA: CDC.

————. 2001. *CDC Fact Book 2000/2001.* [Online information; retrieved 10/15/03.] http://www.cdc.gov/maso/factbook/main.htm.

Davis, C. J. 1999. "Nuclear Blindness: An Overview of the Biological Weapons Programs of the Former Soviet Union and Iraq." *Emerging Infectious Disease* 5 (4): 509–12.

Federal Emergency Management Agency (FEMA). 2002. *Federal Response Plan.* [Online information: retrieved 1/03.] http://www.fema.gov/rrr/frp/.

Fester, U. 1997. *Silent Death,* 2d ed. Port Townsend, WA: Loompanics Unlimited.

Janofsky, M. 1995. "Looking for Motives in Plague Case." *New York Times* May 28, A18.

Okumura, T., K. Suzuki, A. Fukuda, A. Kohama, N. Takasu, S. Ishimatsu, and S. Hinohara. 1998. "Tokyo Subway Sarin Attack: Disaster Management, Part 1: Community Emergency Response." *Academic Emergency Medicine* 5 (6): 613–17.

Török, T. J., R. V. Tauxe, R. P. Wise, J. R. Livengood, R. Sokolow, S. Mauvais, K. A. Birkness, M. R. Skeels, J. M. Horan, and L. R. Foster. 1997. "A Large Community Outbreak of Salmonellosis Caused by Intentional Contamination of Restaurant Salad Bars." *Journal of the American Medical Association* 278 (5): 389–95.

Tucker, J. B. 1996. "Chemical/Biological Terrorism: Coping with a New Threat." *Politics and the Life Sciences* 15 (2): 167–84.

U.S. Department of Health and Human Services (DHHS). 2002. "Critical Benchmarks for Bioterrorism Preparedness Planning." [Online information; retrieved 1/5/04.] http://www.hhs.gov/news/press/2002pres/20020131b.html.

U.S. Department of Homeland Security (DHS). 2003a. *Homeland Security Presidential Directive/HSPD-5*, February 28. [Online information; retrieved 7/03.] http://www.whitehouse.gov/news/releases/2003/02/20030228-9.html.

———. 2003b. *National Response Plan: Initial Plan*. Draft. [Online information; retrieved 7/03.] http://www.nemaweb.org/docs/National_Response_Plan.pdf.

# Checklists

## CHECKLIST 8.1. HEALTHCARE FACILITY PREPARATION FOR CHEMICAL EXPOSURES

❏ Enhance awareness of chemical terrorism among EMS personnel, police officers, firefighters, physicians, and nurses.

❏ Enhance in-house capacity for detecting and responding to chemical attacks.

❏ Ensure education and training of clinical response staff in receiving exposed individuals, including decontamination technique.

❏ Establish decontamination location, supplies, and equipment to decontaminate those in need.

❏ Stockpile appropriate personal protective equipment for clinical staff and responders, and provide training, education, and exercises involving their use.

❏ Stockpile chemical antidotes.

❏ Stock and prepare laboratory staff to utilize bioassays for detection and diagnosis of chemical injuries.

❏ Prepare educational materials to inform and reassure the public during and after a chemical attack.

❏ Participate in communitywide disaster exercises involving chemical exposures.


## CHECKLIST 8.2. HEALTHCARE FACILITY PREPARATION FOR BIOLOGICAL EXPOSURES

❏ Enhance awareness of biological terrorism among emergency medical services personnel, police officers, firefighters, physicians, and nurses.

❏ Enhance in-house capacity for detecting and responding to biological exposures.

❏ Enhance epidemiologic capacity to detect and respond to biological attacks.

❏ Ensure education and training of clinical staff in receiving exposed individuals, including training on preventing the spread of disease once diagnosed in the facility.

- ❏ Stockpile appropriate personal protective equipment for clinical staff and responders, and provide training, education, and exercises involving their use.
- ❏ Establish a supply receipt-and-exchange program for diagnostic reagents with state or local public health agencies.
- ❏ Establish interagency and intraagency communications systems to ensure delivery of accurate information.
- ❏ Enhance bioterrorism-related education and training for healthcare professionals.
- ❏ Prepare educational materials that will inform and reassure the public during and after a biological attack.
- ❏ Stockpile appropriate vaccines and drugs.
- ❏ Establish laboratory molecular surveillance for microbial strains, including unusual or drug-resistant strains.
- ❏ Supply appropriate diagnostic tests, or ensure rapid access to them.
- ❏ Participate in communitywide disaster exercises involving biological exposures.

## CHECKLIST 8.3. CRITICAL BENCHMARKS FOR HOSPITAL BIOTERRORISM PREPAREDNESS PLANNING

- ❏ Designate a senior hospital or corporate official within the healthcare facility or system to serve as director of the bioterrorism preparedness and response program and as a coordinator for hospital- or facility-preparedness planning.
- ❏ Participate in the local, county, and/or state emergency management and/or bioterrorism advisory committee.
- ❏ Participate in the development of regional plans for bioterrorism preparedness and response for a bioterrorist event, infectious disease outbreak, or other public health emergency. Ensure the appropriate integration of your facility into the regional plans.
- ❏ Assess emergency preparedness and response capabilities related to bioterrorism, other outbreaks of infectious disease, and other public health emergencies with a view to facilitating planning and setting implementation priorities.
- ❏ Participate in the state's hospital-bioterrorism-preparedness planning committee, affiliated with the statewide bioterrorism advisory committee (public health based).

❏ Participate in the implementation of rational regional hospital plans that would accommodate at least 500 patients in an emergency.

❏ Assess statutes, regulations, and ordinances within the state that provide for credentialing, licensure, and delegation of authority for executing emergency public health measures.

❏ Develop a plan and identify personnel to be trained to receive and distribute critical stockpile items and manage a mass distribution of vaccine and/or antibiotics on a 24/7 basis.

❏ Develop a plan to receive and evaluate urgent disease reports from the state on a 24/7 basis.

❏ Meet with the closest area epidemiologist to establish a working relationship to facilitate action if a public health crisis occurs.

❏ Participate in the development of a communications systems plan that provides for the 24/7 flow of critical health information between hospital emergency departments, other healthcare facilities, state and local health officials, law enforcement, and first responders.

❏ Enhance internal plans related to risk communications and information dissemination to educate the public regarding exposure risks and effective public response. Maximize the use of media to educate the public and relieve the burden of nonurgent cases arriving at the facility.

❏ Assess training needs with special emphasis on emergency department personnel, infectious disease specialists, public health staff, and other healthcare providers. Institute training as a priority issue for all employees.

*Source*: Adapted from U.S. Department of Health and Human Services (DHHS). 2002. "Critical Benchmarks for Bioterrorism Preparedness Planning." [Online information; retrieved 1/5/04.] http://www.hhs.gov/news/press/2002pres/20020131b.html.

### CHAPTER NINE

# Obtaining and Maintaining Local Interoperability

John D. Hoyle, Sr.

I n June 2001, the federal government held a tabletop terrorism exercise, known as Dark Winter, involving a simulated smallpox attack. In the exercise, the spread of the smallpox and its morbidity and mortality were charted. In testimony to Congress on July 23, 2001, Margaret Hamburg, M.D., former assistant secretary for planning and evaluation at the Department of Health and Human Services (DHHS) stated (Committee on Government Reform 2001):

> Dark Winter...demonstrated how poorly current organizational structures and capabilities fit with the management needs and operational requirements of an effective bioterrorism response. Responding to a bioterrorist attack will require new levels of partnership between public health and medicine, law enforcement and intelligence. However these communities have little past experience working together and vast differences in their professional cultures, missions and needs.

The solution to eliminating this void in interagency cooperation is to work toward achieving interoperability on local, county, and state levels and to coordinate with federal agencies.

---

The views expressed in this chapter are those of the author and do not necessarily represent the views of the U.S. Department of Health and Human Services, the U.S. Public Health Service, or the Government of the United States.

John D. Hoyle, Sr., M.H.A., LFACHE, is director of the Noble Training Center in Ft. McClellan, Alabama.

*Interoperability* is the effective interfacing of all medical and ancillary service providers (e.g., hospitals, public health agencies, emergency medical services [EMS], pharmacies, and medical suppliers) with public safety agencies (e.g., fire, rescue, and police services), Red Cross, Salvation Army, communications centers, public works, and utility companies. These agencies, in turn, must coordinate with political leadership and the media. To be effective, this all-encompassing effort requires each agency to deliberately and rigorously act to identify the strengths, weaknesses, opportunities, and threats (also known as a SWOT analysis) in their community and among themselves. Finally, the agencies must determine the best use of each other's assets for disaster mitigation, preparedness, response, and recovery in various disaster scenarios. This description of interoperability goes far beyond the usual use of the term by public safety agencies, which often simply define it as the ability to communicate— by radio or other means—with each other. While this ability is key to successful interoperability at the scene of a disaster, it is the planning and integration of services that precede the disaster that result in an effective response.

## EARLY EXAMPLES OF INTEROPERABILITY

An early example of military interoperability was the *Blitzkrieg* plan, or "lightning war," used successfully by the Germans in the early years of World War II. During the years between World War I and World War II, the German General Staff developed a doctrine and tactics that combined the infantry, armor, artillery, and support units with the air force, creating one striking force aimed at the enemy. The U.S. military learned from this example and successfully organized integrated techniques in all of its military services that eventually destroyed Germany's ability to wage war. The allied troops' D-Day invasion assembled the mightiest armada of ships, planes, and soldiers in history; it was organized by flag officers and involved troops from many countries. Working together as one unit, they forced their way onto the continent and eventually liberated Europe.

The EMS of the United Kingdom's Ministry of Health, not to be confused with the American EMS, was among the first examples of medical interoperability. During the incessant German bombing of World War II and the attacks by V-1 and V-2 rockets, the British EMS functioned as a planning, control, and operational program that integrated the casualty plan with the various components and levels of healthcare, from first aid to tertiary care and rehabilitation. London, for example, was divided into ten hospital sectors radiating from the city center outward, like a wagon wheel, into the surrounding counties. This organization was fully coordinated with first responders and civil-government authorities. The entire country had an EMS organization based on 12 national regions (Shirlaw 1940; Dunn 1952).

An early case example of medical interoperability in the United States is described in Sidebar 9.1.

## CURRENT INTEGRATION ATTEMPTS

The U.S. military continuously works to improve interservice interoperability into what is now termed Joint Operations, as highlighted in the efforts of the 2003 war to liberate Iraq. Furthermore, its doctrine includes the ability to work with multinational forces and interagency governments in unified, full-spectrum operations (HQDA 2001).

Figure 9.1 illustrates military interoperability through the five elements of combat power—manpower, firepower, leadership, protection, and information—tied together by various principles of war and based on the five tenets of initiative, agility, depth, synchronization, and versatility. These work together in an operational framework to facilitate decisive operations, including offensive, defensive, stabilizing, and supportive actions.

Similarly, DHHS has undertaken a national program to promote improved preparedness and interoperability throughout the United States, known as the Metropolitan Medical Response System (MMRS). The program originated in 1996, and by 2002, a total of 122 cities were enrolled (U.S. DHHS 2002a). The goal of MMRS is "to coordinate the efforts of local law enforcement, fire, hazmat, EMS, hospital, public health and other personnel to improve response capability in the event of a terrorist attack" (U.S. DHHS 2002a).

## EVALUATING COMMUNITY CAPABILITIES

The Department of Health and Human Services issues a contract to a city to develop an MMRS plan with 11 deliverables required for the financial

**Sidebar 9.1. Case Example: Pioneering Interoperability at the Local Level**

Beginning in 1950, the Academy of Medicine in Cincinnati, Ohio (Hamilton County Medical Society), established the Committee on Emergency Medical Services (EMS) to assist the burgeoning civil defense effort. In 1951, the committee submitted a report entitled "Emergency Medical Service for Hamilton County." While this effort was in process, the Hamilton County Office of Civil Defense was engaged in planning for a possible nuclear attack. In 1952, the chief of police requested the Greater Cincinnati Hospital Council (now the Greater Cincinnati Health Council) to submit plans for handling casualties from a civilian disaster.

Working together, the two bodies produced the Natural Disaster Plan, in which 14 hospitals participated. This plan, which spelled out the duties of each agency (including hospitals, the Red Cross, and the Academy of Medicine), was continually refined and was rendered official city policy. The various players continued to meet regularly and studied disasters that had occurred in the United States or abroad. This led to the desire to "crystallize the results of study and planning" (Warner 1968, 140). In 1963, a county disaster drill with 253 high school student "victims" was staged. The following year, the Office of Civil Defense and the Hospital Council conducted a drill with 438 simulated casualties and a host of new players.

One need identified through these exercises was for improved communications with participating hospitals. A dedicated telephone "hot line" system had been in place since 1956 but was subject to interruption by storms and tornadoes. This led the Hamilton County Office of Civil Defense to modify old transceivers for use by hospitals, and the Hospital Radio Net was born in 1963. At this time, participants included 16 hospitals, the U.S. Weather Bureau, the Red Cross, and the Civil Defense headquarters and mobile units, including a boat and a mobile unit owned by the Hospital Council. Membership continued to grow and the group became more diverse by adding city and county fire and police representatives, the health department, and a safety director. The disaster council also assumed responsibility for promoting a mutual-aid agreement among the 40 municipalities in the county and assumed disaster planning beyond the confines of the city of Cincinnati. Disaster drills became countywide in scope.

Participation and capabilities continued to grow. Executives of the County Communications Center joined what was by then known as the Disaster Council, allowing the hospital radio system to be tied into the communications center for quicker communications of conditions and dispatching of ambulances in an orderly manner to hospitals. The Flying Squad, composed of physicians from the Academy of Medicine, was formed to provide on-site medical treatment to trapped or other disaster victims. The Office of Civil Defense modified a semitrailer into a mobile hospital unit. In 1968, a new radio system was purchased and installed in area hospitals. Hospitals outside the county were also invited to participate in the network.

In 2003, 22 hospitals were on the radio net in the tri-state area. The activities of the Disaster Council are ongoing: drills are held, plans are refined, and relationships continue to be strengthened. Today, the Disaster Council has expanded to include the U.S. Coast Guard, utility companies, the metropolitan sewer district, the volunteer hazardous-materials unit, the urban search and rescue unit, the international airport, and the coroner's office.

Furthermore, the Disaster Council has lent its expertise to the development of the local Metropolitan Medical Response System, which includes a plan to receive and distribute pharmaceuticals and supplies from the Strategic National Stockpile, and has participated in airport disaster planning. A third-generation radio system, using 800-megahertz technology, is in the planning stages. The Red Cross contributes a 150-person medical assistance team, and the St. Luke's hospital system support a local disaster medical assistance team, and several regional emergency vehicles. The Greater Cincinnati Health Council now supports, with cooperation from fire and EMS services and the communications centers, a web-based patient diversion system that is currently being expanded to the outlying tri-state counties in Ohio, Kentucky, and Indiana. There are plans to expand the system for the National Disaster Medical System bed-reporting program and to expand other disaster-related applications. The Disaster Council also supports the efforts of, and has many dual members with, the Tri-State Emergency Association, founded in 1982 to promote regional emergency planning and response and to conduct and support multicounty drills.

*Source*: Warner, C. F. 1968. "History of the Hamilton County Disaster Council." Cincinnati, OH: Hamilton County, Ohio, Disaster Planning and Coordinating Council.

reimbursement and supplies for the service. Cities are urged to be comprehensive in their planning and to reach for areas of attention not previously covered in planning efforts. The program offers a number of tools to help cities accomplish this process. Checklist 9.1 at the end of this chapter lists activities concerning community planning efforts involved in MMRS.

The issues highlighted in the checklist contribute to a comprehensive MMRS. It is important that healthcare facilities not wait until an MMRS program comes to their city to begin this level of organization, planning, and preparedness. The health system and emergency services

FIGURE 9.1. MILITARY INTEROPERABILITY AND JOINT OPERATIONS

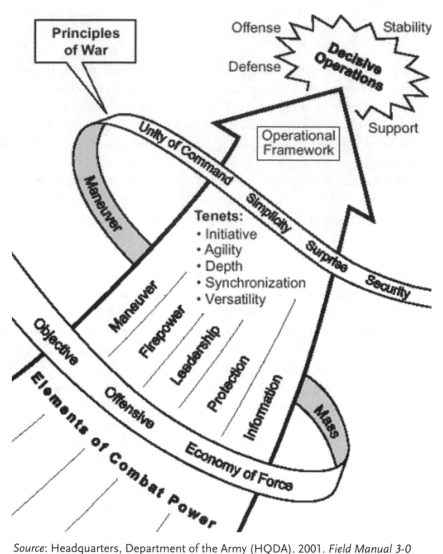

Source: Headquarters, Department of the Army (HQDA). 2001. *Field Manual 3-0 Operations*. Washington, DC: HQDA.

of any municipality can begin the process of improving their ability to effectively handle a mass-casualty incident, whether from natural disaster, pandemic, or terrorism, by reviewing disaster literature, including those items listed in the appendices at the back of this book. The maxim remains true: prior planning prevents poor performance.

An additional tool useful in the evaluation of a hospital's emergency plans is the Hospital Capability Assessment for Readiness

(HCAR), developed by Toby L. Clairmont and the Healthcare Association of Hawaii (CDC 2001). Twelve emergency management functions are assessed in the HCAR, which is "designed to assess capabilities known to be essential factors in the successful employment of hospital organizations in major emergencies" (CDC 2001). Based on the Federal Emergency Management Agency's Capability Assessment for Readiness (used to assess preparedness at the county or state level), the HCAR is a similarly comprehensive assessment tool for healthcare facilities.

## CALL TO ACTION

In the aftermath of the terrorist attacks on 9/11, the American College of Emergency Physicians (ACEP) issued a press release on December 11, 2001, announcing the formation of a new coalition to strengthen community readiness for biological, chemical, and nuclear terrorism and other disasters. Entitled "Partnership for Community Safety: Strengthening America's Readiness," the announcement calls on the federal government to support and sustain comprehensive readiness efforts in the nation's public health departments, hospitals, emergency departments, medical education institutions, nursing profession, and first-responder agencies. To work toward these goals, the partnership has brought together the ACEP, the American Ambulance Association, the American Hospital Association (AHA), the American Organization of Nurse Executives, the American Public Health Association, the Association of American Medical Colleges, the National Association of County and City Health Officers, the International Association of Fire Chiefs, and the National Association of State EMS Directors.

Member organizations agree that weaknesses exist in U.S. medical preparedness and response systems and that additional resources are needed to address the following issues (ACEP 2001):

- Improving the communications infrastructure
- Improving community-based planning
- Increasing community capacity to deal with disasters
- Improving disease surveillance, disease reporting, and field laboratory identification
- Protecting responders from the effects of nuclear, biological, or chemical (NBC) agents

- Increasing and enhancing training programs, continuing education, and community drills for mass-casualty incidents

Two of these recommendations are discussed in the following paragraphs.

*Improving the communications infrastructure* addresses the heart of building interoperability. In most American cities, response organizations, hospitals, and public health agencies are not linked by alternative communications means other than telephones or e-mail. This problem was stated in testimony by the AHA to the DHHS National Committee on Vital and Health Statistics Panel on National Preparedness and a National Health Information Infrastructure (U.S. DHHS, National Committee on Vital and Health Statistics 2002):

> In disasters, particularly those involving a large numbers of casualties, it is critical that hospitals have pre-established communications linkages with other frontline responders that are reliable and interoperable. However, in disasters, most organizations experience problems with interoperability. Communications often degrade as a result of saturated cellular and wireless communications systems that interfere with public safety communications. Public health services must be linked using secure connections to the Internet. High speed, dedicated Internet access should be available for all public and private healthcare facilities and related organizations. There is a critical need for funding to upgrade, modernize and link frontline responder communications systems and to address interoperability problems.

The recommendation to *increase and enhance training programs* is especially important because the new threats posed by terrorists can include NBC agents that are unfamiliar to most medical providers. In addition, the handling of mass casualties has not been studied in U.S. healthcare curricula, nor have the various aspects of community systems and interoperability that must be built for an effective community response to disaster.

## OVERCOMING CHALLENGES

A study performed in Hawaii in 2000–2001 assessed the attitudes and perceived capabilities of physicians and nurses related to working in nonhospital field medical care sites in times of emergency. The results revealed that while the percentages of those who would be willing to work in such a nonhospital setting (an aid station or alternative care center) were high for natural disasters (83 percent physicians, 90 percent nurses), the percentages of those willing to work in specific scenarios were significantly lower, as the following list illustrates:

- Explosion incident—67 percent physicians, 70 percent nurses
- Chemical incident—59 percent physicians, 59 percent nurses
- Biological incident—56 percent physicians, 53 percent nurses
- Contagious epidemic—56 percent physicians, 49 percent nurses
- Radiological incident—52 percent physicians, 45 percent nurses

The study also surveyed the current knowledge, recognition of signs and symptoms, and ability to treat casualties with similar results demonstrated by incident category (Lanzilotti et al. 2002).

If emergency management planners and fire officials are counting on the medical community to staff field medical stations, they will be disappointed to learn the results of this study. Discussion of this issue at an interoperability council meeting would be an excellent way to begin to address similar local issues and could result in improved response.

Clearly, the academic curricula for all healthcare professionals must also contain disaster-preparedness and response information relative to medical specialties. This education should demystify the new threats facing American healthcare providers. Knowledge replaces fear and is necessary to mount an effective community response to disaster (JCAHO 2003). Findings from a recent report on this subject released by the Joint Commission on Accreditation of Healthcare Organizations (JCAHO) are highlighted in Sidebar 9.2.

Realizing the many barriers to community preparedness, JCAHO convened a public policy roundtable of medical and hospital experts to review the situation. This panel made a number of recommendations regarding community-based interoperability, which are summarized below (JCAHO 2003).

1. Initiate and facilitate the development of community-based emergency preparedness programs across the country.
2. Include all appropriate community organizations as key participants to develop the communitywide emergency preparedness program.

In March 2003, the Joint Commission on Accreditation of Healthcare Organizations (JCAHO) released a report entitled *Health Care at the Crossroads: Strategies for Creating and Sustaining Community-Wide Emergency Preparedness Systems*. In this report, JCAHO made the following comments regarding the lack of interoperability:

> The concept of community-wide preparedness systems is new to most healthcare organizations. While most have long prepared and tested disaster plans, healthcare organizations have operated in isolation, and their disaster plans reflect this mindset.
>
> This does not gainsay the continuing extraordinary efforts of the three public safety agencies that this country has long relied on—law enforcement, fire and rescue, and EMS. Nor does it ignore the sometimes heroic efforts of under-funded public health and healthcare provider organizations in managing extremely challenging situations. But in most communities there is no team, nor teamwork, among all these players and other municipal and county leaders. And there is no community emergency preparedness plan, nor program, nor system.
>
> While the cast of emergency preparedness players in a given community can lengthen rapidly, there is no denying the central role that hospitals can and must play in these efforts. However, these are difficult and occasionally overwhelming times for hospitals, even without this expanded responsibility. In fact, many hospitals are struggling to meet the daily demands for their healthcare services.

*Source*: Joint Commission on Accreditation of Healthcare Organizations (JCAHO). 2003. *Health Care at the Crossroads: Strategies for Creating and Sustaining Community-Wide Emergency Preparedness Systems*. Oakbrook Terrace, IL: JCAHO.

3. Encourage the transition of community healthcare resources from an organization-focused approach to emergency preparedness to one that encompasses the community.
4. Provide the community organization with necessary funding and other resources and hold it accountable for overseeing the planning, assessment, and maintenance of the preparedness program.
5. Encourage the pursuit of substantive collaborative activities that will also serve to bridge the gap between the medical care and public health systems.
6. Develop and distribute emergency planning and preparedness templates for potential adaptation by various types of communities.

7. Create redundant, interoperable communications capabilities.
8. Ensure the inclusion of all community emergency preparedness program participants in the plan's tests.

The report continues by saying, "there thus exists a fundamental need to formalize an organization of community resources. That organization should comprise those authorities, agencies, providers, industries and other vital community elements that are critical to mounting an effective emergency response and protecting the community. Community-wide emergency preparedness programs do exist, and some are quite elaborate. However, they are few in number, and almost all exist in large metropolitan areas. By contrast, most of America's communities are 'waiting for someone to call the meeting' " (JCAHO 2003).

## REFERENCES

American College of Emergency Physicians (ACEP). 2001. "Partnership for Community Safety: Strengthening America's Readiness." Press release, December 11. Washington, DC: ACEP.

Centers for Disease Control and Prevention (CDC), Office of Workforce Policy and Planning and the Healthcare Association of Hawaii. 2001. *Hospital Capability Assessment for Readiness*. Version 1.10. [Online information; retrieved 10/15/03.] http://www.phppo.cdc.gov/owpp/assessmenttools.asp.

Committee on Government Reform, Subcommittee on National Security, Emerging Threats, and International Relations. 2001. "Combating Terrorism: Federal Response to a Biological Weapons Attack." 107th Congress, 1st session, July 23. Washington, DC: Committee on Government Reform.

Dunn, C. L. 1952. "Emergency Medical Services." *History of the Second World War*, Vols. I and II. London: Her Majesty's Stationery Office.

Headquarters, Department of the Army (HQDA). 2001. *Field Manual 3-0 Operations*. Washington, DC: HQDA.

Joint Commission on Accreditation of Healthcare Organizations (JCAHO). 2003. *Health Care at the Crossroads: Strategies for Creating and Sustaining Community-Wide Emergency Preparedness Systems*. Oakbrook Terrace, IL: JCAHO.

Lanzilotti, S. S., D. Galanis, N. Leoni, and B. Craig. 2002. "Hawaii Medical Professionals Assessment: A Study of the Availability of Doctors and Nurses to Staff Non-Hospital Field Medical Facilities for Mass Casualty Incidents Resulting from the Use of Weapons of Mass Destruction and the Level of Knowledge and Skills of These Medical Professionals as Related to the Treatment of Victims of Such Incidents." *Hawaii Medical Journal* 61 (8): 162–74.

Shirlaw, G. B. 1940. *Casualty Training, Organization and Administration of Civil Defense Services*. London: Secker and Warburg.

U.S. Department of Health and Human Services (DHHS). 2002a. Metropolitan Medical Response System home page. [Online information; retrieved 10/15/03.] http://www.mmrs.hhs.gov.

———. 2002b. *Metropolitan Medical Response System: 2002 MMRS Contract Deliverable Evaluation Instrument*. Washington, DC: DHHS.

U. S. Department of Health and Human Services (DHHS), National Committee on Vital and Health Statistics. 2002. Statement before the Panel on National Preparedness and National Health Information Infrastructure, February 26–27. Washington, DC: DHHS.

Warner, C.F. 1968. "History of the Hamilton County Disaster Council." Cincinnati, OH: Hamilton County, Ohio, Disaster Planning and Coordinating Council.

# Checklist

## CHECKLIST 9.1. COORDINATING A COMMUNITY RESPONSE

**Organization**

❑ Does the plan include an assessment of the statutes, regulations, and ordinances within the state that provide for credentialing, licensure, and delegation of authority for executing emergency public health measures?

❑ Does the plan identify how to coordinate the response of the public safety, public health, and health services sectors to a nuclear, biological, or chemical terrorist incident?

❑ Is the steering committee led by the state or area emergency management agency (EMA) or other single, officially designated body?

❑ Is the steering committee membership represented by the following:
    ❑ State emergency medical services (EMS)
    ❑ Local EMS
    ❑ Local health department
    ❑ State health department
    ❑ Law enforcement
    ❑ Federal agencies
    ❑ Medical director/examiner
    ❑ National Guard/military
    ❑ Hospital representation (public)
    ❑ Hospital representation (private)
    ❑ American Red Cross
    ❑ Mental health
    ❑ Pharmacy
    ❑ Local EMA
    ❑ Poison control
    ❑ Others

**Communications**

❑ Is the plan integrated with the applicable state plan and regional bioterrorism hospital-preparedness plan?

❑ Does the plan contain command and control procedures?

❑ Does the plan contain notification and alert procedures?

❑ Does the plan detail procedures for notification of hospitals, clinics, and health maintenance organizations (HMOs), etc., that an incident has occurred?

## Patient Transport

Does the plan

❑ include detailed procedures for the emergency medical transportation of victims?

❑ address the capacities and capabilities of emergency and inpatient hospital services, along with predesignated off-site treatment facilities?

❑ include procedures for managing patients arriving at hospitals without prior field treatment/screening or decontamination?

❑ address all available modes of transportation (vehicular, railroad, aircraft, and watercraft) for the forward movements or referral of patients?

❑ identify who in the jurisdiction has the authority to make the decision to move patients?

❑ detail the process for coordination with the state to request a Federal Emergency Management Agency mission assignment for forward movement or referral of patients beyond the state?

## Mass Patient Care

❑ Does the plan detail procedures for rapid expansion of the existing healthcare system capacity and plans for taking care of people in excess of either existing or expanded capacity?

❑ If existing plans include alternate care facilities, secondary assessment centers, or modular emergency medical system components (e.g., acute care facilities, neighborhood emergency health centers, off-site triage/treatment/transport centers), does the plan contain details for staffing, equipping, and providing transportation to and from these facilities?

## Mass-Fatality Management

❏ Does the plan develop or augment existing mass-fatality management plans for providing respectful care and disposition for a large percentage of the population?
❏ Have refrigerated storage locations or provisions been determined for the long-term storage of a large percentage of the population?

## Environmental Surety

❏ Does the plan describe or develop procedures for identifying environmental risk?
❏ Does the plan describe or develop procedures for determining the need for decontamination or vector intervention?
❏ Does the plan establish a process for safe reentry into the suspect area in consultation with local, state, and federal environmental agencies?

## Safety and Security

❏ Does the plan identify procedures to protect hospitals, clinics, and HMOs from contamination from environment or patient sources (e.g., lock-down procedures and patient-decontamination procedures prior to entry)?
❏ Does the plan detail procedures for providing adequate security?
❏ Does the plan identify the availability of adequate personal protective equipment and pharmaceuticals for hospital and clinic providers?
❏ Does the plan specify that adequate pharmaceuticals and equipment (ventilators) are available locally or that agreements are in place to obtain them in a timely manner?

## Response Procedures

Does the plan
❏ provide for three levels of response: (1) up to 100 victims, (2) between 100 and 10,000 victims, and (3) more than 10,000 victims?

❑ include consideration of the following (Category A) biological agents: smallpox, anthrax, plague, botulism, tularemia, and hemorrhagic fever?
❑ include detailed procedures for chemical/agent identification?
❑ include detailed procedures for the transport of contaminated patients and/or remains?
❑ include detailed procedures for antidote administration?
❑ include detailed procedures for victim decontamination?
❑ include procedures for victim triage in the field and prior to entry into the emergency department?
❑ specify that the medical staff have the ability to recognize and treat casualties caused by weapons of mass destruction (WMD)?
❑ detail readily available treatment protocols?
❑ detail procedures to deliver nonmedical supplies to appropriate facilities?
❑ identify training requirements for Metropolitan Medical Response System personnel, including all first responders, emergency medical technicians, paramedics, vehicle drivers, and emergency department and other hospital personnel who will be providing care to victims of a WMD incident?
❑ include initial and refresher training requirements?


## Pharmaceuticals

❑ Has the jurisdiction included the required pharmaceuticals, based on treatment guidelines, to treat 1,000 victims of a WMD event?
❑ Has the jurisdiction included the required pharmaceuticals, based on treatment guidelines, to treat 10,000 victims of a WMD biological event?
❑ Does the pharmaceutical plan integrate the state's plan for the request, receipt, transportation, breakdown, repackaging, storage, and distribution of the Strategic National Stockpile to a local jurisdiction?

*Source*: U.S. Department of Health and Human Services (DHHS). 2002b. *Metropolitan Medical Response System: 2002 MMRS Contract Deliverable Evaluation Instrument.* Washington, DC: DHHS.

### CHAPTER TEN

# Integrating Civilian and Military Medical Resources and Response Capabilities

Donna F. Barbisch

A s the nation's disaster-management capabilities evolve, building civilian and military medical interoperability is critical. Although both systems independently provide essential medical services to their enrolled populations, they differ in experience and approach to managing medical disasters.

The U.S. military has a long history of managing healthcare needs in complex combat and disaster environments. Military medical strength is built on clear and well-defined objectives, distinct lines of authority, consistent capability, well-organized planning, and established training criteria—all of which leads to predictable outcomes regardless of location. In contrast, civilian medical disaster-management capability varies from community to community. As part of our nation's capabilities, the military plays a role in providing medical support when civilian resources are overwhelmed.

What can and should the military medical community be prepared to provide in the domestic environment? Does the military have a need for support from the civilian community? This chapter explores these questions by examining the organizational differences in the military and civilian medical communities and providing insight into opportunities for mutual benefit. Although the military's hierarchical structure does not always translate well to the civilian environment, military management

Donna F. Barbisch, D.H.A., M.P.H., CRNA, is chief executive officer of Global Deterrence Alternatives in Washington, DC, and a major general in the United States Army Reserve.

processes may offer templates for civilian application. The issues related to the appropriate use of military medical assets for domestic support is examined in this chapter, as well as the often-overlooked need for civilian support to military communities. This chapter also identifies the process for accessing military support to synchronize planning and response initiatives.

## MILITARY MEDICAL ORGANIZATION AND OPERATIONAL CAPABILITY

The military medical system has two primary missions: (1) to provide healthcare services and support to members of the Armed Forces during military operations (operational medicine) and (2) to provide healthcare services and support for the entire enrolled population—military members, their families and dependents, and retirees (infrastructure support).

The military's managed care program, known as TRICARE, is a complex military benefits system with approximately 8 million beneficiaries and 465 military treatment facilities (91 hospitals and 374 clinics) located across the nation and around the world (U.S. GAO 1999). TRICARE is linked with civilian healthcare through provider networks, making it the largest managed care organization in the United States. The TRICARE program shares similar challenges with its civilian counterparts when dealing with the threats facing American healthcare. Military TRICARE resources generally work with the civilian community at the local level.

Operational medicine has as its primary goal optimizing battlefield-casualty management. The operational mission sets military healthcare apart from civilian healthcare in its focus on battlefield conditions. To meet the strategic wartime objectives and improve human performance, operational medicine has a formal command-and-management structure based on combat operations and potentially large numbers of casualties. Personnel maintain a high state of readiness to provide a full spectrum of medical support services. The system optimizes the health of service members before engaging in hostile environments, provides care onsite (where the injury occurs) at specified locations along evacuation routes, and makes every effort to return members to their predeployment state of health. Personnel train to perform critical medical services while serving in potentially hostile environments under extraordinary conditions. Deeply embedded in operational medicine is a full range of support systems that enable military medical services and facilities to seamlessly surge to meet complex healthcare objectives during combat operations.

## Military Command and Management Processes

Military management structure assigns responsibility and authority to meet mission objectives. The military has a clear and distinct chain of command and line of authority. Command and control are essential elements of the art and science of warfare that effectively decrease ambiguity during disasterlike conditions of combat.

Commanders are held accountable for maintaining standards in planning, directing, coordinating, and controlling personnel and operations. The system supports continual feedback with a process to align resources and correct deficiencies. While structured somewhat differently from the presidentially mandated incident management system, military staff is organized along the functional elements of personnel, intelligence, operations, logistics, civil-military operations, and signal (automation, network management, and information security).

### Planning and Coordination

The operational structure of military medical support is based on the projected combat or operational situation. A clearly delineated, formal planning process evolves from deliberate planning (long range) or crisis action planning (a form of planning while doing during an emergency) depending on time constraints for the required action. The military decision-making process is an organized and defined path to reach analytical solutions that will predictably achieve the desired objective (HQDA 1997).

Military medical planning defines the coordination that must occur across a spectrum of functional areas, referred to in military terms as battle operating systems. These include command and control, communications, computers, intelligence, hospitalization, evacuation, laboratory services, logistics, blood management, preventive medicine, and combat stress control. Coordination of these functional areas requires a strategic overview of the entire theater of operations (U.S. GAO 2001).

## Personnel Management

Military personnel systems balance deployment needs with the need for maintaining the TRICARE system. A cascading system exists to fill critical positions in operational units as necessary. Medical personnel are assigned to one of three categories: an operational combat unit, a TRICARE or fixed facility unit, or a combination wherein personnel work in their fixed-facility but train and deploy when necessary to support combat operations. As the combat priority is filled, the military vacancies left behind are filled through a system of backfill using assigned reserve, civilian, or contract support. Sidebar 10.1 illustrates this support system.

*Surge Capacity*

Military reserve components have the mission to expand the capability of the active component when called on to do so. They train on a regular basis with their active component counterparts and are held to the same high standards. The reserve components consist of federally assigned reserve forces and the National Guard. The National Guard, while having a federal mission, is primarily organized under state law whereby it serves at the pleasure of the governor. The National Guard of one state can access another state's National Guard assets through mutual-aid agreements. Although it has significant manpower, the National Guard does not focus on medical assets; collectively the Air and Army National Guards have only 10 percent of the physicians and 8 percent of the nurses assigned within the reserve structure (U.S. DoD 2001).

The military medical reserve structure is organized to support the two separate missions of its medical department: fulfilling the backfill mission of TRICARE and other nondeploying active-duty organizations (medical training, planning, policy positions, etc.) and deploying in support of an operational mission. Reserve components comprise 51 percent of the military medical strength (U.S. DoD 2001). This includes 56 percent of nurses, 42 percent of doctors, 43 percent of veterinarians, 29.5 percent of medical service corps members, and 50 percent of enlisted medical personnel. Table 10.1 illustrates the breakdown by corps.

The Commissioned Corps of the Public Health Service (PHS) also may be called to support the Department of Defense (DoD) under certain circumstances. PHS also provides medical support to the Coast Guard, which is organized under the Department of Homeland Security (DHS) during peacetime but may transfer to DoD to support declared war or national security emergencies.

These reserve components are a critical link between the military and the civilian community. In addition to the capability they provide for the military, having military-trained personnel in the civilian medical community provides a unique opportunity for community healthcare systems to capitalize on that military training and organizational skill. CEOs would be wise to identify their reserve personnel and tap their expertise. In the event of a military mobilization, healthcare organizations can reduce the impact of vacancies created by deploying reserve personnel by developing a backfill system.

*Training and Assessment*

Quality and capability are paramount in the military culture and are ensured through training and assessing skills and readiness. Members of military medical departments must maintain readiness at all times to

## Table 10.1. Department of Defense (DoD) Medical Personnel

|  | DoD Active Totals | DoD Reserve Totals |
|---|---|---|
| *Officers* | | |
| Nurses | 15,408 | 19,404 |
| Doctors | 12,585 | 8,956 |
| Veterinarians | 417 | 310 |
| Medical service personnel | 7,555 | 7,697 |
| *Officers total* | 35,965 | 36,367 |
| | | |
| *Enlisted* | | |
| Medics | 70,355 | 51,536 |
| Ready reserves | — | 19,117 |
| | | |
| **Totals** | 106,320 | 107,020 |

*Source*: U.S. Department of Defense (DoD). 2001. *Fiscal Year 2001 Health Manpower Statistics Report*. Washington, DC: DoD.

deploy to harsh environments and provide combat care. Training encompasses the full range of readiness from personal physical fitness and leadership to critical clinical skills. The military maintains continual monitoring processes to train, assesses readiness, identifies shortfalls, corrects deficiencies, and reassesses readiness. Mandatory quarterly reports flow from the smallest unit to the most senior levels in the chain of command to maintain accountability. Each commander's success is measured by stringent training standards.

## Equipment and Logistics Support

The military standardizes equipment and logistics-support packages for similar kinds of units. For example, every combat-support hospital has the same table of organization and equipment (TOE) so that each is essentially the same. An example of a standard combat-support hospital and its capability is shown in Figure 10.1. An individual can move from one unit to the next and know how the organization functions, know the command relationships (who is in charge of what), and know what type of equipment is available.

From the standard profile, planners can substitute one combat-support hospital for another in a given plan with assurance of providing the same capability. To optimize operational capability, equipment is packaged and

FIGURE 10.1. MILITARY MEDICAL-ASSET CAPABILITY TEMPLATE

| Combat-Support Hospital | |
|---|---|
| **Personnel** | 605 |
| **Mobility** | 15% |
| **Basis of allocation** | 2.4 hospitals per division |

**Mission**: To provide hospitalization for all types of patients within the theater of operations.

**Capacity: 296 beds**

| Type | 92 Bed (partial) | 296 Bed (full) |
|---|---|---|
| Personnel | 229 | 605 |
| ICU beds | 12 | 96 |
| Intermediate beds | 40 | 160 |
| Neuropsychology-dedicated beds | | 20 |
| Minimal care beds | 40 | 40 |
| OR tables | 4 | 8 (total of 144 OR table hours/day) |
| Mobility | 50% | 15% |
| Deployment | 48 hours | 72 hours |

**Capabilities**: Deployable hospital packages tailored to meet operational requirements. Provide emergency treatment to receive, triage, and resuscitate casualties; command and control; consultation services for inpatients and outpatients; pharmacy; psychiatry; community health services; clinical lab; blood banking; radiology; physical therapy; nutrition care services; and medical administrative and logistical services. *No Laundry Services.* The attached medical specialty teams enhance the hospital capabilities in dealing with infectious disease, neurosurgery, and head and neck surgery.

**Additional nonmedical support available:** The hospital has a dining facility capable of feeding several hundred people, a full motor pool, fuel trucks, water trucks, and a wrecker. It has a plumbing system, its own power generation team, and biomedical-equipment-repair facilities. Two radiology suites provide enhanced x-ray capabilities, and the hospital has full lab and blood-bank capabilities. Its communications section is equipped with the advanced long-range Harris radio system for worldwide connectivity.

*Note*: ICU = intensive care unit; OR = operating room

*Source*: Headquarters, Department of the Army (HQDA). 1994b. *Army Field Manual 8-10-14: Employment of the Combat Support Hospital, Tactics, Techniques, and Procedures.* [Online information; retrieved 8/03.] http://www.adtdl.army.mil/cgi-bin/atdl.dll/fm/8-10-14/toc.htm.

stored to be accessed and deployed in a time-phased process that coordinates the arrival of equipment with the arrival of personnel. Equipment may differ somewhat from service to service, but standards are evolving to ensure interoperability across the services.

Civilian hospitals can adapt baseline standards in assessing communitywide response needs. Developing a facility-capabilities profile similar to that shown in Figure 10.1 can assist community planners in assessing comparable capabilities among area healthcare facilities. Some information can be extrapolated from hospital associations and public health data. However, much of the existing data are based on licensure and financial reporting, requiring a clarification in terms such as "staffed beds."

## Communications

A system exists to manage and control information capability and services across geographical boundaries from the operations-support area to the forwardmost combat areas. Signal operations include automation and network management and information security. The military objective in a theater of operations is to have a single entity to manage the protocols and coordinate the interfaces between different parts of the medical system, such as radio frequencies, user directories, commercial systems, and multinational forces. Although different services may have different communications protocols, the objective is to seamlessly cross jurisdictional boundaries and effectively maintain operations.

## Facilities

The number of healthcare facilities that support military operations is determined by projected casualty rates extrapolated from historical data. During operational missions, predetermined plans identify the number of medical assets necessary to support the operational mission (HQDA 1994a). Through the use of planning assumptions regarding the number of casualties, acuity level, and ability to evacuate, planners revise the amount of hospitalization and holding capacity necessary as the situation changes. Comprehensive threat assessments, which include environmental and public health factors, drive the location of facilities.

Deployable facilities provide the flexibility of positioning definitive healthcare close to the area of impact.

## Policies and Procedures

Detailed systems drive the development of policy and procedures from the most senior levels within DoD down to the tactics, techniques, and procedures at the corpsman level. Policies and procedures flow from the statutory and regulatory requirements of the military. DoD directives identify broad policy guidelines, whereas joint publications direct overlapping operational service guidelines. Each service develops its own regulations that guide the development of field and training manuals. Consistency and interoperability are key in achieving overall objectives. Deliberate planning processes facilitate the development of policies that provide a basis for quality and consistency.

## EXPANDING MILITARY OPERATIONAL CAPACITY

With an emphasis on quality of service and cost containment, military medical-management systems are evolving to build collaborative systems with other healthcare partners. Ongoing initiatives to consolidate services and reduce redundancy are improving efficiency while maintaining the unique mission requirements of military healthcare.

Specifically, sharing agreements between DoD and the Department of Veterans Affairs (VA) aim at building on the strengths of the VA to optimize federal healthcare. The VA and DoD are engaged in sharing agreements for buying or selling services, joint ventures, TRICARE, pharmaceuticals and medical/surgical supplies, shared staffing, advanced technology, education and training, and consolidated procurement. As efficiencies improve and redundancy is eliminated, interdependence provides opportunities for improved asset visibility. The downside of reducing redundancy is the threat of overreliance on the same assets to fill critical needs in times of emergency.

In addition, the VA/DoD Contingency Hospital System and the National Disaster Medical System (NDMS) provide healthcare backup to DoD in the event of war or national emergency (U.S. DoD 2001). DoD maintains medical operational plans that coordinate the receipt, distribution, and treatment of returning military casualties. The VA/DoD Contingency Hospital System plan describes how VA-staffed hospital beds would be made available to treat returning military casualties (U.S. VA 2001). NDMS, described in Chapter 7, is a mutual-aid program that supports both military and civilian needs when medical systems are overwhelmed. The different systems were designed to support specific needs of returning military casualties as they relate to priority of care and fiduciary responsibility. For example, if a soldier returns as a military casualty to be treated in a VA medical center, the priority under the VA/DoD Contingency Hospital System plan is higher than if treated under TRICARE. Additionally, the funding allocation differs, affecting the facilities' bottom line. As the systems evolve, issues related to the priority of care and fiduciary responsibility must be clearly defined.

### Appropriate Use of Military Medical Assets

During the initial use of the Federal Response Plan in 1992, the Army's 44th Medical Brigade was called on to support civil authorities when those authorities were overwhelmed during Hurricane Andrew. The military medical response provided significant organizational structure and clinical support to the civilian medical response. As civil authorities regained capability, the 44th Medical Brigade redeployed to ready itself for its next military mission.

Military doctrine dictates that military assets should never be the first option in a civilian domestic response; the military's significant medical capability is organized to support combat operations. DoD recognizes the obligation for domestic support but is not organized, staffed, or equipped for initial domestic support.

As commander in chief of the Armed Forces, the president can order the military to provide domestic support in national emergencies. However, until or unless the military mission changes, the forces are organized around projected requirements for specific military contingencies. Having the *capability* to provide support should not be equated with the *responsibility* for initial support. All military assets, active and reserve, exist to support projected military missions. If needed for civil support, current planning dictates that the military is the last support in and the first out. Access to military support is addressed later in this chapter.

## Coordinating Local Military and Community Medical Assets

When military assets are located in the community, as in the case of military treatment facilities or military medical reserve units, what role exists for them in community planning? Coordination and synchronization begin with communicating existing capability and recognizing existing constraints. The first responsibility of the military is to support operational missions. As such, they may not be initially available to the community.

Military commanders, however, are a community asset and should be involved in community disaster planning. Supporting arrangements and memoranda of understanding may be appropriate, with the requisite review of senior command and legal counsel. On the other hand, the needs of the military community for civilian support are often overlooked. Disasters involving military facilities may require significant civilian assets; thus, the needs of the military should be considered and addressed in local planning. Every military commander has the authority to direct his or her assigned forces to support imminently serious situations to save lives, prevent human suffering, or mitigate great property damage. That authority must follow proper procedure and cannot be used to subvert the routine, albeit "emergency," requests.

## HOW TO ACCESS MILITARY MEDICAL SUPPORT

Military support for civil emergencies exists at two distinct state and federal levels. At the state level, National Guard assets are accessible through state emergency-preparedness processes and are generally coordinated through the state emergency management agency (EMA). Community medical planners should review existing regional plans that identify access to National Guard assets. A common error in community planning is assuming National Guard support without coordinating potential needs with National Guard leadership.

Under a federally declared disaster, access to federal military medical assets is generated through an official civil agency such as the public health department or EMA. Requests for assistance may be generated by a civilian healthcare facility to the local EMA or public health department. If local assets are overwhelmed or committed, requests for assistance are forwarded to the state EMA or health department.

If state assets become overwhelmed or are committed (e.g., through National Guard and mutual-aid agreements with other states), the state can request federal assistance through DHS. Requests are sorted for appropriateness to different federal agencies. Military requests go through the Office of the Secretary of Defense and the North America Command (NORTHCOM) to organize the DoD response. (NORTHCOM was established in 2002 to meet the evolving demands of homeland defense.) Operational support is coordinated through the Joint Task Force for Civil Support. The process can be executed in relatively short order. Figure 10.2 illustrates the flow of requests for assistance and how federal military assets are accessed to assist a disaster response at the local level.

Military planning is evolving as NORTHCOM assumes responsibility for executing homeland defense plans. Although very few federal military assets are assigned a primary role for domestic support operations, plans are currently being developed that allow medical personnel or units that might be designated to the civil support mission to become a part of the planned force structure.

It is important to note that requests to DoD for military support should be for a specific *capability* rather than for a specific unit. For example, if a public health department needs additional hospital assets and is aware of a particular unit in the local region, the request must still go forward as a request for the capability to care for a defined number of patients at a defined acuity level. Requests should never identify a specific military unit.

The organizational approach to accessing military medical support under a federal disaster declaration is different from when no federal declaration exists. Reimbursement is paramount in constrained fiscal environments; thus, without a federal disaster declaration, medical facilities run the risk of providing medical care without compensation. NDMS, through memoranda of agreement, may provide some level of support. The reimbursement criteria are specific, requiring documentation of requests and authorizations. FEMA manages reimbursement under federally declared disasters.

## Legal Authority

The use of military personnel to support medical requirements is primarily a function of planning and programming the national military structure. The military serves at the pleasure of the president—the commander

FIGURE 10.2. ACCESSING FEDERAL MILITARY ASSETS

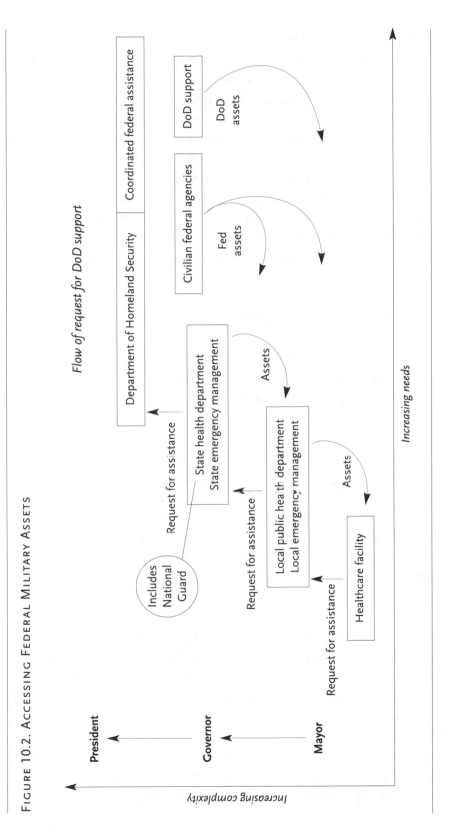

in chief—with the support of Congress. Contrary to portrayals by the entertainment industry, the military is not programmed to march into a city and take over. Statutory and regulatory guidance dictates that military assets are support functions and, when engaged, fall under the direction of civil authorities.

Limitations on the use of the military to enforce the law are referred to in the Posse Comitatus Act of 1878 (Title 18 USC, 1385). In the case of medical support, where law enforcement is not the issue, Posse Comitatus becomes moot. National Guard personnel under state authority (as opposed to federal authority) are exempt from Posse Comitatus and may be engaged by the governor, as they were to provide airport security throughout the United States following the 9/11 attacks.

## Multiple Events and Priority of Mission

The current configuration of military assets aligns the force to support the national military and security strategies of the United States. The National Military Strategy (U.S. Government, The White House 2002) states,

> The Armed Forces are the Nation's military instrument for ensuring our security. Accordingly, the primary purpose of U.S. Armed Forces is to deter threats of organized violence against the United States and its interests, and to defeat such threats should deterrence fail. The military is a complementary element of national power that stands with the other instruments wielded by our government. The Armed Forces' core competence is the ability to apply decisive military power to deter or defeat aggression and achieve our national security objectives.

The size of DoD's medical force is designed to support projected military actions. If multiple events occur simultaneously, DoD balances the risk and allocates force structure appropriately. The medical structure is part of the total force capability. If the nation requires domestic military medical support at the same time it is launching combat operations, the priority for military medical assets will be driven by national security concerns and will be determined by the president. All local planning should consider that military assets may not be available for local use if national security requires them elsewhere.

# REFERENCES

Headquarters, Department of the Army (HQDA). 1994a. *Army Field Manual 8-55: Planning for Health Service Support.* [Online information; retrieved 7/03.] http://www.adtdl.army.mil/cgi-bin/atdl.dll/fm/8-55/toc.htm.

———. 1994b. *Army Field Manual 8-10-14: Employment of the Combat Support Hospital, Tactics, Techniques, and Procedures.* [Online information: retrieved 8/03.] http://www.adtdl.army.mil/cgi-bin/atdl.dll/fm/8-10-14/toc.htm.

———. 1997. *Army Field Manual 101-5: Staff Organization and Operations.* [Online information; retrieved 8/03.] http://www.adtdl.army.mil/cgi-bin/atdl.dll/fm/101-5/f540.pdf.

U.S. Department of Defense (DoD). 2001. *Fiscal Year 2001 Health Manpower Statistics Report.* Washington, DC: DoD.

U.S. Department of Veterans Affairs (VA), Emergency Management Strategic Healthcare Group. 2001. *FY-2001 Annual Report.* [Online information; retrieved 8/03.] htttp://www.va.gov/emshg/docs/FY01_Annual_Report.w.doc.

U.S. General Accounting Office (GAO). 1999. *Defense Health Care: Tri-Service Strategy Needed to Justify Medical Resources for Readiness and Peacetime Care.* GAO/HEHS-00-10. Washington, DC: GAO.

———. 2001. *Doctrine for Health Services Support in Joint Operations.* Joint Publication 4-02, July 30. [Online information; retrieved 7/03.] http://222.dtic.mil/doctrine/jel/new_pubs/jp4_02.pdf.

U.S. Government, The White House. 2002. *The National Security Strategy of the United States of America.* [Online information; retrieved 8/03.] http://www.whitehouse.gov/nsc/nss.html.

# PART IV

*Exploring Special Areas
of Concern*

### CHAPTER ELEVEN

# Legal and Ethical Considerations in Disaster Situations

Section I by William R. Wayland, Jr.
Section II by Marjorie H. Brant

L aw, medicine, and ethics intersect when life's most challenging questions are raised. Under what circumstances do we impose compulsory treatment? What are the appropriate parameters of the patient-safety movement? How do we identify and address the racial, ethnic, and economic disparities that exist with regard to treatment and access to healthcare? How do healthcare professionals and institutions prepare and respond to natural or man-made acts that result in massive numbers of persons being injured, killed, or infected? How do we balance and preserve personal freedoms when there are broad public health implications to the exercise of those freedoms? Often, values and allegiances seem to compete or conflict. As the time-honored ethical code of the medical profession recognizes, the physician is responsible to many constituencies: patients, society, other health professionals, and self. It is not surprising, then, that disaster preparedness has both legal and ethical implications for healthcare organizations and raises many challenging questions.

---

William R. Wayland, Jr., J.D., M.S.H.H.A., is the author of Section I of this chapter, "Legal Aspects of Disaster Preparedness." He is principal at the law firm of McKoon, Williams & Gold in Chattanooga, Tennessee. Marjorie H. Brant, J.D., is the author of Section II of this chapter, "Ethical Considerations in Disaster Situations." She is an attorney and former general counsel for Columbia Gas of Kentucky in Lexington and Columbia Gas of Ohio in Columbus.

## SECTION I: LEGAL ASPECTS OF DISASTER PREPAREDNESS

Ongoing compliance with increasing governmental regulation and the process of formulating policy to anticipate specific legal issues that may arise during an actual civil disaster are both important legal aspects of disaster preparation by healthcare institutions. To ensure compliance, governmental regulations focus almost entirely on provider monitoring, reporting, and standards of preparedness. The heightened awareness of terrorist threats in the United States will stimulate more such regulation over the next few years.

Anticipating possible legal issues arising from a healthcare provider's response to an actual disaster, however, involves understanding the tension between public health needs and individual rights. Healthcare institutions must constantly review relevant policies and, through ongoing education and practical exercises, foster preparedness and awareness of their employees and physicians about these issues.

### Regulatory Reporting Requirements

Even more than the horrific destruction of the World Trade Center towers on 9/11, the ensuing assault with anthrax-contaminated mail exposed weaknesses in America's public health policy and laws. In response, the Centers for Disease Control and Prevention requested that Johns Hopkins University and the Center for Law and the Public's Health at Georgetown University prepare the Model State Emergency Health Powers Act (known as the Model Act) (Gostin 2002). By the end of 2002, more than 20 states had enacted legislation based in whole or in part on the Model Act (Center for Law and the Public's Health 2002).

Section 301 of the Model Act requires healthcare providers to report any illness or health condition that may cause a public health emergency, including diseases caused by biological agents, within 24 hours of their discovery. Each report must include details of the patient's condition, age, address, occupation, and other information needed by state authorities to locate and identify any other affected persons (Center for Law and the Public's Health 2001).

The Model Act imposes a new twist on reporting requirements in that all pharmacists, including hospital-based outpatient pharmacists, are required to monitor and report "unusual trends in pharmacy visits" that may indicate a public health emergency. These trends include unusual numbers or types of prescriptions and even unusual sales of over-the-counter medications (Center for Law and the Public's Health 2001).

Whether or not the jurisdiction of a particular provider has adopted the Model Act, all states maintain some regulatory scheme to monitor and report infectious diseases that potentially pose a public health emergency. Each healthcare facility must refer to its own state's statutes.

## Federal Standards of Preparedness

Some hospitals and other healthcare organizations meet Medicare's Conditions of Participation (COPs) through state surveys and certification by any number of designated state agencies, but most typically by a state health department. Disaster preparedness standards contained in Medicare's COPs are far from comprehensive. The facility must have "detailed written plans and procedures to meet all potential emergencies and disasters, such as fire, severe weather, and missing residents," and "train all employees in emergency procedures when they begin to work in the facility, periodically review the procedures with existing staff, and carry out unannounced staff drills using those procedures" (42 CFR 483.75(m)).

In general, state agencies have not elaborated on this standard. However, as part of the Balanced Budget Act of 1997, hospitals seeking certification from a state agency as a critical access hospital (CAH) under Medicare's rural hospital flexibility program are now required to maintain written procedures for managing patients, personnel, records, and the public traffic in its facilities. The CAH disaster plan must be developed in consultation with qualified experts and include procedures for transferring casualties and records, notifying emergency personnel, and providing ongoing training and drills for all personnel associated with the CAH "in all aspects of disaster preparedness. . . . All new personnel must be oriented and assigned specific responsibilities regarding the facility's disaster plan within two weeks of their first workday" (42 CFR 485.64). Guidelines specify a number of performance expectations to ensure a CAH is guarding the safety of patients in nonmedical emergencies (42 CFR 485.623).

## The Legal Effect of Accreditation

By calendar year 2000, approximately five of every six hospitals maintained participation in Medicare through accreditation by the Joint Commission on Accreditation of Healthcare Organizations (JCAHO) or the American Osteopathic Association (AOA) (CMS 2000). With a few exceptions, hospitals accredited by JCAHO or AOA are deemed in compliance with Medicare COPs for hospitals (42 CFR 488.5).

Hospitals and other healthcare providers that seek and maintain such accreditation as a basis for Medicare participation assume a higher duty of care and public health responsibility. No hospital should choose to renounce its accreditation because of increased legal risk. Nonetheless, a hospital that represents to others that it complies with JCAHO or AOA standards but in fact fails to comply risks institutional liability based on that failure. (JCAHO emergency management standards are further discussed in Chapter 4.)

Several cases have referred to JCAHO standards to determine the standard of care owed to the patient by a hospital facility. For example, the Supreme Court of Arizona found a duty to treat patients presenting for emergency treatment based on JCAHO requirements (*Thompson v. Sun City Community Hospital* 1984), as detailed in Sidebar 11.1. The U.S. Ninth Circuit Court of Appeals held that a hospital is directly liable for corporate negligence in failing to use reasonable care in selecting competent medical staff as that duty of care is defined by JCAHO (*Rembis v. Anderson* 1991). A Texas Court of Appeals held that the standards set by JCAHO could be used to help determine the appropriate standard of care for a hospital (*Denton Regional Medical Center v. LaCroix* 1997). However, in a subsequent Texas case, another appellate court found that JCAHO standards were formulated as goals and not as minimal standards of care or conduct (*Mills v. Angel* 1999).

In some cases, bona fide compliance with JCAHO standards may be used as a legal defense (see, e.g., *Access Now, Inc. v. Ambulatory Surgery Ctr. Group, Ltd.* 2001). Notwithstanding some case law to the contrary, an institution that voluntarily subjects itself to JCAHO standards must at a minimum use its best efforts to comply with those standards, including its emergency management standards.

JCAHO emergency management standards are more detailed than both the basic Medicare COPs and the standards required for CAH designation. As healthcare institutions began to review their own preparedness following the events of September and October 2001, many administrators came to believe that JCAHO had made extensive changes to the standards in reaction to terrorist attacks (HANYS 2002). In truth, the amendments to the standards are small but reflect an increased focus on the healthcare institution's role as a responsible but subordinate player in a larger, coordinated public health response.

Read as a whole, JCAHO emergency management standards suggest an affirmative duty to actively cooperate with public health authorities. Private healthcare facilities are expected to provide crowd and traffic control, plan logistics for critical supplies, identify and provide transport to other care sites, and provide family support activities (JCAHO 2002a). Each of these activities, and many others mentioned in the standards, are normally assumed by the state or federal emergency management agencies. Compliance with JCAHO standards means an assumption of some traditional governmental services but without expectation of reimbursement. The subject of reimbursement is covered in Chapter 12.

## Public Health Needs Versus Individual Rights

Formulating policies to address specific conflicts between the rights of the individual and the public in an extreme public health emergency or large-scale disaster may seem like a futile exercise. Fine legal distinctions with respect to individual civil rights at times must be subordinate to the health and safety of individuals.

Nevertheless, policy development, employee education, and practical exercises have always served healthcare facilities well. Healthcare providers must consider these difficult issues if for no other reason than to defend institutional decisions made under the stress of a real-time public health emergency or large-scale disaster.

### Patient Confidentiality Issues

Private patient information has never enjoyed any significant constitutional protection in relation to the fundamental interest of each state in the health of its citizens. In 1905, the U.S. Supreme Court set forth the legal principle on which public health initiatives are based (*Jacobson v. Massachusetts* 1905):

> the police power of a state must be held to embrace . . . such reasonable regulations . . . as will protect the public health and the public safety. . . There are [many] restraints to which every person is necessarily subject for the common good. On any other basis organized society could not exist with safety to its members.

Notwithstanding the inherent power of government, most states maintain some statutory scheme for protecting the confidentiality of the medical information that they compile. As with reporting requirements, these protections vary in content and complexity from jurisdiction to jurisdiction.

Some privacy standardization has recently been imposed on providers by the Health Insurance Portability and Accountability Act of 1996 (HIPAA). HIPAA standards preempt any contrary state law or regulation, allowing stricter state laws on privacy to stand, but do not restrict disclosures for "public health activities" (42 USCS § 1320d-7(b) 2002). Therefore, careful compliance with HIPAA standards and traditional state privacy standards should not restrain such comprehensive reporting of patient information as may be necessary to protect the public and the reporting institution.

HIPAA also contains other useful exceptions to the nondisclosure of patient information, including disclosure of "protected health information to authorized federal officials for the conduct of lawful intelligence, counter-intelligence, and other national security activities" (45 CFR 164.512(k)(2)). Furthermore, a healthcare provider is allowed to disclose protected patient information if the provider believes in good faith that the disclosure is "necessary to prevent or lessen a serious and imminent threat to the health or safety of a person or the public" (45 CFR 164.512(j)(1)(i)).

## Other Individual Rights

The civil and constitutional rights of American citizens have commonly suffered infringement from the exigencies of war or perceived threats to national security. In the case of a widespread public health threat, providers may expect to be "drafted" into a larger public health response, including a policing role. Providers may be expected to actively assist local, state, and federal officials in restraining the basic freedom of movement of its patients, visitors, and employees in case of quarantine. Furthermore, providers may be compelled to administer medical treatments to patients or employees who not only refuse to consent but actively resist the treatment.

The surgeon general, with approval of the secretary of the Department of Health and Human Services (DHHS), may promulgate rules for the apprehension, detention, or conditional release of individuals "for the purpose of preventing the introduction, transmission, or spread of . . . communicable diseases" (42 USCS § 264(b)). Currently, individuals with suspected cases of cholera, diphtheria, infectious tuberculosis, plague, smallpox, yellow fever, viral hemorrhagic fevers, or SARS (severe acute respiratory syndrome) are subject to apprehension and detention by federal officials (3 CFR Executive Order 13295, 2003).

Based on the legal duty to a mentally impaired patient, healthcare facilities have some experience in restraining the free movement of mentally incompetent individuals. However, widespread quarantines in response to a biological attack could require hospitals to police the entrance and exit of isolation units or of entire facilities. Discharge against medical advice, patient restraint, patient consent, and similar hospital policies should be reviewed to anticipate directives from public health officials as well as court orders.

One of the most controversial aspects of the Model Act is the power assumed by states under section 504 to compel the involuntary vaccination or treatment of individuals during a public health emergency (Center for Law and the Public's Health 2002). Numerous individuals and organizations were outraged by this section of the model legislation (see, e.g., Staver 2002). A review by the author of relevant state law prvisions in June 2003 revealed that except for statutes directed to the protection of minors and incompetent persons, only nine states had enacted legislation that allowed compulsory vaccination or treatment during a public health emergency. These state statutes vary in detail, and none have been tested in a court of law.

Only Arizona and Georgia grant powers to health officials to compel vaccinations in times of an extreme public health emergency (A.R.S. § 36-787; O.C.G.A. § 38-3-51). Delaware, Florida, Maryland, Minnesota, Wisconsin, and Wyoming empower public health authorities to quarantine individuals who refuse immunization (20 Del. C. § 3137; Fla. Stat. § 381.00315; Md. Ann. Code art. 41, § 2-202; Minn. Stat. § 12.39; Wis. Stat. § 252.041; Wyo. Stat. § 35-4-113). Maine grants such power to health officials only if there are "no less restrictive alternatives available to protect the public health and safety" (ME 22 M.R.S. § 820).

The constitutionality of these statutes has not yet been tested. Based on the history of similar statutes, one would expect a court of law to weigh the police powers of the state, and its inherent interest in protecting the health of its citizens, against the rights of the individual, including the personal, constitutional right to refuse treatment. The Supreme Court of the United States has "assumed, and strongly suggested, that the Due Process Clause protects the traditional right to refuse unwanted . . . medical treatment" (*Washington et al. v. Glucksberg et al.* 1997). To meet the constitutional standard, any treatment imposed by a state on an unwilling citizen almost certainly must be a last resort. Isolation or quarantine must not be a reasonable alternative.

## Liabilities from Smallpox Vaccination and New Protections

The passage of the Homeland Security Act of 2002 (U.S. Congress 2002) has intensified the intrinsic conflict of individual rights and the police powers of the government. Hospitals, healthcare providers, and their representative organizations expressed serious concerns about potential liability arising from participation in the smallpox vaccination program authorized by the act. When the secretary of the Department of Homeland

Security issued such a declaration of countermeasures on January 24, 2003 (68 FR 4212), opposition to the program increased. Section 304 of the act exempted persons or entities that administer the smallpox vaccine following a declaration of countermeasures, but healthcare employers and workers retained substantial risk of liability to individuals who might be harmed by the vaccine (42 USCS § 233).

The compensation limits for workers suffering a smallpox vaccination injury were viewed as inadequate by representative organizations. An April 2003 survey by the American Federation of Labor–Congress of Industrial Organizations (AFL-CIO 2003) determined that worker compensation laws in 19 states would cover a smallpox vaccination injury, 17 states would not provide coverage, and coverage in the remaining 14 states was then yet undetermined. Thus, in many cases the employer would absorb the costs of injury, directly or indirectly through premium increases or legal costs (NACCHO 2003).

The Homeland Security Act also sparked concern about liability to patients or other third parties who become infected with the smallpox vaccinia from a vaccinated healthcare worker. The smallpox vaccinia used in the United States is a live virus that posses minimal risks to a healthy individual. Because it is possible for a recently vaccinated individual to transmit the vaccinia to another individual ("contact vaccinia"), healthcare providers were particularly concerned about their potential liability to those individuals (Neff et al. 2002).

In an effort to address these and other concerns, Congress enacted the Smallpox Emergency Personnel Protection Act of 2003 (SEPPA), which President George W. Bush signed into law on April 30, 2003. SEPPA amends certain provisions of the Homeland Security Act and provides that a healthcare worker who is vaccinated pursuant to an emergency response plan approved by the secretary of the Department of Homeland Security and who has volunteered prior to the time the secretary may publicly announce an active case of smallpox anywhere in the world becomes a "covered individual" and thus is entitled to compensation under SEPPA (U.S. Congress 2003).

Any other person who contracts the vaccinia virus from a covered individual is also entitled to compensation under the no-fault program. If an injured individual is eligible for coverage under SEPPA, an action against healthcare institutions and individual providers is barred (2003 H.R. 1770). Unquestionably, SEPPA expanded the rights of workers and persons injured by smallpox vaccination as well as clarified and expanded the immunity of healthcare institutions and workers who participate in the program.

Notwithstanding the expanded rights and protections to healthcare institutions and workers under SEPPA, by the end of June 2003, an expert panel advised the president that the then-current vaccination program not be expanded. Several government officials also reported privately that the program had come to a virtual standstill (Connolly 2003). The concern of healthcare executives and their legal counsel must be that such "overnight" shifts in law and policy may become commonplace.

The Homeland Security Act directs the secretary of DHHS to work with the secretary of the Department of Homeland Security to set priorities, establish preparedness goals, and develop a coordinated strategy. The secretary of DHHS "shall develop specific benchmarks and outcome measurements for evaluating progress toward achieving the priorities and goals" (6 USCS § 184). These new priorities and goals may be expected to further elevate the standard of care for the public's health and the burden of compliance for healthcare providers.

### Effect of Disaster Response on Common Legal Risks

*Environmental Issues*

Except that in some cases enforcement of existing law is now linked to homeland security, compliance with environmental laws is not generally affected by the newest regulations. The U.S. Nuclear Regulatory Commission (2003) has already increased its enforcement actions against nuclear materials licensees, which in some cases involves revocation of licenses and assessment of civil monetary fines.

Reasonable but comprehensive preparations for containing the runoff of decontamination solution must still be made. The legal implications likely will be driven by an analysis of the reasonableness of the actions taken to control the runoff. Decontamination runoff may be viewed essentially as a hazardous-materials issue. Questions that should be raised include the following:

- What was the substance?
- Were adequate precautions taken to minimize the risk of further contamination of people or the environment by the runoff?

- Where does runoff go? To a water-treatment facility or into an open stream?
- Were steps taken to reduce the amount of runoff, such as a lined containment pool or pond, or were absorptive barriers provided?

Under the Good Samaritan provisions of the Comprehensive Environmental Response, Compensation, and Liability Act (CERCLA), no person shall be liable for damages resulting from rendering care in accordance with the National Contingency Plan (NCP) or at the direction of an on-scene coordinator of an NCP. However, healthcare providers remain liable for their own negligence (42 USCS § 9607(d)(1)).

The only protection given to healthcare providers from CERCLA liability in case of a large-scale emergency results if the provider is under the specific directives of an NCP or its coordinator. If facilities are not reasonably prepared to render assistance to persons contaminated by hazardous substances, or if any facility or provider acts outside the scope of an NCP, customary liability standards apply.

*Reimbursement Issues*

There would seem to be a clear ethical prohibition against predicating action on an assessment of whether reimbursement could be obtained. (Such ethical implications are discussed below in Section II of this chapter, "Ethical Considerations in Disaster Situations.") As discussed earlier, some courts consider the financial resources of the patient to be an "arbitrary" standard on which to base healthcare delivery decisions (*Thompson v. Sun City Community Hospital* 1984). A court could view decisions based on the likelihood of reimbursement in the same manner. Whether the exigencies of a response to a mass disaster would excuse an organization's failure to comply with procedural steps normally required for reimbursement likely would be a discretionary decision for the reimbursing agency.

*Malpractice Liability*

With the exception of Good Samaritan laws in some states, the potential for malpractice liability of a healthcare provider does not change in response to a natural disaster or terrorist attack. Most Good Samaritan laws do not extend immunity to persons (or facilities) who have a duty to render care under the particular circumstances. No reported case has granted immunity to a hospital facility or persons acting within the scope of their employment under any such law. Healthcare facilities are accountable to licensure standards and, in some cases, accreditation standards, including those related to disaster preparedness.

To be liable for a patient's injuries, the provider must be deemed to have a duty to care for that patient and must have failed to meet the relevant standard of care under the circumstances, which failure actually resulted in the injury to the patient. Under the Emergency Medical Treatment and Active Labor Act (EMTALA), all hospital institutions that participate in Medicare have a duty to treat and stabilize every person who presents in the hospital's emergency department (42 USCS § 1395dd). The duty of care is a flexible standard, however.

Good Samaritan laws are intended to give protection from legal liability in the context of emergency response. However, the fact that there was an emergency or disaster situation does not suspend the concept of reasonableness or the standard of care to provide a person who gives treatment (actor) with blanket immunity. One must still act within the reasonable limits of one's knowledge and skill. A physician acting under emergency/disaster conditions (e.g., with limited equipment or inadequate resources) would not be held to the same standard as would a physician of like knowledge and skill who provided treatment under significantly better conditions. The first physician, however, must not act with abandon or disregard for the welfare of the patient and hope to justify unreasonable actions on the basis of exigent circumstances.

Hospitals are expected to be reasonably prepared, although no healthcare facility can prepare for the infinite number of scenarios that could arise to challenge its capabilities during a large-scale natural disaster or terrorist attack.

### Refusal to Treat

In the event of a terrorist attack of a biological nature, a hospital may also have to tackle issues of staff who refuse to treat for fear of disease or agent transmission. The critical legal issue may be the basis for the refusal to treat and the timing of the refusal. If treatment has begun, any relevant Good Samaritan law and general negligence theory may apply. In brief, once one has begun to render aid, one cannot merely stop and leave the victim in a more precarious position or worse off than the person was before being given aid.

If treatment has not begun and there is a selective refusal to treat, the basis for that refusal becomes important, as does whether it is the refusal of an individual doctor or an institution. An institutional refusal would be either that of a doctor who is the agent of the institution or as a matter of institutional policy. An individual's refusal might violate ethical canons and result in licensure action but not result in legal liability. The institution and individuals who function as its agents must abide by any statutory or constitutional mandates (e.g., antidiscriminatory bans) that apply, as well as by relevant ethical and licensure issues.

### Volunteer Physicians and Other Professionals

Medical personnel volunteer in disasters. This act occurs in every disaster in communities across this country, as it does overseas. Volunteer professionals (physicians, nurses, pharmacists, and others) are those not on staff who report to the hospital in a disaster situation volunteering their services to assist. To prepare for such a situation, the facility should implement a screening process during nondisaster times to review the credentials of those indicating they would like to be "local volunteers" and should develop a method to integrate them into the response of the facility in mass-casualty situations.

When this action does not occur prior to an event, the circumstances of the disaster might make the process more or less exacting and more or less time consuming. If circumstances make screening impossible, the facility might elect to limit potential legal exposure by restricting the volunteer professional to duties that have a reduced likelihood of adversely affecting the health and well-being of the patient.

It is wise to preidentify medical resources that may be available in disasters and develop a system to notify and use these professionals when disasters occur. Their preinvolvement with your facility (whether through facility tours, in-service meetings or continuing education sessions with hospital personnel, or precredentialing) will greatly increase their utility in disaster situations.

### Roles and Responsibilities of the Board

With respect to an organization's preparedness for the extreme conditions occasioned by a natural disaster or a terrorist attack, the roles and responsibilities of the governing body are not defined by law. Without that definition, healthcare organizations face some increased legal risk. Because preparation to confront a remote risk costs time and resources, leadership of the board in the area of disaster preparedness is indispensable.

To avoid liability resulting from the new accreditation and regulatory environment, a governing body should monitor compliance with accreditation, regulatory, and statutory requirements as it now monitors other aspects of corporate compliance. For larger healthcare institutions, particularly tertiary-care trauma centers, it may be necessary to form a distinct committee to monitor the ongoing preparation to meet the demands of a large-scale disaster.

### Preparing Through Practice

In response to the great variety and changing standards of public health responsibility, hospitals must develop policies and principles to guide future decisions made during an actual public health emergency. All hospital policies relating to public health and emergency response must be continuously reviewed in light of evolving standards and proliferating regulation.

Sidebar 11.2 gives sample case-method exercises with hypothetical scenarios that healthcare managers, physicians, and critical emergency services personnel may use to practice their responses to issues they may be forced to confront. Of necessity, the hypothetical scenarios only touch on the limitless variety of potential risks. Furthermore, the suggested answers do not consider applicable state law or future regulations. At a minimum, hospital counsel should approve, and probably participate in, such exercises.

### SECTION II: ETHICAL CONSIDERATIONS IN DISASTER SITUATIONS

The ethical imperative for healthcare organizations to participate in emergency preparedness is embedded in the historical development of

**Sidebar 11.2. Case Examples: Hypothetical Cases and Legal Responses to Emergency Situations**

| Hypothetical Case | Suggested Legal Response | Statute or Regulation |
|---|---|---|
| Emergency services personnel respond quickly to a call for a patient seen running frantically from his apartment. The patient has a runny nose, is sweating, is short of breath, and staggers but is still conscious and can answer in English. He demands the drug atropine by name and insists that the ambulance immediately take him from the site. | Possible accidental release of toxic gas should be reported immediately to authorities, including all relevant patient information. | 45 CFR 164.512 allows good-faith disclosure for national security or to protect the health or safety of another. |
| A patient staggers into a hospital emergency department (ED) with a severe cough. ED personnel immediately observe obvious symptoms of smallpox. Patient sits down in the crowded waiting room and then gets up to leave before being evaluated. | The patient may be restrained against his will based on imminent risk to public health, but not without some legal risk to ED personnel. | 42 USCS § 264 and 48 FR 56927 allow federal officials to restrain. If a public health emergency is in effect, state statute may allow restraint. ED personnel may need to justify personal actions as common-law defense of others or necessity defense. |
| Hundreds of patients are streaming through a facility's clinic for a state-mandated emergency smallpox vaccine. One individual escorted by a police officer refuses because he says he is a Vulcan. The facility has no open beds, and the officer says the public emergency means no one is available to guard the individual. | Hospital personnel may or may not be able to administer the vaccine based on the patient's incompetence, the reasonableness of locating a guardian, and the availability of alternatives. | The state statute authorizing vaccinations, if any, must be consulted. |

medical ethics, the ethical codes and policy statements of numerous professional medical organizations, and the accreditation standards of JCAHO and AOA. Although there may be a philosophical question of whether organizations can be held ethically accountable for their actions, the degree of coordination and the close affinity between practicing professionals and the organization in the decision-making process suggest that healthcare organizations should be held ethically accountable (AMA 2000).

Numerous professional healthcare organizations have adopted individualized codes of ethics or issued ethical policy guidelines. Individual professionals are the primary focus of professional codes of ethics and are thus obliged to use their expertise in service to their communities (AMA 2000). It is this ethical imperative that supports vigorous engagement in emergency preparedness.

Healthcare organizations, like the professionals they employ, are held accountable to act in ways deserving public trust, and although they must act in a way that validates individual rights, they must also focus on patient populations (AMA 2000). Although some healthcare organizations may have defined "community" in ways that encourage select membership (e.g., defining community so as to exclude the costly sick [AMA 2000]), a broader, more inclusive definition is reasonable and appropriate in the context of ethical standards. Service to the community makes disaster preparedness an ethical responsibility.

## Ethical Codes, Policies, and Standards Supporting Service to the Community

Several professional medical associations and accrediting organizations obligate healthcare professionals or organizations to provide service to their communities or the public, which includes preparing for, responding to, and mitigating the possible effects from large-scale disasters. The codes of ethics of some of these organizations are discussed below. This obligation is contained within their respective ethical codes, policy statements, or standards. In the words of the American Medical Association (AMA 1994), although ethical values and legal principles are usually closely related, "ethical obligations typically exceed legal duties...and in exceptional circumstances of unjust laws, ethical responsibilities should supersede legal obligations." Disaster preparedness is an ethical responsibility of individual medical professionals and healthcare organizations.

### American College of Healthcare Executives

The American College of Healthcare Executives' (ACHE 2000) policy statement *Healthcare Executives' Responsibility to Their Communities* provides that the healthcare executive's responsibility to the community encompasses a commitment to improving the community's health status and working for the betterment of the community at large. It is the healthcare executive's responsibility to take a leadership role in serving the community through support of organizational initiatives and civic affairs. Evidence of participation and leadership is required to advance within ACHE. The list below highlights those leadership actions cited by ACHE that are considered to be imperative in disaster planning and preparedness:

- Advocating and participating in collaborative efforts with other community healthcare providers and social service agencies
- Working with other concerned organizations and individuals to develop effective measures of the community's health status
- Leading their organization in collaborative efforts to address health concerns by working with public health and other governmental agencies, businesses, associations, educational groups, religious organizations, elected officials, and others
- Participating in local assessments of community need
- Volunteering to meet on behalf of the organization with the public, with policymakers, and with key stakeholders to define community healthcare priorities

Ethical decision making is the balancing of the needs and interests of the individual, the organization, and society. ACHE's (2002) policy statement *Ethical Decision Making for Healthcare Executives* describes healthcare executives' responsibility to address ethical issues with broad community and societal implications. Two of the recommended actions in particular support ethical decision making in the context of disaster preparedness:

- Develop organizational mechanisms that can deal with the spectrum of ethical concerns—medical, social, and financial.
- Promote diverse input into ethical considerations by including groups that bring unique and valuable perspectives to the discussion of ethical issues.

ACHE professional policy statements include a number of responsibilities of the healthcare executive that relate to personal, facility, organizational, and community preparedness. ACHE policies can be viewed at http://www.ache.org/policy/index.cfm.


### American Medical Association

AMA's (2001) *Principles of Medical Ethics*, the Reports of the Council on Ethical and Judicial Affairs, and the Opinions of the Council of Ethics and Judicial Affairs together constitute AMA's Code of Medical Ethics. Two of the nine principles help define the physician's ethical responsibility toward the community:

- A physician shall recognize a responsibility to participate in activities contributing to the improvement of the community and the betterment of public health (principle VII).
- A physician shall support access to medical care for all people (principle IX).

AMA's (2003) official policy statement on organized medicine's role in the national response to terrorism commits AMA to work with appropriate public health, law enforcement, hospital, and emergency response agencies and associations, as well as the pharmaceutical industry and media, to do the following:

- Develop coordinated plans and strategies that identify the specific needs, roles, contributions, and participation of organized medicine and individual physicians in disaster planning and emergency response to terrorist attacks.
- Identify procedures for the rapid detection, early reporting, and medical management of affected individuals.

- Urge medical schools and residency programs to develop curricula and training programs for medical students and residents regarding medical and public health aspects of biological and chemical terrorism, as well as community disaster planning and emergency response procedures, in the event of such terrorism.

### American College of Emergency Physicians

Supplementing the general ethical obligations that are common to all physicians, the American College of Emergency Physicians' (ACEP 2002)[1] *Principles of Ethics for Emergency Physicians* sets forth the following specific ethical obligations for emergency physicians:

- Emergency physicians have a social role and the responsibility to act as healthcare providers of last resort.
- Emergency physicians have a social duty to render emergency aid outside the normal healthcare setting to save life.
- Emergency physicians are a resource for the community in disaster management, public health, and related areas.

ACEP recognizes that emergency medicine requires multidisciplinary cooperation and teamwork and that emergency physicians owe a duty to society as well as to the individual patient. The central tenets of that duty include the following:

- Access to emergency medical care is a fundamental right.
- Adequate in-hospital and outpatient resources must be available to guard emergency patients' interests.
- Emergency physicians should promote prudent resource stewardship without compromising quality care for all patients.
- There is a duty to respond to out-of-hospital emergencies and disasters.

Thus, emergency physicians have an ethical duty to respond to emergencies in the community and to offer assistance as a special resource. When the resources of a healthcare facility are overwhelmed by epidemic illness, mass casualties, or disaster, the emergency physician must make triage decisions to benefit the greatest number of potential survivors based on both the need and the likelihood of survival.

### Joint Commission on Accreditation of Healthcare Organizations

JCAHO defines an emergency as a natural or man-made event that suddenly or significantly disrupts the environment of care, disrupts care or treatment, or changes or increases demand for the healthcare organization's services. In January 2001, the JCAHO disaster preparedness standards were modified to introduce the concepts of emergency management and community involvement into the management process in its Environment of Care (EC) standard 1.4 (JCAHO 2002a). Following the terrorist attacks of 9/11, JCAHO added a requirement that organizations communicate and coordinate with each other (JCAHO 2002b).

EC.1.4 requires hospitals and ambulatory care, behavioral health, home care, and long-term-care organizations to develop a management plan that ensures effective response to emergencies by addressing the four phases of emergency management: mitigation, preparedness, response, and recovery (implementation of the plan is mandated by EC.2.4). Furthermore, standard EC.2.9.1 requires facilities to execute the management plan by conducting emergency management drills (JCAHO 2002a). Certain obligations and activities are specified for each phase of emergency management; these are described in more detail in Chapter 4.

### American Osteopathic Association

AOA represents America's osteopathic physicians and surgeons and also accredits the Colleges of Osteopathic Medicine, osteopathic internships and residency programs, and healthcare facilities. AOA's (1998) *Code of Ethics* includes the following support for active participation in community disaster management:

- In emergencies, a physician should make his or her services available (§ 3).
- A physician shall recognize a responsibility to participate in community activities and services (§ 14).

There are no easy answers to the questions that arise when law, ethics, and medicine intersect. Indeed, often there may be no definitive answers. Regulatory compliance, accrediting standards, statutory directives, and professional codes of conduct provide guidance and help to define and produce what our society deems to be acceptable and expected behaviors. Post 9/11, there is a heightened awareness of the potential for man-made disasters and a heightened concern that American institutions, including our healthcare institutions, may not be able to meet the challenges posed by that potential. Disaster preparedness has taken on a new definition and a new urgency.

## NOTE

1. See FRED Online (the Federation Repository of Ethics Documents Online) for a collection of full-text codes of ethics and ethics-related policies provided by state and specialty medical associations in AMA's Federation.

## REFERENCES

*Access Now, Inc. v. Ambulatory Surgery Ctr. Group, Ltd.*, 146 F. Supp. 2d 1334, 2001 U.S. Dist. LEXIS 23091 (S.D. Fla. 2001).

American College of Emergency Physicians (ACEP). 2002. *Principles of Ethics for Emergency Physicians*. [Online article; retrieved 10/16/03.] http://www.ama-assn.org /ama/pub/article/7665-4671.html

American College of Healthcare Executives (ACHE). 2000. *Healthcare Executives' Responsibility to Their Communities*. [Online policy statement; retrieved 10/16/03.] http://www.ache.org/policy/Respon.cfm.

———. 2002. *Ethical Decision Making for Healthcare Executives*. [Online policy statement; retrieved 10/16/03.] http://www.ache.org/policy/decision.cfm.

American Federation of Labor–Congress of Industrial Organizations (AFL-CIO). 2003. "State and Federal Smallpox Compensation." [Online article; retrieved 6/17/03.] http://www.afl-cio.org/.

American Medical Association (AMA). 1994. "The Relation of Law and Ethics." [Online statement; retrieved 10/16/03.] *Code of Ethics* E-1.02. http://www.ama-assn.org/ama /pub/category/8312.html.

———. 2000. *Organizational Ethics in Healthcare: Toward a Model for Ethical Decision-Making by Provider Organizations*, 4. [Online report; retrieved 10/16/03.] Report for the National Working Group on Health Care Organizational Ethics convened by the

Institute for Ethics at the American Medical Association. http://www.ama-assn.org/ama/upload/mm/369/organizationalethics.pdf.

———. 2001. *Principles of Medical Ethics*. http://www.ama-assn.org/ama/pub/category/2512.html.

———. 2003. *Organized Medicine's Role in the National Response to Terrorism*. [Online report; retrieved 10/16/03.] Report 10 of the Council on Scientific Affairs (A-00). http://www.ama-assn.org/ama/pub/article/2036-2929.html.

American Osteopathic Association (AOA). 1998. *Code of Ethics*. http://www.aoa-net.org/MembersOnly/code.htm.

Center for Law and the Public's Health at Georgetown and Johns Hopkins Universities. 2001. Model State Emergency Health Powers Act (Model Act). [Online report; retrieved 11/12/02.] http://www.publichealthlaw.net/MSEHPA/MSEHPA2.pdf.

———. 2002. "Model State Emergency Health Powers Act State Legislative Activity." [Online information; retrieved 11/12/02.] www.publichealthlaw.net.

Centers for Medicare & Medicaid Services (CMS). 2000. *The CMS Chart Series*. [Online information; retrieved 6/29/03.] http://www.cms.hhs.gov/charts/default.asp.

Connolly, C. 2003. "Panel Urges Caution on Smallpox Inoculation." *Washington Post* June 20: A09.

*Denton Regional Medical Center v. LaCroix*, 947 S.W.2d 941, 950 (Tex. App.—Fort Worth 1997, writ denied).

Gostin, L. O. 2002. "Public Health Law: A Renaissance." *Journal of Law, Medicine & Ethics* 30 (Summer): 136–40.

Healthcare Association of New York State (HANYS). 2002. *JCAHO Rumor Buster*, July. [Online publication; retrieved 11/20/03.] http://www.hanys.org/auth/dir2/rumorbuster/rumorbuster702.pdf.

Jacobson v. Massachusetts, 197 U.S. 11, 38–39, 25 S. Ct. 358, 366, 49, L. Ed. 643 (1905).

Joint Commission on Accreditation of Healthcare Organizations (JCAHO). 2002a. "Emergency Management Standards—EC.1.4 and EC.2.9.1." [Online information; retrieved 10/16/03.]. http://www.jcrinc.com/subscribers/perspectives.asp?durki=2914.

———. 2002b. *Facts About the Emergency Management Standards*. [Online information; retrieved 10/16/03.] http://www.jcaho.org/accredited+organizations/health+care+network/standards/ems+facts.htm.

*Mills v. Angel*, 995 S.W.2d 262 (Tex. App.—Texarkana 1999, no pet.).

National Association of County and City Health Officials (NACCHO). 2003. "Smallpox Pre-event Vaccination: Liability and Compensation Concerns." ASTHO/NACCHO Smallpox Liability and Compensation Working Group Paper. Washington, DC: NACCHO.

Neff, J. M., J. M. Lane, V. A. Fulginiti, and D. A. Henderson. 2002. "Contact Vaccinia—Transmission of Vaccinia from Smallpox Vaccination." *Journal of the American Medical Association* 288 (15): 1901–05.

*Rembis v. Anderson*, 1991 U.S. App. LEXIS 24844 (9th Cir. U.S. Ct. App July 31, 1991).

Staver, M. D. 2002. "Proposed Emergency Health Powers Law Threatens Civil Liberties." [Online article; retrieved 10/16/03.] *Jerry Falwell's National Liberty Journal.* http://www.nljonline.com/jan02/staver.htm.

*Thompson v. Sun City Community Hospital*, 141 Ariz. 597; 688 P.2d 605; 1984 Ariz. LEXIS 252 June 12, 1984 (Supreme Court of Arizona 1984).

*United States Code Service* (USCS). 2002. Various cases. New York: Matthew Bender and Company, Inc.

U.S. Congress. House of Representatives. *Homeland Security Act of 2002.* P.L. 107-296, 116 Stat. 2135 (2002).

U.S. Congress. House of Representatives. *Smallpox Emergency Personnel Protection Act.* P.L. 108-20 (2003).

U.S. Nuclear Regulatory Commission (NRC). 2003. "Fact Sheet on Nuclear Security Enhancements Since Sept. 11, 2001." [Online fact sheet; retrieved 6/23/03.] www.nrc.gov/reading-rm/doc-collections/fact-sheets/security-enhancements.html.

*Washington et al. v. Glucksberg et al.*, 521 U.S. 702; 117 S. Ct. 2258; 117 S. Ct. 2302 (1997).

### CHAPTER TWELVE

# Availability of Disaster Assistance from the Federal Emergency Management Agency[1]

Ernest B. Abbott

In the event of a serious terrorism event—one involving significant threat to life and public health and significant damage to property—the governor of the state in which the incident occurs will almost certainly request federal help. After receiving this gubernatorial request, the president can then declare a "major disaster" or "emergency" under the Robert T. Stafford Disaster Relief and Emergency Assistance Act of 1988, as amended (Stafford Act).[2]

This chapter outlines the basic issues that are raised when hospitals and other healthcare organizations attempt to qualify for federal disaster grants from the Federal Emergency Management Agency (FEMA). It does not address the interaction between these programs and assistance programs available for individuals (including individual insurance coverage) nor public health preparedness and response programs administered and funded by federal agencies other than FEMA.

## DECLARING A DISASTER

FEMA's disaster assistance programs are activated only upon a Stafford Act declaration by the president. Although healthcare administrators will

---

Ernest B. Abbott, Esq., is of the FEMA Law Associates in McLean, Virginia.

generally not have a role in the process of obtaining a declaration, understanding how the process works is useful. It is also useful to understand the critical role that state governments play in administering emergency assistance.

The Stafford Act does not provide any independent authority to the federal government to address directly the emergency conditions in an affected state. The act only authorizes the federal government to "assist" state and local governments in their efforts to address the situation. Direct federal authority to act in response to specific terrorist or health threats may well be found in other statutory authorities. Even in that regard, the Stafford Act remains extremely significant because funds to pay for any actions taken under Stafford Act programs to assist state and local governments, either directly or by providing financial assistance in the form of federal grants, are already appropriated and available for expenditure in the Disaster Relief Fund.[3]

### Emergency Declarations

Emergency declarations activate federal resources to help state and local governments (and not-for-profit institutions like hospitals and other healthcare organizations) "save lives, protect property and public health and safety, and lessen or avert the threat of catastrophe."[4] These declarations are intended for situations in which prevention of a disaster is still possible, by, for example, evacuating populations in advance of a hurricane, sandbagging structures to protect them from predicted flooding, or vaccinating a population threatened by a disease outbreak. The emergency authorities are restricted to those actions necessary to reduce the imminent threat of harm; emergency declarations do not allow reimbursements to help pay for the recovery or rebuilding from resulting loss or damage. There is no restriction on the type of emergency that can trigger an emergency declaration. Emergencies have been declared in the past to pre-position equipment to help fight wildfires, assist in spraying mosquitoes carrying West Nile encephalitis, construct detention facilities for a massive influx of illegal immigrants, help find all of the parts of the Space Shuttle Columbia after its breakup over Texas, and help fund snow-removal efforts after record or near-record snowfalls.

With one very significant exception, the president can declare an emergency *only* if the governor of the affected state asks the president for a declaration, tells the president that the "situation is beyond the resources of state and local government,"[5] and activates the state's emergency plan.

The exception mentioned above is narrow and quite important, particularly with respect to potential terrorist events involving weapons of mass destruction. The president "may" exercise any of the Stafford Act's emergency authorities (to assist state and local governments) when he

> determines that an emergency exists for which the primary responsibility for response rests with the United States because the emergency involves a subject area for which, under the Constitution or laws of the United States, the United States exercises preeminent responsibility and authority. In determining whether or not an emergency exists, the President shall consult with the governor of any affected States, if practicable.[6]

Unilateral presidential declarations are quite rare, particularly because governors have tended to request declarations even in situations where a president could have acted without a request. Incidents on federal property (such as the bombing of the Murrah Federal Building in Oklahoma City in 1995 and the attack on the Pentagon on 9/11) qualify for unilateral declarations. Emergencies involving nuclear materials are clearly the preeminent responsibility of the United States under the Atomic Energy Act. Because the responsibility for national defense rests with the federal government, the United States is likely to take the view that any terrorist incident is a matter of preeminent federal responsibility.

## Major Disaster Declarations

"Major disaster" declarations not only activate emergency authorities to protect against imminent harm, they also trigger federal grant and "in-kind" assistance programs to help victims recover from disaster loss and damage. A major-disaster declaration will not necessarily be available in some terrorist scenarios. A disaster can only be declared if caused by a natural catastrophe (including any hurricane; tornado; storm; high water; wind-driven water; tidal wave; tsunami; earthquake; volcanic eruption; landslide; mudslide; snowstorm; or drought or, regardless of cause, any fire, flood, or explosion).[7]

A terrorist event that does not involve a fire or explosion and cannot be classified as a natural catastrophe cannot be declared a major disaster. However, it is not clear how important this limitation will be in practice. For example, faced with a catastrophic outbreak of smallpox or anthrax spread by a terrorist, it is easy to imagine a president finding that an epidemic resulting from release of the biological agents anthrax or smallpox—diseases found in nature—is a "natural catastrophe."

Again, the president can only declare a major disaster after the governor of a state

1. asks the president to do so,
2. activates the state's emergency plan, and
3. advises the president that the situation is beyond the state's capability.

The declaration process is handled by FEMA, and FEMA has developed procedures for recommending to the president whether a declaration is appropriate. Immediately after a disaster event occurs, a damage assessment team of state and FEMA officials tours the disaster area and prepares a preliminary damage assessment identifying the impact and magnitude of damage to individuals, businesses, the public sector, and the community as a whole.[8] The governor includes the data from this joint assessment in his or her request for a declaration, and these data are used by the president (with a recommendation from FEMA) in deciding whether to declare a disaster and, in the event of a declaration, which disaster assistance programs should be activated.

Under the Stafford Act, if the president declares a major disaster and activates the Public Assistance Program, the federal government generally will make a grant covering "not less than 75 percent" of certain emergency costs (such as police overtime and debris removal) incurred by eligible entities and the cost of "repairing, restoring, reconstructing, or replacing" virtually any public facility.[9] These costs must be incurred by the event triggering the disaster declaration and must have been incurred (or the facility located) in a county that is included in the disaster declaration. Even though Congress may supplement existing assistance programs with new legislation following a major terrorist disaster, many of the rules governing existing programs are transferred to new legislation.

FEMA programs can provide a great deal of direct assistance to parts of the healthcare system, and it may indirectly fund other costs incurred by healthcare providers that are ineligible for direct assistance. In fact, the way in which hospital and emergency care administrators respond to terrorism events involving weapons of mass destruction can have substantial impact on whether costs incurred and damages suffered are reimbursable by FEMA. Not only does the type of assistance vary significantly for different healthcare institutions, but the Stafford Act and related regulations require applicants to comply with numerous physical and/or financial mitigation rules.

## DETERMINING ELIGIBILITY

The Federal Emergency Management Agency uses a three-part analysis to determine what projects are eligible for assistance and what amount of assistance should be awarded. First, FEMA determines whether the particular person—the legal entity—applying for assistance is eligible for assistance under the Stafford Act. Next, FEMA reviews whether particular work is eligible. Finally, FEMA reviews whether the costs incurred in performing the eligible work are reasonable or should be disallowed. Because grants are provided only to those who apply for them, administrators are encouraged to at least start the process. Sidebar 12.1 provides information on how to begin. The following sections describe which healthcare entities can apply for direct assistance from FEMA.

### Public Organizations

Every healthcare facility that is owned by a state or local government or public authority is an eligible applicant under the Public Assistance Program. Federal assistance under the Stafford Act (§ 406) is provided "to assist state and local governments" in their response to a disaster; if a facility is a government facility, it is eligible even if the facility is primarily supported by attendance fees (such as a stadium or theater).

### Not-for-Profit Organizations Open to the General Public

The Stafford Act also authorizes FEMA to provide assistance to not-for-profit institutions, providing what FEMA calls "essential government-type services to the general public," including schools, utilities, emergency services such as volunteer fire companies and medical and custodial care facilities.[10] Thus, a not-for-profit organization that operates a hospital, emergency care facility, or nursing facility open to the public generally can be eligible for FEMA assistance.

FEMA looks closely at the identity of the not-for-profit applicant to be sure it qualifies. To be eligible for assistance, not only must that applicant own or operate a facility providing essential government-type services, but that facility must be open to the general public. Not-for-profit hospitals have been surprised by rigid application of these two criteria, as shown in Sidebar 12.2.

### For-Profit Organizations

In contrast to not-for-profit entities, for-profit hospitals are simply ineligible for direct assistance under the Stafford Act. However, a for-profit institution participating in the healthcare system's response to a federal

**Sidebar Figure 12.1. Initial Application for Public Assistance Following a Disaster**

| FEDERAL EMERGENCY MANAGEMENT AGENCY<br>**REQUEST FOR PUBLIC ASSISTANCE** | O.M.B. No. 3067-0151<br>Exprires April 30, 2001 |
|---|---|

**PAPERWORK BURDEN DISCLOSURE NOTICE**

Public reporting burden for this form is estimated to average 10 minutes. The burden estimate includes the time for reviewing instructions, searching existing data sources, gathering and maintaining the needed data, and completing and submitting the forms. You are not required to respond to this collection of information unless a valid OMB control number is displayed in the upper right corner of the forms. Send comments regarding the accuracy of the burden estimate and any suggestions for reducing the burden to: Information Collections Management, Federal Emergency Management Agency, 500 C Street, SW, Washington, DC 20472, Paperwork Reduction Project (3067-0151). NOTE: Do not send your completed form to this address.

| APPLICANT *(Political subdivision or eligible applicant.)* | DATE SUBMITTED |
|---|---|

COUNTY *(Location of Damages. If located in multiple counties, please indicate.)*

**APPLICANT PHYSICAL LOCATION**

STREET ADDRESS

| CITY | COUNTY | STATE | ZIP CODE |
|---|---|---|---|

**MAILING ADDRESS (If different from Physical Location)**

STREET ADDRESS

| POST OFFICE BOX | CITY | STATE | ZIP CODE |
|---|---|---|---|

| **Primary Contact/Applicant's Authorized Agent** | **Alternate Contact** |
|---|---|
| NAME | NAME |
| TITLE | TITLE |
| BUSINESS PHONE | BUSINESS PHONE |
| FAX NUMBER | FAX NUMBER |
| HOME PHONE *(Optional)* | HOME PHONE *(Optional)* |
| CELL PHONE | CELL PHONE |
| E-MAIL ADDRESS | E-MAIL ADDRESS |
| PAGER & PIN NUMBER | PAGER & PIN NUMBER |

Did you participate in the Federal/State Preliminary Damage Assessment (PDA)? ☐ YES ☐ NO

Private Non-Profit Organization? ☐ YES ☐ NO

If yes, which of the facilities identified below best describe your organization? _____

Title 44, CFR, part 206.221(e) defines an eligible private non-profit facility as: "...any private non-profit educational, utility, emergency, medical or custodial care facility, including a facility for the aged or disabled, and other facility providing essential governmental type services to the general public, and such facilities on Indian reservations." "*Other essential governmental service facility* means museums, zoos, community centers, libraries, homeless shelters, senior citizen centers, rehabilitation facilities, shelter workshops and facilities which provide health and safety services of a governmental nature. All such facilities must be open to the general public."

Private Non-Profit Organizations must attach copies of their Tax Exemption Certificate and Organization Charter or By-Laws. If your organization is a school or educational facility, please attach information on accreditation or certification.

| Official Use Only: FEMA-_____-DR-_____-____ FIPS# _____ | Date Received: |
|---|---|

FEMA Form 90-49, SEP 98        REPLACES ALL PREVIOUS EDITIONS

*Source:* Federal Emergency Management Agency (FEMA). 1998. "Request for Public Assistance." [Online form; retrieved 10/17/02.] *Public Assistance Application Handbook*, Publication No. 323. http://www.fema.gov/pdf/rrr/pa/apphndbk.pdf.

disaster can, if its activities are properly requested and documented, be an indirect beneficiary of federal assistance by performing work for compensation for eligible applicants.

A good example of the issues raised by the ineligibility of for-profit entities for disaster assistance is the terrorist attacks on the World Trade Center on 9/11. On that day, casualties were immense and initially were feared to be far higher. A call went out for all available ambulances to come to triage centers being established for the wounded. These ambulances included public ambulances, not-for-profit ambulances, ambulances normally operating under contract with not-for-profit hospitals (which may have had no other connection with the disaster), and for-profit ambulances working with for-profit hospitals or nursing homes.

For any of the costs of the for-profit ambulances and other entities to be eligible for federal assistance under FEMA's programs, FEMA had to find a request for assistance from an eligible public or not-for-profit entity and then assume an agreement under which the requester would pay for and be reimbursed for its service.

Another issue raised by the ineligibility of for-profit entities arises from the conversion of not-for-profit hospitals into for-profit hospitals.

The 1994 earthquake in Northridge, California, caused hidden structural damage to a number of not-for-profit hospitals in the Los Angeles area, requiring years of engineering evaluation and major construction before the damage could be repaired or the hospital facilities replaced. As long as the hospital remained a not-for-profit hospital through the grant process, it was eligible for assistance. After construction was complete and the hospital placed in service, there were no restrictions on the ability of the not-for-profit hospital to sell its hospital facilities—in far better condition than it had been prior to the disaster—to for-profit hospital chains. Hospital administrators negotiating a conversion to for-profit status at the time of or shortly after a disaster event had to be sure not to cause this conversion to occur too soon and lose disaster benefits.

**Critical Services**

Prior to enactment of the Disaster Mitigation Act of 2000, all disaster assistance under the Public Assistance Program was independent of the financial capability of the applicant. If an eligible applicant incurred eligible costs as a result of a federal major-disaster event, that applicant would receive a federal grant—not a loan—covering the federal share of eligible costs.

The Disaster Mitigation Act of 2000 added a new provision to the Stafford Act stating that if a facility is owned by a not-for-profit organization and does not provide "critical services," the organization is eligible for federal grants to repair, restore, reconstruct, or replace facilities only if it cannot get a low-interest disaster loan.[11] The low-interest loans are provided by the Small Business Administration (SBA) under Section 7(b) of the Small Business Act.[12] Under this act, to be eligible for FEMA grants, an applicant that does not provide critical services must apply for an SBA loan and either be deemed ineligible or have received the maximum amount available from SBA.

The new Stafford Act provision defines "critical services" as including power, water (including water provided by an irrigation organization or facility), sewer, wastewater treatment, communications, and emergency medical care. In its rules, FEMA has added nursing homes to the list of critical services. A definition of "emergency medical care" was also included in the rules:

Emergency medical care includes essential direct patient care to persons and includes hospitals, clinics, outpatient services, and nursing homes. Owners and operators of these critical service facilities may apply directly to FEMA for assistance.[13]

At present, FEMA has not made a distinction between facilities providing emergency medical care and those providing long-term medical care or even cosmetic medical procedures. Given FEMA's definition of emergency medical services, hospitals, clinics, outpatient services, and nursing homes should seek grant assistance from FEMA rather than explore SBA low-interest loans.

## WHAT COSTS ARE ELIGIBLE

Eligible healthcare providers can receive direct assistance in the following two categories:

1. Emergency costs incurred to address imminent threats of harm to life, property, and the public health and safety
2. Costs to repair, restore, reconstruct, or replace damaged facilities

Although other FEMA assistance programs may indirectly assist healthcare providers (for example, by providing funds to allow individuals to pay emergency medical bills[14] or by funding crisis counseling services[15]), they are not discussed here.

### Emergency Services Costs

After the president has declared an emergency or a major disaster, those eligible applicants that incur the cost of many types of emergency work caused by the disaster are eligible for federal disaster assistance. These costs can include the following:

- "Work to save lives and protect property" incurred by performing, on public or private lands or waters, any work or services essential to saving lives and protecting and preserving property or public health and safety, including search and rescue; emergency medical

care; emergency mass care; emergency shelter; and provision of food, water, medicine, and other essential needs, including movement of supplies or persons
- Provision of temporary facilities for schools and other essential community services
- Dissemination of public information and assistance regarding health and safety measures
- Provision of technical advice to state and local governments on disaster management and control
- Reduction of immediate threats to life, property, and public health and safety[16]

To qualify for assistance, an emergency cost must be incurred because of the declared disaster event; this "causation" requirement is strictly interpreted for emergency costs. For example, regular-time pay and benefits of an applicant's workforce (FEMA calls this "force account labor") would have been incurred with or without the disaster; these costs are not eligible for FEMA assistance. Overtime pay for force account labor performed as a result of the disaster is eligible. Both regular pay and overtime pay for temporary employees hired as a result of the disaster are also eligible costs. The variety of possible emergency costs that a disaster could generate for hospitals, clinics, and ambulances are virtually endless. Just a few examples are shown in the list that follows:

- Overtime costs of staff doctors, nurses, and attendants
- Contract costs for emergency doctors, nurses, and attendants
- Administering inoculations required to protect against spread of disease caused by the disaster
- Medical supplies and equipment actually consumed or contaminated in treating patients who were or believed themselves to be victims of the disaster event
- Operation of emergency generators
- Increased security
- Debris removal
- Temporary reinforcement/restoration of damaged physical facilities to restore ability to provide emergency medical care

Again, the primary rule used in evaluating eligibility for reimbursement of emergency costs is whether these costs indeed were incurred in a declared county while addressing immediate threats to life, property, or the public health and safety.

The eligibility of broad categories of emergency costs for reimbursement will by no means cover all related losses and other economic impacts. Under the Stafford Act, FEMA reimburses "costs" suffered as result of a disaster. The meaning of the word "costs" may appear obvious, but it is so important to understanding the process that it requires elaboration. First, a cost is only incurred when someone must pay for something. A cost—at least as interpreted by FEMA—is not created when a disaster event keeps money from coming in. That means loss of revenue is not a cost. In the context of a healthcare catastrophe, if patients with a highly communicable disease are treated or quarantined at one hospital and as a result other patients refuse to go to that hospital, the hospital's loss of revenue, however debilitating, is not reimbursable by FEMA.

"Costs" also implies a legal responsibility to pay for the services. In the world of major disasters, FEMA must distinguish between services that were donated by people and organizations that swarm to the scene and volunteer to help out and those that were performed by paid service providers. Donated resources are not costs and thus are ineligible for reimbursement even if the donor subsequently asks for reimbursement.

**Repair and Replacement Costs**

In addition to the costs of emergency protective measures described above, qualified applicants are eligible for grants covering the federal share—which ranges from 75 percent to 100 percent—of the cost of bringing damaged facilities back into predisaster condition. This includes costs for repair, restoration, reconstruction, and replacement of damaged facilities. *Facilities* include both real property (such as hospital and laboratory buildings and related administrative, utility, and maintenance structures) and personal property (such as motor vehicles, medical equipment, and medical supplies).

FEMA is required by statute to give a generous interpretation of what it takes to restore a structure to predisaster condition; this can be very significant, particularly for older structures. Thus, the Stafford Act provides that the eligible cost estimate for public assistance grants should be developed

- on the basis of the design of the facility as the facility existed immediately prior to the major disaster and
- in conformity with codes, specifications, and standards (including floodplain management and hazard-mitigation criteria required by the president or under the Coastal Barrier Resources Act) applicable at the time the disaster occurred.[17]

This means that damaged hospital and building systems must be repaired in accordance with the building codes and specifications in the community that were in effect as of the date of the disaster.

FEMA regulations[18] specify which "codes and standards" trigger federal funding of improvements over the preexisting condition of a structure. The objective of the regulation is to fund code upgrades where the community requires that all new construction meets these standards and not to fund upgrades where it appears that the code applies only, or principally, where federal funding is available.[19]

In addition, FEMA may be persuaded in its discretion to fund "cost-effective" upgrades to a structure, which will have the effect of reducing future disaster damage.[20] The theory behind this flexibility of discretion is that it does not make sense to spend federal funds to reconstruct a facility to be just as susceptible to collapse as it was before the disaster.

FEMA has also grappled with situations in which an applicant really does not want to rebuild the damaged structure, even with code upgrades. Given the pattern of growth in the community, perhaps a community hospital should be rebuilt in a different location to be more accessible to additional neighborhoods. Perhaps a small hospital should be replaced by a network of smaller clinics. Changing the nature of the facility to be rebuilt will not cut off federal disaster-relief funding,[21] but it may have a significant impact on how much funding is actually received. The Stafford Act makes a distinction between "replacement" of facilities substantially destroyed by a disaster (by building a new facility in another location) and determining to use disaster relief funds generated by damage to an eligible facility to construct another type of facility filling another type of community need (e.g., replacing a community center with a school). The latter is considered an "alternate" or "in lieu of" project subject to a 10 percent to 25 percent reduction in federal funding.[22]

The primary rule to remember is that FEMA funding is generally limited to the cost to repair or replace the structure that was damaged, in accordance with code upgrades, but additional FEMA funding may be available with appropriate structuring of the project.

*Eligible Work Complication: Legal Responsibility Doctrine*

The ineligibility of the private sector for disaster assistance is not limited to emergency operating costs but extends also to reimbursement of property damage (whether a facility is physically damaged by an earthquake or requires decontamination as a result of treating victims of a biological or chemical terrorist attack). FEMA regulations establish that for eligible public applicants that contract with ineligible for-profit entities to transfer control of a structure—for example, by lease or in a construction contract—assistance is available to the eligible applicants only to the extent that they are "legally responsible" for performing the work.[23]

Thus, if a hospital signs a construction contract to rehabilitate the hospital wing, control of that wing normally transfers to the contractor, and the contractor has "legal responsibility" to repair any damage in the wing—whether caused by a construction mishap or by a major disaster. In this situation, no FEMA assistance will be available, even if the contractor's insurance is inadequate to repair damage to the wing. Similarly, if a hospital leases some of its facilities to private physicians or private laboratory service providers, and the lease provides that the lessees are responsible for damage to the leased premises, then those hospital-owned facilities will not be eligible for assistance even if the physicians and their insurers cannot or will not fund repairs.

## GRANT REQUIREMENTS AND REASONABLENESS

Understandably, FEMA disaster assistance is not a blank check. Grant funds are provided to applicants for eligible work, but only reasonable costs for this work are reimbursable. Controlling costs in the disaster environment is difficult indeed. The disaster itself causes shortages, which can trigger price increases and sometimes price gouging. All applicants should use care in their procurement of FEMA-funded projects as if the funds were their own. Furthermore, all applicants should keep in mind that all federal grants are subject to audit.

## Federal Competition Clause

The Public Assistance Program is a federal grant program and therefore subject to the Common Rule specifying uniform administrative requirements for grants to states and local governments.[24] All Public Assistance Program grants are made to the state government, which administers subgrants to eligible local government and not-for-profit entities. The subgrants made to eligible healthcare providers are grants to reimburse eligible costs they have incurred. If a healthcare provider's contracts do not comply with federal grant requirements, it runs the risk of a FEMA determination that its costs are not eligible for federal assistance.

Probably the most important arena for conflict in the area of federal competition is the "emergency exception." FEMA requires that contracts be competitively bid, unless "the public exigency or emergency for the requirement will not permit a delay resulting from competitive solicitation."[25] But beware of this exception. An organization cannot assume that competitive procurements can be safely ignored just because the president has found the situation to be of such severity that it is "beyond the capability of local resources" to respond, nor can they be ignored because assistance is being sought for what FEMA regulations call Category A and B "emergency work." FEMA will not necessarily agree that sole-source (versus competitive) procurement is appropriate.

A good rule to remember is that any contractual commitments made during the chaotic initial stages of the disaster should be of short duration. Limit these commitments to work that can be handled while some form of competitive analysis, appropriate to the emergency environment, is concurrently conducted. If it is possible to prepare contingent contracts for emergency services or supplies prior to the disaster—when procurement staffs have the time to develop proposals and to solicit bids on them—by all means do so.

## Work Performed Under Mutual-Aid Agreements

Healthcare organizations may have executed agreements defining terms and conditions of when one provider will assist another in the event that a local event causes facilities and resources to be overwhelmed. These agreements, if in writing and between eligible applicants, will generally be treated as mutual-aid agreements whose costs are eligible for assistance. (In the absence of a written agreement, FEMA will deny reimbursement of costs incurred because the work was performed without an expectation of payment; the work will essentially be treated as donated.)

Intergovernmental agreements and agreements solely between not-for-profit institutions provide the primary model for mutual aid. Under these mutual agreements, each party agrees that should it be requested to respond, and should it agree to and be able to do so in the aftermath of an event, the responding party will provide services and the requesting party will pay for the cost of those services (including overhead) and accept any liabilities incurred in providing them. FEMA does not require that mutual-aid agreements be subjected to competitive bidding (discussed above). However, if an agreement involves for-profit institutions, care should be taken to ensure that costs are not disqualified on grounds that the arrangement should have been put out for competitive bidding. For-profit hospitals participating in community-preparedness exercises and activities should try to establish how compensation for both exercises and response activities will be handled and try to gain express recognition in preparedness plans that their mutual-aid agreements will qualify for either direct or indirect funding.

## Duplication of Benefits

Federal disaster assistance cannot duplicate benefits available from other sources. This prohibition applies not only to benefits available from federal or state grant programs, but also to insurance benefits. The Stafford Act requires that

> [t]he President . . . in consultation with the head of each Federal agency administering any program providing financial assistance to persons, business concerns, or other entities suffering financial losses as a result of a major disaster or emergency, shall assure that no such person, business concern, or other entity will receive such assistance with respect to any part of such loss as to which he has received financial assistance under any other program or from insurance or any other source.[26]

This prohibition is not even limited to duplicative assistance that an applicant in fact receives; it also extends to assistance that FEMA believes to be available to the applicant. These provisions quite frequently lead to disputes over how much assistance is in fact "available to" an applicant and therefore how much is deducted from "eligible cost" for a federal disaster grant.

Wherever insurance or other government assistance and FEMA-eligible costs and damage overlaps, an applicant must take special care in documenting efforts to recover costs under other policies and programs and to track separately proceeds received to reimburse "FEMA-eligible" and "FEMA-ineligible" losses. For example, this would be necessary in instances where a single-limit insurance policy combines coverage for ineligible losses (such as business interruption) and FEMA-eligible property damage.

On occasion, FEMA has taken the position that it will not fund particular projects to repair damage to a facility if Congress has granted to another federal-agency-specific authority to do so. Thus, FEMA does not fund grants to repair roads that are part of the Federal Highway System, which is funded by the Department of Transportation; FEMA does not fund repair of levees that are the responsibility of the Corps of Engineers; and FEMA has entered into an agreement with the Environmental Protection Agency to divide responsibility for costs in hazardous-materials releases. To the author's knowledge, FEMA has not yet reached similar agreements for how to coordinate its funding with that of the Department of Health and Human Services.

Healthcare providers should take note when FEMA indicates that its funding cannot be provided because it duplicates funding that is *authorized* by other federal programs. Only if funds are in fact *appropriated* and *available* should funding be denied as a duplication of benefit. Do not give up, however, if FEMA disallows significant costs without clear legal or regulatory support. Disasters exhibit such great variation in the nature of damage that it can be difficult for FEMA to apply its policies to particular cases. Decisions disallowing costs can be appealed within FEMA.

Although FEMA's disaster assistance programs are structured as discretionary programs, disappointed applicants have two potential arenas to address FEMA decisions or policies that deny assistance for disaster losses. First, Congress not infrequently enacts special legislation to deal with "special needs" created by a disaster that are not addressed by the general Stafford Act programs. Second, applicants can seek judicial review of FEMA decisions. Although FEMA has sovereign immunity when making discretionary decisions about what kind of assistance to provide in a disaster, courts have found aspects of FEMA's disallowance of assistance to be reviewable.

## RECOMMENDATIONS FOR A SUCCESSFUL APPLICATION PROCESS

To best ensure that the FEMA reimbursement lifeline is available—and not pulled back after audits are conducted years later—service providers should review and follow the tips provided in the following list.

- Apply for FEMA assistance as soon as possible after the disaster event—certainly within 30 days.
- Ensure that federal grant requirements, and particularly competitive bidding procedures, are followed for all procurements funded by FEMA grants.
- Be sure that FEMA understands the limitations and restrictions governing all "other" assistance, such as insurance, that is available to the institution. Identify and segregate any costs that are not eligible for FEMA assistance but that are eligible for insurance benefits or other assistance.
- Document expenditures and develop systems to document the eligibility of the work performed.
- Develop good relations with FEMA and state officials so that they understand your disaster costs. Do not be afraid to appeal a disallowed cost if you feel that it is eligible.

All of the actions involved in emergency preparedness—training; conducting exercises; identifying emergency procurement needs; reviewing insurance requirements; and developing lists of employees and relationships with key suppliers, customers, and officials—will have the greatest impact on an organization's success in responding to major disasters, whether natural or nonnatural in origin. Once a healthcare organization is hit by a disaster, FEMA funding is a lifeline that can allow the organization to provide critical medical services in the disaster environment and beyond.

## NOTES

1.  On March 1, 2003, pursuant to the Homeland Security Act of 2002, the Federal Emergency Management Agency (FEMA) became part of the then-new Department of Homeland Security (DHS), and the authority of FEMA and its director was transferred to the secretary of Homeland Security. As of this writing, FEMA has continued to operate under the name "Federal Emergency Management Agency"; FEMA's director also serves as undersecretary of DHS. To avoid confusion during this transition period, this chapter continues to use the terms "FEMA" and "director" as the agency administering the disaster-relief programs of the Stafford Act.

2.  The Stafford Act is codified at 42 U.S.C. § 5121 et. seq. The Stafford Act was significantly amended by the Disaster Mitigation Act of 2000 [P.L. 106-390, 114 Stat. 1552 (2000)]. FEMA's regulations implementing the Stafford Act are found in the Code of Federal Regulations, Title 44, Part 206.

3.  Each year, Congress appropriates to FEMA (now in DHS) an amount for "disaster relief." For example, in the Department of Homeland Security Appropriations Act for Fiscal Year 2004, Congress appropriated "for necessary expenses in carrying out the Robert T. Stafford Act Disaster Relief and Emergency Assistance Act, $1,800,000,000, to remain available until expended" (P.L. 108-90, Oct. 1, 2003). Traditionally, if the amount remaining in the Disaster Relief Fund is low enough that FEMA's ability to respond to disaster events may be jeopardized, Congress enacts an emergency supplemental appropriations bill. See, for example, the Emergency Supplemental Appropriations Act of 1999 [P.L. 106-31, 113 Stat. 54 at 73 (1999)].

4.  Stafford Act § 502(a), 42 U.S.C. § 5192(a).

5.  Stafford Act § 501(b), 42 U.S.C. § 5191(b).

6.  Stafford Act § 501(b), 42 U.S.C. § 5191(b).

7.  Stafford Act § 102(2), 42 U.S.C. § 5122(2) (emphasis added).

8.  44 CFR § 206.33 (2003).

9.  Stafford Act § 406, 42 U.S.C. § 5172.

10. 44 CFR § 206.221 (2003).

11. Stafford Act § 406(a)(3), 42 U.S.C. § 5172(a)(3), added by the Disaster Mitigation Act of 2000, P.L. 106-390, 114 Stat. 1552 (Oct. 30, 2000).

12. Small Business Act, § 7(b), codified at 15 U.S.C. § 363(b).

13. 66 Fed. Reg. 22443; 44 CFR § 206.226(b) (emphasis added).

14. Stafford Act § 408(a)(3), 42 U.S.C. § 5183.

15. Stafford Act § 416, 42 U.S. C. § 5174.

16. Stafford Act § 403, 42 U.S.C. § 5170b(a)(3).

17. Stafford Act § 406(e)(1); 42 U.S.C. § 5172(e)(1).

18. 44 CFR § 406(c) (2003).

19. See Second Appeal Analysis, FEMA-1008-DR-CA, PA ID # 000-92040; University of California, Los Angeles, DSR # 02623; Royce Hall (UC Seismic Safety Policy), March 10, 1998.

20. Stafford Act § 406(e)(1)(A)(ii), 42 U.S.C. § 5172(e)(1)(A)(ii) (2003).

21. Stafford Act § 406(c), 42 U.S.C. § 5172(c) (2003).

22. Stafford Act § 406(c), 42 U.S.C. § 5172 (c) (2003).

23. 44 CFR § 206.223(a)(3) (2003).

24. 44 CFR Part 13.

25. 44 CFR § 13.36(d)(4)(i) (2003).

26. Stafford Act § 312(a), 42 U.S.C. § 5155(a).


## REFERENCES

Code of Federal Regulations, Title 44, Part 13 (2003).

Code of Federal Regulations, Title 44, Part 206 (2003).

Source: Federal Emergency Management Agency (FEMA). 1998. "Request for Public Assistance." [Online form; retrieved 10/17/02.] Public Assistance Application Handbook, Publication No. 323. http://www.fema.gov/pdf/rrr/pa/apphndbk.pdf.

———. 2002. FEMA Second Appeal Division; 1379-DR-TX; PA ID # 201-U917N-00; Thermal Energy Cooperative PW # N/A; Applicant Eligibility Determination; 08/16/2002.

*Robert T. Stafford Disaster Relief and Emergency Assistance Act*, as amended, codified at U.S. Code 42, §§ 5121 et. seq. of 2000, Pub. L. No. 106-390, U.S. Statutes at Large 114 (2000): 1552.

### CHAPTER THIRTEEN

# Lessons from the Israeli Experience

Jakov Adler

A though Israel does not profess to hold the answers to preparation for mass-casualty disasters or events that may involve weapons of mass effect (WME), decades of preparation and experience have engrained the necessity of medical preparedness into the culture of the country. Israel's history of healthcare facility preparation for chemical attacks dates to the early 1970s. Coupled with a regular and rigorous schedule of drills, training, and exercises, often of massive proportion, the healthcare sector's level of preparedness is among the best in the world. The American healthcare system can benefit from the lessons from Israel provided in this chapter as it plans for, responds to, and mitigates current threats and future challenges.

Before the establishment of the State of Israel, hospitalization and primary healthcare were provided by private organizations as well as facilities operated by the General Worker's Sick Fund (presently Clalit Health Services). After 1948, the British Mandatory (government) hospitals were transferred to the Israeli government. Planning to manage casualties in war situations was initiated during the 1950s, and hospitals were required to establish internal standard operating procedures (SOPs) for planning, preparing, and managing war casualties. Sidebar 13.1 provides some background information on Israel's demographics. A historical time line is provided in Table 13.1, which summarizes major events that have forged a culture of disaster preparedness in Israel.

Jakov Adler, M.D., is emergency medical advisor for the Israeli Ministry of Health in Tel Aviv, Israel, and a colonel (ret.) for the Israeli Defense Forces.

With the increase of major terrorist activities in Jerusalem in the 1970s, hospitals in Jerusalem established their first SOPs to manage mass casualties during terrorist attacks, which later became a model for all Israeli hospitals. After the 1973 Yom Kippur War, a potential threat for a chemical attack against Israel was recognized. In 1975, the Ministry of Health appointed a planning committee that established the doctrine and steps for the preparedness and management of chemical warfare casualties in all general hospitals.

In the early 1990s, the Ministry of Health once again appointed a committee of medical experts—this time, to establish a plan for an integrated, national-trauma management system, which included minimal requirements for prehospital and hospital care. In 1994, the committee presented its recommendations, including the designation of six regional trauma centers, and the following year a trauma registry was initiated in these trauma centers.

## ISRAELI HEALTH SERVICES

There are 25 acute care general hospitals in the country, all located in cities and urban centers from the northern border to the Gulf of Aqaba in the

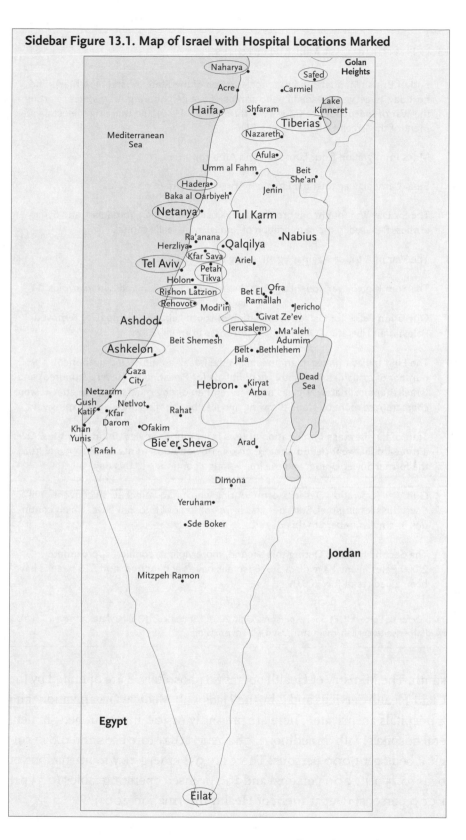

**Sidebar Figure 13.1. Map of Israel with Hospital Locations Marked**

## TABLE 13.1. HISTORICAL ISRAELI MILESTONES

| | |
|---|---|
| 1948 | End of British Mandate and the proclamation of the State of Israel (14 May). The next day, Israel was invaded by the armies of five neighboring Arab states, starting the War of Independence (May 1948 through July 1949) and marking the establishment of the Israeli Defense Forces (IDF). |
| 1948–52 | Mass immigration from European and Arab countries. |
| 1956 | Sinai Campaign against the Egyptian Army in the Sinai Peninsula. |
| 1967 | The Six Day War, fought on three fronts against the Egyptian, Jordanian, and Syrian armies. Resulted in the reunification of Jerusalem, Israel's capital. |
| 1968–70 | The War of Attrition against Egypt, along the Suez Canal. |
| 1973 | The Yom Kippur War, fought against the invading Egyptian and Syrian armies. |
| 1982 | Operation Peace for Galilee (occupation of south Lebanon by the IDF) removed Palestinian Liberation Organization terrorists from Lebanon. |
| 1987–89 | The First Intifada (Palestinian uprising in the Israeli-administered territories). The number of casualties during this first intifada for Palestinians (several hundred) and Israelis (approximately 50) was much lower than during others because attacks were characterized more by stone throwing and less by shooting and use of explosives. |
| 1989 | Start of largest mass immigration of Jews from former Soviet Union countries. Over a three- to four-year period, more than one million immigrants came to Israel from the former Soviet Union, and the immigration continues to this day. |
| 1991 | Gulf War (Operation Desert Storm), during which Iraq launched 39 conventional Scud missiles at Israel. Start of mass immigration of Ethiopian Jews, which continues in small numbers to this day. |
| 2001– present | The Second Intifada. During this second, more violent, conflict, approximately 2,000 Palestinians have died, 5,616 Israelis have been injured, and 816 Israelis have been killed (as of July 2003). |

*Source*: Israeli Defense Forces (IDF) Spokesperson's Unit. 2003. "Statistics." [Online data; retrieved 7/1/03.] http://www.idf.il/newsite/english/main.stm. Used with permission.

south. The Ministry of Health operates 11 hospitals, 8 are operated by the Clalit Health Services and 2 by the Hadassah Medical Organization, and 4 hospitals are private. There are presently 14,300 inpatient beds in general hospitals, with an additional 982 general day-care beds and 0.827 surgical beds per 1,000 persons. There are 951 emergency room stations or beds (0.15 per 1,000 persons) and 399 licensed operating tables (0.53 per 1,000 persons) (Department of Health Information 2001).

In a war, the capacity of all hospitals can be increased by 30 percent to 40 percent, expanding the number of beds in the wards, using "surge capacity" treatment space, and increasing the number and work hours of medical personnel. The number of beds for the sick and lightly injured can further be augmented by deploying additional beds in hotels, as extensions to the hospitals. The number of licensed physicians is one of the highest among Western countries. In 2000, Israel had 375 physicians per 100,000, whereas the United States had 279 per 100,000 (WHO 2000).

The National Health Insurance Law, put into effect in January 1995, provides for standardized medical services, including hospitalization and full healthcare services for all citizens and residents of Israel. All medical services are supplied by the country's five health management organizations (HMOs), which provide primary and family healthcare and specialist care in outpatient clinics. The five HMOs include the following:

1. Ministry of Health—provides hospitalization to about 45 percent of the population and is the largest HMO
2. Clalit Health Services—operates clinics and 30 percent of all hospitals and is the second largest HMO
3. Meuchedet (United) Sick Fund
4. Macabi Sick Fund
5. Leumi (National) Sick Fund

## EMERGENCY MEDICAL SERVICES SYSTEM

Since 1930, ambulance services have been provided in cities, villages, and settlements by the voluntary Magen David Adom (MDA) organization, which became the medical section of the Hagana, the predecessor of the Israeli Defense Forces (IDF). In July 1950, the Magen David Adom Law was passed by the parliament, entrusting the organization to carry out all of the functions of a national Red Cross society.

In the late 1970s, an American physician conducted the first paramedic course in Israel. Since that time, several hundred paramedics have been trained by MDA, which presently operates some 370 regular ambulances and 100 mobile intensive care unit vehicles staffed by either a physician, paramedic, and medic/driver or a paramedic, medic/driver, and volunteer. The ambulances operate from 11 regional stations and some 100 substations located in villages and settlements. In addition, 30 armored ambulances, protected against light weapons, have recently been introduced into settlements in the territories and some 180 ambulances are sublet and operated by industrial enterprises and villages. Although the numbers fluctuate depending on the security situation and changing needs, approximately 700 MDA ambulances are presently operating in the country.

The Emergency Medical System (EMS) is controlled from the 11 regional centers and the MDA headquarters in Tel Aviv. All the regional ambulance centers and their ambulances have radio communication with the general hospitals and trauma centers in their respective areas. Radio communication can be established with the medical department of the Home Front Command (HFC), as well as the police and IDF.

## THE STRUCTURE AND FUNCTION OF HEALTHCARE IN EMERGENCIES

The National Health and Hospitalization Authority (NHHA) is responsible for the planning, preparedness, and operation of the health system in the country during emergencies. (Figure 13.1 details the structure of NHHA.) Central operational control of all general hospitals during emergencies is delegated by NHHA to the HFC chief medical officer (CMO). The HFC CMO is responsible for training and coordinating hospital operations in emergencies on behalf of the Ministry of Health.

### Military-Civilian Cooperation

Under law, all fit citizens serve in IDF from the age of 18 to 21 (three years for men and two years for women) in compulsory military service. After that age, they continue to serve annually for up to 40 days in the reserves until age 45.

The three IDF medical units (battalion aid stations, medical companies, and field surgical teams) can all be mobilized in emergencies to support the civilian population. HFC, a latter-day civil defense organization, is part of IDF and under the command of the IDF chief of staff. HFC is mainly built of reserve units from search and rescue battalions with technical and medical support units that are activated in times of emergency. Civilian emergency and rescue organizations (such as fire services, the

FIGURE 13.1. STRUCTURE AND AUTHORITY OF NHHA

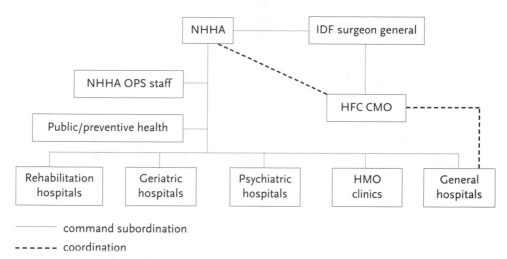

command subordination

- - - - - - coordination

Note: HFC CMO = Home Front Command chief medical officer; HMO = health management organization; IDF = Israeli Defense Forces; NHHA = National Health and Hospitalization Authority; NHHA OPS staff = Ministry of Health Emergency Division's staff.

police, and MDA) are also coordinated by HFC headquarters. This unified command system ensures the full coordination of all national EMS resources.

Tasks required in planning for terrorism and dealing with emergency casualties are shown in Checklists 13.1 (for the NHHA) and 13.2 (for general hospitals) at the end of this chapter.

During a terrorist attack, hospitals function in emergency mode and temporarily cease all regular operations. Casualty loads are often extensive in the affected areas because of self-evacuation of victims. Hospitals may receive large numbers of victims within a very short time (minutes) or with no warning time, depending on their proximity to the incident. Admission and hospitalization capacities of various facilities may differ and are based on previous admissions and time of day.

The HFC CMO may allocate hospital beds and initiate interhospital transfers to increase utilization and efficiency of all facilities. It has also been determined from prior experiences that the reinforcement of hospitals with medical staff from other facilities is less effective than secondary transfer of patients from the primary receiving facility.

Because of large numbers of victims and continued risks to the victims from secondary explosions or further exposure to an attack, treatment at the site of an incident will be limited only to life-saving procedures. Evacuation will be mainly by "scoop and run," as time and proximity to the exposure pose additional risks.

## TERRORISM IN ISRAEL

Israel has experienced repeated terrorist attacks against its civilian population during the last century. Terrorism has taken different forms along the decades, from the murders of women, children, and the elderly during the Hebron pogroms in the late 1920s to attacks against the first settlers in the 1930s to attacks during and following the establishment of the State of Israel in 1948.

Terrorism has escalated since 2001, during the last two years of the Second Intifada (*intifada* is defined as both "uprising" and "shaking off"), causing hundreds of civilian deaths and thousands of injuries among the Israeli and Palestinian populations. (Statistics related to causes of death among Israelis are provided in Table 13.2.). Hospitals had to adapt quickly to the sudden influx of large numbers of casualties with a very short warning time or no warning at all.

All civilian fatalities (71 percent of all fatalities) were caused by conventional weapons, with suicide bombings being the most frequent cause (53 percent), followed by assault weapon shootings (22 percent). Explosions in confined spaces—mainly in buses—caused a high incidence of fatalities, predominantly by blast injuries, burns, and penetration of nails and other metallic objects lacing the explosive charge. The majority of casualties occur in urban areas, and in most cases MDA ambulances or private vehicles evacuate victims to the nearest hospital.

During this period, the Palestinians sustained more than 2,000 fatalities (IDF Spokesperson's Unit 2003). IDF provides medical first aid to all Palestinians when Palestinian Red Crescent ambulances are not available. Some of the injured are transferred to Israeli hospitals for further surgical treatment, as needed.

## TREATING PSYCHOLOGICAL CASUALTIES

Attacks on unprotected civilians have had a severe psychological effect on the Israeli population. People are changing their behavior and daily

## TABLE 13.2. CAUSES OF DEATH AMONG ISRAELI CIVILIANS AND SECURITY FORCES SINCE START OF SECOND INTIFADA, SEPTEMBER 29, 2000, TO JULY 21, 2003*

| Type of Attack | Civilians | Security Forces | Total |
|---|---|---|---|
| Rock throwing | 2 | 0 | 2 |
| Stabbing | 6 | 0 | 6 |
| Running over by car | 1 | 7 | 8 |
| Lynching | 17 | 2 | 19 |
| Shooting—drive-by | 28 | 9 | 37 |
| Shooting—vehicle from ambush | 58 | 11 | 69 |
| Shooting—at towns and villages | 15 | 3 | 18 |
| Shooting—at military installations | 0 | 26 | 26 |
| Shooting—general/other | 87 | 92 | 179 |
| Bombs—suicide | 318 | 31 | 349 |
| Bombs—car | 15 | 23 | 38 |
| Bombs—mortar | 0 | 1 | 1 |
| Bombs—other | 24 | 35 | 59 |
| Other | 1 | 4 | 5 |
| **Total** | **572** | **244** | **816** |

* During this period of time, 3,965 civilians and 1,651 security personnel were injured.

*Source*: Adapted from Israeli Defense Forces (IDF) Spokesperson's Unit. 2003. "Statistics." [Online data; retrieved 7/1/03.] http://www.idf.il/newsite/english/main.stm. Used with permission.

routine to avoid public places, such as restaurants and coffee shops, where deadly attacks have occurred. The use of bus transportation has decreased, and other modes of transportation, such as private vehicles and taxicabs, are preferred.

The numbers and rates of people suffering from acute fear and early posttraumatic stress disorder (PTSD) who refer to hospitals during the first days after a terrorist attack increase constantly, as the repeated exposure to stress accumulates. In several larger incidents, the number of casualties suffering from early PTSD surpassed the numbers of the physically injured. Hospitals are expanding care of psychologically stressed casualties who are evacuated by EMS immediately after the attack or who self-refer in the following days.

Psychological teams, which include psychiatrists, clinical psychologists, and social workers, are immediately mobilized by an internal call-up of staff in the hospitals and reinforced by staff from government psychiatric hospitals, psychiatric health clinics, and city emergency departments. During an incident, these teams provide information to admitted patients

and their relatives and psychological support to patients admitted to the
emergency department (ED) or hospitalized. The team triages casualties
in the ED, and those patients without physical injuries are then referred
to a separate treatment area. Patients are encouraged to share their experiences and are reassured on the legitimacy of their reactions. Most patients are released after a couple of hours and receive further verbal and
written instructions for assistance and follow-up in the community health
centers.

Written instructions, prepared by the Mental Health Services, are distributed to all patients released from hospitals following a terror attack.
They are available in English, Arabic, Hebrew, and Russian. A sample
handout is provided in Figure 13.2. In addition, written instructions are
provided to parents whose children have been exposed to traumatic
events, with instruction on how to diagnose acute stress reactions and
how best to manage them at home.

The psychological teams participate in debriefing sessions after terror
incidents and provide supportive care to EMS personnel and the hospital staff as well. Hospital and community health workers (nurses, psychologists, and physicians) participate in education workshops organized

## FIGURE 13.2. PATIENT INFORMATION SHEET FOR POSTTRAUMATIC STRESS DISORDER

**Ministry of Health**                                       **Mental Health Services**

### Information Sheet
### Acute Stress Response

Following a traumatic event, such as bombing, physical attack or a car accident, most people find returning to normal life to be difficult. Some of the most common problems include:

- Sleeping difficulty. Both falling asleep and sleeping through the night.
- Nightmares: not only of the traumatic event, but other nightmares of violence and helplessness.
- Recurring images of the event.
- Sadness.
- Irritability.
- Lack of interest in work or social life.
- Decreased appetite.
- Anxiety.
- Fear or phobias.
- Guilt.

These symptoms are NORMAL. They are the mind's way or dealing with the horror of the event.

For almost everyone these symptoms will start improving within a few days. In fact, people who react in this way very strongly early on, tend to return to normal life quickest.

The most effective way to deal with these symptoms and feelings is to be around people who care about you. SPEAK ABOUT IT. Most people get better simply by knowing that what they are experiencing is normal and by having caring people around to listen to them.

Often, for the first day or two, people feel fine and then, either suddenly or gradually, these symptoms develop. Most people find this very frightening. Once again, this is a normal reaction to trauma and will most likely start improving within a few days. A small number of people find these symptoms unbearable and do not start feeling better after a few days. The most common problem is lack of sleep. If you do not see any improvement within about a week, then go see your family doctor. After discussing it with you, (s)he may recommend counseling in order to help with the recovery. In rare instances, the anguish is so severe that the person feels hopeless. This can be especially difficult when there is no one to turn to. In such cases it is recommended to call for emergency consultation.

Refuah Shleima*

Name: _____

Tel:_____

*Get Well Soon.

*Source*: Ministry of Health Psychiatric Service; used with permission.

by either the Ministry of Health or health providers in the management of PTSD cases, and they participate in all annual mass-casualty exercises in the hospital to which they are assigned.

## TRAINING AND EXERCISES

All general hospitals in Israel are required to conduct a mass-casualty event exercise annually. "Conventional" and mass-toxicology exercises in war alternate so that each specific event is drilled every third year. Based on the achievement of the previous exercise, a different exercise scenario is conducted (e.g., a biological attack). The dates of the exercises are usually known in advance to allow the hospitals time to prepare for the event. Frontal lectures (formal lectures presented to a large audience) and group training sessions for individual hospital teams complement sectorial exercises (the training of nurses, technicians, or physicians separately from each other).

Occasionally, a "surprise" exercise may be held with no advance warning or only a few minutes' warning. Although these exercises are more realistic, they are not used too often. The sudden disruption to patient care is detrimental, and objections are raised from recalled personnel.

The exercises are conducted by the HFC's medical department, which assists hospitals in preparation and monitors the exercise. Simulated casualties are recruited from the IDF basic-training camps. The casualties are brought to the entrance of the hospitals by MDA ambulances and army vehicles.

In past years, some of the "casualties" were army medical doctors in training. Their task was to provide immediate feedback on the treatment provided by the medical teams in the ED. This use of "feedback casualties" has been discontinued in recent years, as it was deemed to interfere with the main organizational objectives of the exercise.

After conclusion of the exercise, the hospital administration conducts a structured internal debriefing session, at the end of which lessons learned are discussed with the HFC CMO. The repeated exercises are accepted by the hospitals, EMS, and the primary healthcare services with full understanding of their importance. The ongoing terrorism and resulting casualties increase the awareness and positive motivation of the health workers. Primary lessons learned from hospital drills and exercises are summarized in Table 13.3.

## TABLE 13.3. LESSONS FROM ISRAELI HOSPITAL TRAINING AND EXERCISES

| Category | Lessons Learned |
|---|---|
| Administrative | Increase commitment of hospital administration and department heads. |
| | Set aside appropriate funding for training and exercises. |
| | Improve assessment of performance measures and levels. |
| Security | Control media access to casualties and restrict identifying pictures of victims prior to notification of family members. |
| Process | Table-top exercises improve skills of medical personnel and managers. |
| | Increase team drills and frequency of new personnel training. |
| | Increase coordination with community and national emergency services. |
| | Conduct exercises without warning in evening hours. |

### Simulation Training of Medical Personnel

The Israeli Association of Surgeons introduced advanced trauma life support (ATLS) training in Israel in 1989. The Medical Training Center of IDF conducts several courses annually for young Army physicians and for IDF reservists. Reserve physicians from hospitals and prehospital health services are required to pass the course.

Recently, the ATLS course has become mandatory for surgeons in training for all surgical specialties. Through mid-2002, 7,024 trainees participated and 5,500 successfully passed the course. In the late 1990s, a medical simulation center was established in a major medical center. The Center for Medical Simulation, at Haim Sheba Medical Center, trains and conducts exercises with emergency medical staff from hospitals and with army physicians in the treatment of emergent trauma and medical cases, using the most advanced simulation techniques. Several hundred physicians and nurses have undergone this training.

## PRESENT STATUS OF PREPAREDNESS FOR WME EVENTS

NHHA dictates that all general hospitals be prepared for a mass-casualty event in which the demands on the hospital exceed its normal capacity. Trained to receive a large number of casualties within a short warning time, hospitals are required to be prepared for the following:

- Conventional events (e.g., terrorist bombings/shootings or major road accidents)
- Toxicological (chemical) mass-casualty events
- Radiological events, with release and contamination by radiological substances
- Biological events caused by intentional (terrorist or war related) or accidental or natural spread of a biological substance (toxin) or an infectious-disease epidemic

Each hospital must establish an emergency planning team, headed by the medical director or chief executive officer of the facility. The team includes the director of medicine and surgery, the head of the ED, the chief nurse, the hospital administrator, the chief pharmacist, the chief engineer, the head of security, and other officials as needed. The hospital plan is coordinated with the HFC and local police headquarters and is approved by the HFC CMO.

Hospital SOPs define the preparations of the medical wards, the ED, hospital support systems, the call-up of additional personnel, the flow of patients, the admission policy of regular patients, patient registration and recording, information and social services, mortuary services, and the identification of victims and security. The hospital command-and-control center coordinates all hospital operations and activities; handles reporting and public relations; and coordinates with the police, EMS, HFC, and the relevant health authorities.

After every mass-casualty incident a debriefing is conducted in which problems encountered and lessons learned are discussed.

### Preparedness for Toxic-Agent Response

Unconventional weapons capable of causing mass casualties have not been used against Israel. Israel is, however, perceived to be under a potential threat in a future war or through an act of terrorism. Chemical weapons were produced and weaponized by many of Israel's past and present potential enemies, necessitating the protection of IDF and the civilian population against such weapons.

In 1976, NHHA established a professional committee to investigate the preparedness of all general hospitals and to present recommendations for upgrading their readiness against a chemical weapons threat.

The committee assigned the following tasks for the reorganization of hospitals, with proposals to be implemented over several years:

- The decontamination of casualties near the entrance to the hospitals
- The preparedness of sufficient staff resources for the decontamination and treatment of large numbers of casualties
- The preparation of means for medical treatment, taking into account that a large number of casualties will be referred to the hospitals after receiving first aid by the civil defense medical units or may be self-referred without any previous treatment or decontamination.
- The separation of areas for treatment of chemical casualties from areas dedicated to regular patients

The committee visited all 25 general hospitals in the country and held discussions with the hospital administration to make decisions regarding the reorganization of the hospital. The members of the committee surveyed the hospitals' facilities, examining their layout and capability to receive patients and provide intensive medical and pharmacological treatment to chemical casualties. The committee assessed all general hospitals for the capabilities listed in Checklist 13.3.

Next, the committee examined the personnel assigned to the hospital in emergencies (de facto posting). According to these parameters, the final and maximum number of casualties to be admitted during an emergency was established, and each hospital was requested to prepare its SOP.

Subsequently, each hospital estimated the necessary funds required to implement the program. The Ministry of Health allocated the necessary funds in a staged program over the next years. The program was implemented, and all hospitals were involved in exercises before the outbreak of the Persian Gulf War in 1991, when the threat of a chemical attack by Iraqi Scud missiles became a possibility.

## CURRENT HOSPITAL-LEVEL RESPONSE PLANS

Current plans to respond to unconventional weapons call for an HFC medical company to be deployed near the hospital's entrance, sorting the incoming victims and providing supplementary first aid to the treatment provided by mobile HFC medical platoons and MDA ambulance teams in the affected area.

In a sudden, unexpected terrorist attack, there will be no warning period, and casualties may present at the ED within minutes of exposure. For such an event, a smaller decontamination (decon) facility will be established at the entrance to the ED in several hospitals, which can be operational with available hospital staff within minutes.

In case chemical or biological casualties present in the EDs, without any knowledge of the possible exposure, the ED will probably be contaminated and all patients will have to be moved to an alternative site for observation. The teams in the ED will don protective equipment for the treatment of these casualties. Any new casualties presenting to the hospital will undergo decontamination and triage at the entrance. Even administrative and maintenance personnel have been trained to decontaminate patients at the entrance to the hospitals and can be called by beepers (group call) or the internal loudspeaker system. The HFC teams are reservists and will become active only after 48 to 72 hours. They will deploy only in a war situation.

### Mass-Decontamination Centers

Persons not showing signs of poisoning will be observed for several hours in a special holding area and released home if their residential area is not in a contaminated zone. Those who develop signs of chemical intoxication will be immediately decontaminated in a mass-decon center at the entrance to the hospital, then admitted for further treatment. (Budgeting for the construction of the decon facility, the procurement of medical equipment and drugs, and the training and exercises are provided by the Ministry of Health for all medical facilities on an annual basis.) The decon centers are usually constructed at the entrance to the ED, in a parking lot, or at any other convenient location (see Figure 13.3).

Routine procedure in wartime calls for all casualties to undergo "dry" and "wet" decontamination before entering the hospital. Water for the decon process is provided in adequate amounts from the regular water supply system and is delivered through shower heads and hoses mounted to the ceiling of the facility. The need for heated water is not usually a problem in Israel's climate. The water supply pipes are fixed to the ceiling of covered parking lots. In open areas, they are mounted on stands or on fences or walls. The plastic hoses with spouts and with connectors are kept in storage next to the decon facility. Wastewater from the

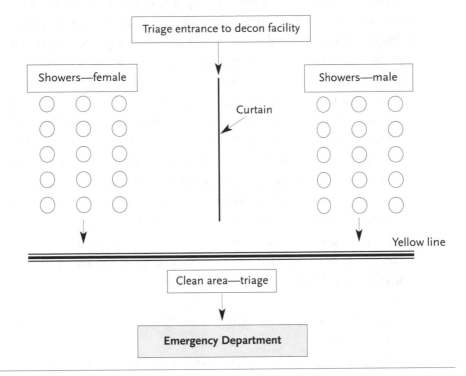

process is allowed to flow into the regular sewage system, assuming that most toxic material will be neutralized by the detergents used to clean the casualties and diluted sufficiently so as not to pose any threat to the environment.

An HFC military-assistance unit operates the decon center. All hospital and HFC staff operating outside the hospital will be fully protected with gas masks and light protective suits until the "all clear" signal is sounded. Hospital personnel within the facility will don their gas masks only if they are operating in nonprotected areas. Personnel are easily identified by their title/role ("MD," "RN," "Decontaminator," "Police," etc.) visibly placed on both sides of their personal protective garments.

## Surge Capacity

During an emergency, such as a war or missile attack, most hospital beds (except those used for emergent cases) will be vacated and additional beds will be prepared in corridors, dining rooms, and other open areas for the admission of large numbers of medium and severe casualties. Oxygen supply and suction lines have been preinstalled in the walls of overflow or surge areas such as cafeterias, waiting rooms, and large auditoriums. A large number of mobile ventilators are stocked in each of the hospitals for the treatment of severe cases. Trolleys with all necessary equipment and antidotes in sufficient amounts are also stored in each hospital.

The discharging of the regular patients and vacating of beds take about six to eight hours. Therefore, these preparations will be made only in emergency situations such as a war. In previous wars, the expansion of hospital beds was maintained for several months. Urgent or emergent patients were admitted to hospitals and treated in makeshift departments according to the flow of casualties from the front lines. In some instances, smaller hospitals were assigned for the treatment of civilians.

Psychological support and social services are provided to all hospitalized patients and their relatives. Social services are available to accomplish the following tasks:

- Provide information to patients and the public at the hospital information center
- Assist in locating family members in different hospitals
- Assist released patients with transportation, and facilitate their return to the community
- Establish child care centers in the hospitals for hospital personnel

Lessons from the 1991 Gulf War stressed the importance of child care centers in hospitals, as parents, especially mothers, were not comfortable leaving their children at home while working in the hospital during their shifts.

## THE LOOMING BIOLOGICAL THREAT

The emerging bioterrorism threat, amplified by the October 2001 mailings of anthrax spores in the United States as well as attempts by radical and extremist terrorist groups or states to weaponize biological agents, have led to increased efforts in the Western world to protect its population.

The Israeli health authorities have attempted to anticipate these scenarios for several years. The national disease-surveillance system has been upgraded based on real-time reports from the prehospital health services and from hospitals as well as veterinary services, laboratories, and pathological institutes. Epidemiological teams will immediately investigate any deviation from the baseline incidence of flu-like symptoms or clusters of disease. The recent outbreaks of West Nile fever, which is endemic in Israel, served as a model for testing and upgrading the surveillance system. Sufficient amounts of vaccines and antibiotic drugs have been stored and can be distributed to the affected or exposed population within days.

Certain hospitals have been designated to admit the victims of a biological-agent attack. These hospitals will receive additional drugs, personal protective equipment, and other necessary medical equipment (such as respirators). Training programs have been initiated and exercises are being held to upgrade the readiness of the entire health system. In addition to the hospitals and community health system, the IDF and HFC medical system will be instrumental in an emergency, assisting in distribution of drugs and in mass vaccinations. Schools, primary health clinics, and other locations have been identified for use in vaccinating the population within days, if needed. By early 2003, the author has observed that some 17,000 primary and hospital health workers had been revaccinated against smallpox.

In any major emergency, such as a war or an attack using WME, all human and material resources will be mobilized. The Israeli government will proclaim a state of emergency, and a decision may be made to transfer command and control of the response activities to the emergency authorities. In such an instance, all national essential services may be mobilized, including all health services. All health personnel who are not drafted to active military service will be called up and ordered to work at their assigned post.

## REFERENCES

Department of Health Information, Health Information and Computer Services, State of Israel Ministry of Health. 2001. Selected data, Jerusalem, September.

Israeli Defense Forces (IDF) Spokesperson's Unit. 2003. "Statistics." [Online data; retrieved 7/1/03.] http://www.idf.il/newsite/english/main.stm.

World Health Organization (WHO). 2000. Health Statistics Annual. Geneva, Switzerland: WHO.

# Checklists

## CHECKLIST 13.1. MAIN TASKS OF NHHA

❏ Plan for maximum utilization and expansion of hospital beds.

❏ Effectively manage and mobilize manpower volunteers.

❏ Procure, store, and maintain drugs and equipment in the hospital and supplied by the Emergency Division of the Ministry of Health.

❏ Participate in central budgeting for emergency (war and terrorism) preparedness and operations by the Ministry of Health.

❏ Prepare facility standard operating procedures based on a uniform operational doctrine.

❏ Perform annual training and exercises in all general hospitals.

❏ Inspect facilities, audit procedures, manage resources, and review operational capability on a regular basis.

## CHECKLIST 13.2. MAIN TASKS OF GENERAL HOSPITALS

❏ Receive, sort, and manage casualties.

❏ Decontaminate chemical and bacteriological casualties.

❏ Provide definitive care to biological and chemical casualties.

❏ Provide laboratory support to epidemiological investigation in biological events.

❏ Perform surgery on the injured.

❏ Hospitalize and provide intensive care to severe cases.

❏ Provide psychological and social support to casualties and relatives.

❏ Ensure continued medical care and rehabilitation to the affected population.

## CHECKLIST 13.3. ASSESSING HOSPITAL CAPABILITIES FOR HANDLING VICTIMS OF WME

❏ Location and condition of existing decontamination facilities and plans for upgrading

❏ Available staffing in hospitals for decontamination activities

- ❏ Required equipment for decontamination
- ❏ Drugs and medical equipment necessary for resuscitation and management of chemical casualties
- ❏ Personal protective equipment (including gas masks and protective suits) for medical and auxiliary personnel
- ❏ "Safe areas" that can be protected against chemical or toxic substances to accommodate patients who cannot be protected by standard gas masks
- ❏ Establishment of a professional planning team for the preparedness and readiness of the hospital and training of its staff
- ❏ Planning for the acquisition of additional resources, such as vehicles
- ❏ Communication, water sources, and equipment for decontamination facilities.
- ❏ Establishment a training-and-exercise program

# Glossary of Acronyms

| | |
|---|---|
| ACEP | American College of Emergency Physicians |
| ACHE | American College of Healthcare Executives |
| AEGL | acute exposure guideline limit |
| AHA | American Hospital Association |
| AMA | American Medical Association |
| AOA | American Osteopathic Association |
| ASTM | American Society of Testing and Materials |
| ATLS | advanced trauma life support |
| | |
| CAH | critical access hospital |
| CAR | Capability Assessment for Readiness |
| CBRNE | chemical, biological, radiological, nuclear, and (high yield) explosives |
| CDC | Centers for Disease Control and Prevention |
| CEM | comprehensive emergency management |
| CERCLA | Comprehensive Environmental Response, Compensation and Liability Act |
| CEO | chief executive officer |
| CMO | chief medical officer |
| CMS | Centers for Medicare & Medicaid Services |
| COP | Conditions of Participation (CMS) |
| CQI | continuous quality improvement |
| | |
| DHS | Department of Homeland Security |
| DHHS | Department of Health and Human Services (also abbreviated as HHS) |
| DHS | Department of Homeland Security |
| DoD | Department of Defense |

| | |
|---|---|
| EC | Environment of Care (as related to JCAHO standards) |
| ED | emergency department |
| EMA | emergency management agency |
| EMAC | Emergency Management Assistance Compact |
| EMP | emergency management program |
| EMS | emergency medical services/Emergency Medical System (Israel) |
| EMT | emergency medical technician |
| EMTALA | Emergency Medical Treatment and Active Labor Act |
| EOC | emergency operations center |
| EOP | emergency operations plan |
| EPA | Environmental Protection Agency |
| ESF | emergency support function |
| | |
| FCC | Federal Coordinating Center |
| FEMA | Federal Emergency Management Agency |
| FMEA | failure modes and effects analysis |
| FMECA | failure modes, effects, and criticality analysis |
| FRP | Federal Response Plan |
| | |
| GAO | General Accounting Office |
| | |
| HAN | Health Alert Network |
| HAZMAT | hazardous materials |
| HAZWOPER | Hazardous Waste Operations and Emergency Response |
| HCAR | Hospital Capability Assessment for Readiness |
| HEICS | Hospital Emergency Incident Command System |
| HFC | Home Front Command (Israel) |
| HIPAA | Health Insurance Portability and Accountability Act of 1996 |
| HMO | health management organization (Israel) |
| HRSA | Health Resources and Services Administration |
| HVA | hazards vulnerability analysis |
| HVAC | heating, ventilation, and air conditioning |
| | |
| ICS | incident command system |
| IDF | Israeli Defense Forces |
| IDLH | immediately dangerous to life and health |

| | |
|---|---|
| JCAHO | Joint Commission on Accreditation of Healthcare Organizations |
| JIT | just-in-time |
| | |
| LEPC | local emergency planning committee |
| | |
| MAA | mutual-aid agreements |
| MaHIM | Medical and Health Incident Management (system) |
| MDA | Magen David Adom (Israel) |
| MMRS | Metropolitan Medical Response System |
| MOU | memorandum of understanding |
| | |
| NBC | nuclear, biological, and chemical |
| NCP | National Contingency Plan |
| NDMS | National Disaster Medical System |
| NFPA | National Fire Protection Association |
| NHHA | National Health and Hospitalization Authority (Israel) |
| NIOSH | National Institute for Occupational Safety and Health |
| NMRT | National Medical Response Team |
| NMRT-WMD | National Medical Response Team–Weapons of Mass Destruction |
| NORTHCOM | U.S. Northern Command |
| NRC | National Research Council |
| NRP | National Response Plan |
| | |
| OSHA | Occupational Safety and Health Administration |
| | |
| PAPR | powered air-purifying respirator |
| PDD | Presidential Decision Directive |
| PPE | personal protective equipment |
| PTSD | posttraumatic stress disorder |
| | |
| RDD | radiological dispersal device |
| | |
| SARA | Superfund Amendments and Reauthorization Act |
| SARS | severe acute respiratory syndrome |
| SBA | Small Business Administration |
| SCBA | self-contained breathing apparatus |
| SEPPA | Smallpox Emergency Personnel Protection Act of 2003 |

| | |
|---|---|
| SNS | Strategic National Stockpile (formerly National Pharmaceutical Stockpile) |
| SOP | standard operating procedure |
| SWOT | strengths, weaknesses, opportunities, and threats (analysis) |
| | |
| TIC | toxic industrial chemical |
| TIM | toxic industrial material |
| TOE | table of organization and equipment |
| | |
| VA | Department of Veterans Affairs |
| | |
| WMD | weapons of mass destruction |
| WME | weapons of mass effect |

# Resources and Guidance for Effective Community-Based Disaster Planning

## AOA/AACOM Task Force on Bioterrorism Resources

American Osteopathic Association/American Association of Colleges of Osteopathic Medicine Task Force on Bioterrorism Resources. http:/www .aoa-net.org/Executive/allresource.

This task force was formed in October 2001 with a mission to educate osteopathic physicians to recognize and respond to biological (and other) agents that may be used in an attack and to assist in responding to questions and concerns of patients and the general public. The task force has done the following:

- Compiled a resource list of biological and chemical terrorism resources on the web and provided links to those sources
- Compiled facts, a response plan, and guidelines for the smallpox threat
- Compiled "links" to emergency contact numbers for state health departments and contact numbers for state public health laboratories

## Partnership for Community Safety

Coalition for Partnership for Community Safety: Strengthening America's Readiness. http://hospitalconnect.com/partnershipforsafety.

The Partnership for Community Safety is a coalition formed to advocate strengthening community readiness for biological, chemical, and nuclear terrorism and other disasters. In addition to working to help shape national policy, the member organizations pledge to collaborate to "retool disaster plans and focus on increasing the capacity for frontline responders, to reduce duplication of effort, and to develop a "bank" of best practices. The coalition has identified the following areas of need:

- Improve communications infrastructure
- Improve community-based planning
- Increase community capacity to deal with disaster
- Improve disease surveillance and reporting and field laboratory identification systems
- Protect responders from effects of biological, chemical, and nuclear agents
- Increase and enhance training programs, continuing education, and community drills for mass-casualty incidents

### AMA Council on Scientific Affairs Report No. 11

American Medical Association Council on Scientific Affairs (May 2001). *Report 11: Medical Preparedness for Terrorism and Other Disasters (1-00)*. http://www.ama-assn.org/ama/pub/print.

This report attempts to identify preparedness and response issues for physicians and medical societies in dealing with acts of terrorism and other disasters. It concludes that overall preparedness can be enhanced by collaboration with local and state health departments; continuing medical education; physician participation in disaster care planning by healthcare facilities; and coordination with community resources such as fire and police, emergency medical technicians, utilities, schools, government officials, and large employers. The report covers the following areas:

- Discussion of types of terrorism, analogous natural disasters, and the medical response
- Critical needs in preparing a medical response
- Physician preparedness

- Healthcare facility and community preparedness
- The role of the Federation of Medicine, academic medicine, and federal agencies
- Extensive references for further research and reading

It makes the following recommendations:

1. Create a public-private entity to collaborate with the medical educators and specialty medical societies to
    - develop disaster medical education curricula;
    - develop information resources on disaster medicine;
    - work cooperatively with other interested organizations to develop model plans for community medical response to disasters; and
    - address timely, accurate reporting of dangerous diseases by community physicians to public health authorities.
2. Encourage the Federation of Medicine to become involved in planning for the medical component of disaster response.
3. Encourage JCAHO and state licensing authorities to include an evaluation of hospital plans for terrorism and other disasters as part of the periodic accreditation and licensure process.


**AMA Report 26 of the Board of Trustees**

American Medical Association ( 2001). *Report 26 of the Board of Trustees: AMA Leadership in the Medical Response to Terrorism and Other Disasters (BOT Rep. 26, 1-01)*. http://www.ama-assn.org.

   This report chronicles the past activities of the AMA, its current actions, and its future direction. Seven recommendations were made.

1. Condemn terrorism in all its forms and provide leadership in coordinated efforts to improve the medical and public health response to terrorism and other disasters.
2. Work with appropriate federal, state, local, and medical specialty societies to
    - enhance the medical and public health response,
    - develop a comprehensive strategy to ensure surge capacity to address mass-casualty care,

- implement communications strategies,
- convene local and regional best practice/lessons learned workshops,
- hold annual symposia to share new scientific knowledge and information regarding enhanced medical and public health disaster responses, and
- develop joint educational programs.

3. Recommend the appointment of a medical professional to the Department of Homeland Security.
4. Urge Congress to adequately fund and support relevant research on agents, vaccines, and antidotes.
5. Educate physicians to increase awareness of signs of possible use of chemical and biological agents and how to respond.
6. Participate directly with state, local, and national public health, law enforcement, and emergency management authorities to develop and implement disaster preparedness and response protocols in communities, hospitals, and practices.
7. Maintain and update a comprehensive Internet-based resource on disaster medicine and emergency response.


### AMA Report, *Organizational Ethics in Health Care*

American Medical Association (June 2000). *Organizational Ethics in Health Care: Toward a Model for Ethical Decision Making by Provider Organizations.* Research project for the National Working Group on Health Care Organizational Ethics convened by the Institute for Ethics at the AMA. http://www.ama-assn.org/ama/pub/category/2735.html.

This is a scholarly report with a twofold purpose: (1) to try to determine what should be considered ethical conduct for a healthcare organization and (2) to outline a model for ethical decision making that draws guidance from business ethics, professional ethics, and contemporary law and social policy and to identify standards that appear ambivalent or inadequate to meet present and future societal and individual healthcare needs. It identifies three ethical guideposts, or priorities, for healthcare organizations.

1. Healthcare of patients
2. Professional expertise in clinical matters

3. Six independent considerations, including "public health" and "benefit to community," that must be part of the ethical decision making process but whose relative importance depends on the facts and circumstances of the ethical issue.

This report concludes that an organization that pays no attention to public health is operating with a narrow and naïve understanding of healthcare, but it need not devote as much of its resources to public health services as it devotes to patient care to behave ethically.

## AHA Report on Hospital Preparedness for Mass Casualties

American Hospital Association (June 2000). *Hospital Preparedness for Mass Casualties*. http://www.hospitalconnect.com/ahapolicyforum.resources /disaster.html.

This report is a summary of an invitational forum, held in March 2000, that brought together a diverse group of hospital and government personnel to develop recommendations and strategies for mass-casualty preparedness for hospitals. The report's recommendations and strategies are relevant to mass-casualty incidents regardless of cause, and fall into the following four arcas:

1. Communitywide preparedness
   - By definition, mass casualty incidents will overwhelm the resources of individual hospitals.
   - The public will view the hospital as a vital resource for diagnosis, treatment, and the follow-up of physical and psychological care.
   - Hospitals must expand their preparedness focus to include external and community-level planning.
   - Hospitals must expand their preparedness focus to consider potential need to evacuate, quarantine, or divert incoming patients.
   - In multihospital communities, hospitals must collaborate and develop a real-time database of emergency capabilities, includ-ing an unduplicated count of staff.
2. Staffing
   - Hospitals must develop a communitywide "reserve staff" of physicians, nurses, and hospital personnel who have retired,

changed careers, or work in healthcare but outside of direct patient care. This will also require adequate funding to train and update the skills of the reserve staff.

- Hospitals should advocate the development of cross-jurisdictional licensure under defined emergency conditions.
- Hospitals should consider the criteria for temporary privileges during emergency or disaster situations.

3. Communications
- Redundant systems are necessary and must be tested and drilled.
- A single medical spokesperson must be identified and supported with medical expertise.
- A communitywide system is needed for locating patients with a single point of contact.

4. Public policy
- As a community, stakeholders need to develop a financial framework to pay for the planning, education, supplies, and training that will be necessary.
- Federal statutory changes must occur to protect hospitals from technical violations of the EMTALA.

### JCAHO White Paper, *Health Care at the Crossroads*

Joint Commission on Accreditation of Healthcare Organizations (2003). *Health Care at the Crossroads: Strategies for Creating and Sustaining Community-wide Emergency Preparedness Systems.* http://www.jcaho.org/news +room/press+kits/emergency+prep.htm.

The purpose of this white paper is to frame the issues that must be addressed in developing communitywide preparedness and to delineate federal and state responsibilities. Hospitals will play a central role while facing a healthcare system with diminished capacity, personnel shortages, and immense financial pressures. The report organizes its recommendations into three categories and for each category provides tables that outline "tactics" and assigns "accountability" for accomplishment of the tactics. The recommendation categories follow.

- Enlisting the community in preparing the local response
- Focusing on aspects of the preparedness system that will preserve the ability to care for patients, protect staff, and serve the public

- Establishing accountability, oversight, and leadership to sustain a communitywide preparedness system.

## JCAHO Special Issue of *Perspectives*

Joint Commission on Accreditation of Healthcare Organizations (December 2001). *Perspectives: Emergency Management in the New Millennium*. Vol. 21, No. 12. Available online at http://www.jcrinc.com/subscribers/perspectives.asp
?durki=1122&site=10&return=1627.

This special issue of the JCAHO newsletter Perspectives was dedicated to emergency management and is available free for download as a PDF file. The following subjects are dealt with in this special issue:

- Mobilizing America's healthcare resources
- The need for a national bioterrorism response
- Using JCAHO standards as a starting point to prepare for an emergency
- Revised Environment of Care standards
- What the survey process expects of your organization
- Analyzing your vulnerability to hazards
- Adapting tools to the task ahead
- Developing practical emergency management education programs
- Preparing for a mass-casualty event
- Disseminating lessons learned from a terrorist attack
- Managing people and resources effectively
- The power of preparation
- Talking to each other in a crisis
- Caring for our own
- Nuclear, biological, and chemical decontamination
- Common symptoms of exposure to contaminants
- Responding effectively in the midst of a natural emergency
- Emergency management resources

*Source*: Created by M. H. Brant for use in this book.

# Health and Medical Web Resources for Disaster-Related Information

This appendix is directed toward the administrator and/or planner and does not focus on medical care or clinical guides, agent identification sites, or sites for patient care processes or equipment. It represents only a small number of references available via Internet access, as items are added continuously. This listing was accurate at the time of publication.

| CATEGORY | AGENCY | WEB SITE |
|---|---|---|
| *Healthcare Association or Related Web Sites* | | |
| ACHE | American College of Healthcare Executives | www.ache.org |
| AHA | American Hospital Association | www.aha.org |
| AMA | American Medical Association | www.ama-assn.org |
| ANA | American Nurses Association<br>• Bioterrorism and Disaster Response | http://www.ana.org<br>http://nursingworld.org/news /disaster/response.htm |
| JCAHO | Joint Commission on Accreditation of Healthcare Organizations | www.jcaho.org |
| *Government Agencies* | | |
| Multiagency disaster web site | DisasterHelp.gov | https://disasterhelp.gov |
| AHRQ | Agency for Healthcare Research and Quality<br>• Bioterrorism and Emergency Infections Site | www.ahrq.gov<br><br>www.bioterrorism.uab.edu/index.htm |
| ATSDR | Agency for Toxic Substances and Disease Registry; U.S. Public Health Service, DHHS | www. atsdr.cdc.gov |

| CATEGORY | AGENCY | WEB SITE |
|---|---|---|
| CDC | Centers for Disease Control and Prevention<br>See also: U.S. DHHS<br>Search also for: | www.cdc.gov |
| | • Bioterrorism information for healthcare | www.cdc.gov/ncidod/hip/Bio/bio.htm |
| | • Emergency Preparedness and Response branch (bioterrorism web site, general) | www.bt.cdc.gov/index.asp |
| | • Healthcare Infection Control Practices Advisory Committee (HICPAC), *Guideline for Environmental Infection Control in Healthcare Facilities*, 2001 | www.cdc.gov/ncidod/hip/enviro /env_guide_draft.pdf |
| | • National Institute of Occupational Safety and Health | www.cdc.gov/niosh/homepage.html |
| | • Business Emergency Management Planning | www.cdc.gov/niosh/topics/prepared/ |
| | • Strategic National Stockpile Program | www.bt.cdc.gov/stockpile/index.asp |
| | • Mass Trauma Preparedness and Response site | www.cdc.gov/masstrauma/default.htm |
| DHHS | Department of Health and Human Services<br>Includes: AHRQ, ATSDR, CDC, FDA, HRSA, NIH | www.hhs.gov |
| | • Metropolitan Medical Response System (MMRS) | www.mmrs.hhs.gov |
| | • Health Resources and Services Administration | www.hrsa.gov |
| DHS | Department of Homeland Security<br>See also: FEMA | www.dhs.gov/dhspublic |
| | • Office for Domestic Preparedness (ODP) | www.ojp.usdoj.gov/odp |
| | • National Disaster Medical System (NDMS) | http://ndms.dhhs.gov/index.html |
| DoD | Department of Defense<br>• Global Engineering Infections Surveillance and Response System (GEIS-Web) | www.defenselink.mil<br>http://141.236.12.246/ |
| DOE | Department of Energy | www.energy.gov |

| CATEGORY | AGENCY | WEB SITE |
|---|---|---|
| DOJ | U.S. Department of Justice<br>• Federal Bureau of Investigation<br>• Office of Domestic Preparedness (now under DHS) | www.usdoj.gov<br>www.fbi.gov<br><br>www.ojp.usdoj.gov/odp |
| DOT | Department of Transportation<br>• Office of Hazardous Materials Safety | www.dot.gov<br><br>http://hazmat.dot.gov |
| EPA | Environmental Protection Agency<br>See also:<br>• Office of Emergency Prevention, Preparedness and Response (OEPPR)<br>• *Radiological Emergency Response Plan*, 2000 | www.epa.gov/ceppo<br><br><br>www.epa.gov/radiation/rert/docs/rerp-1-00.pdf |
| FDA | Food and Drug Administration, bioterrorism information<br>• Counterterrorism<br><br>• Manuals and publications | <br><br><br>www.fda.gov/oc/opacom/hottopics/bioterrorism.html<br>www.fda.gov/opacom/7pubs.html |
| FEMA | Federal Emergency Management Agency<br>See also:<br>• Office of National Preparedness (ONP)<br>• Critical Infrastructure Protection Information Center<br>• Emergency Management Guide for Business and Industry<br>• U.S. Fire Administration (USFA) | www.fema.gov<br><br><br>www.fema.gov/nwz02/nwz02_03a.shtm<br>www.usfa.fema.gov/fire-service/cipc/cipc.shtm<br><br>www.fema.gov/library/bizindex.shtm<br><br><br>www.usfa.fema.gov/ |
| GAO | General Accounting Office, reports on terrorism and aspects of preparedness | www.gao.gov |
| HRSA | Health Resources and Services Administration<br>See also: DHHS | www.hrsa.gov |
| NIH | National Institutes of Health<br>• National Institute of Mental Health<br>• *Mental Health and Mass Violence*, 2002 | www.nih.gov<br><br><br>www.nimh.nih.gov/research/massviolence.pdf |

| CATEGORY | AGENCY | WEB SITE |
|---|---|---|
| NIOSH | National Institute of Occupational Safety and Health (see CDC) | www.cdc.gov/niosh/ |
| NLM | National Library of Medicine<br>• Search for bioterrorism information | www.nlm.nih.gov/ |
| OSHA | Occupational Safety and Health Administration<br>See also: OSHA Emergency Preparedness and Response resources<br>• *Hospitals and Community Emergency Response— What You Need to Know,* 1997<br>• Publications and fact sheets | www.osha.gov<br><br><br><br>www.osha-slc.gov/Publications /OSHA3152/osha3152.html<br><br>www.osha-slc.gov/pls/publications /pubindex.list |
| SBA | Small Business Administration, disaster loans | www.sba.gov/disaster_recov/index .html |
| VA | Veterans Administration, Emergency Management Strategic Healthcare Group (EMSHG)<br>See also:<br>• *Emergency Management Program Guidebook,* 2002 | www.va.gov/EMSHG<br><br><br><br>http://www1.va.gov/emshg/apps/emp /emp.htm |
| White House | Homeland security topics | www.whitehouse.gov/homeland/ |
| *Other Agencies/States* | | |
| ARC | American Red Cross | www.redcross.org |
| DHS (California) | California Department of Health, *California Hospital Bioterrorism Planning Guide,* 2002 | www.dhs.cahwnet.gov/BioTerrorism %20Headline/Revised%20BT%20 Response%20Master%20document.pdf |
| KHA | Kentucky Hospital Association, *Bioterrorism Reference Materials for Hospitals* | www.kyha.com/prepare.htm |
| MIPT | National Memorial Institute for the Prevention of Terrorism (Oklahoma City, OK) | www.mipt.org/index.html |
| NOD | National Organization on Disability<br>• *Guide on Special Needs of People with Disabilities,* 2002 | www.nod.org/pdffiles/epi2002.pdf |

| CATEGORY | AGENCY | WEB SITE |
|---|---|---|
| PERI | Public Entity Risk Institute | www.riskinstitute.org |
| TMA | Texas Medical Association Bioterrorism Resource Center | www.texmed.org/has/bioterrorism.asp#prepare |
| **Academic Centers** | | |
| | Center for Law & the Public's Health, Georgetown and Johns Hopkins universities | www.publichealthlaw.net |
| | Harvard School of Public Health | www.hsph.harvard.edu/index.html |
| | Johns Hopkins University Center for Civilian Biodefense Studies | www.hopkins-biodefense.org |
| | Saint Louis University School of Public Health Center for the Study of Bioterrorism | http://www.bioterrorism.slu.edu/ |
| | University of California–Los Angeles Center for Public Health and Disasters | http://www.ph.ucla.edu/cphdr/ |
| | University of Colorado Natural Hazards Center | www.colorado.edu/hazards |
| | University of Delaware Disaster Research Center | www.udel.edu/DRC |
| | University of North Carolina School of Public Health | www.sph.unc.edu/about/webcasts |
| | University of Pittsburg Center for Biosecurity | http://www.upmc-biosecurity.org/ |
| **Associations—Weapons of Mass Destruction Information** | | |
| AAP | American Academy of Pediatrics<br>• "Children, Terrorism and Disasters" | www.aap.org<br><br>www.aap.org/terrorism/index.html |
| ACEP | American College of Emergency Physicians<br>• *Positioning America's Emergency Health Care System to Respond to the Act of Terrorism*, 2002 | www.acep.org<br><br>www.acep.org/library/pdf/terrorismResponse.pdf |
| ACP/ASIM | American College of Physicians/ American Society of Internal Medicine, "Bioterrorism Resources" | www.acponline.org/bioterror/?chapinc |
| APIC | Association for Professionals in Infection Control and Epidemiology<br>• "Bioterrorism Resources" | www.apic.org<br><br>www.apic.org/bioterror/ |

| CATEGORY | AGENCY | WEB SITE |
|---|---|---|
| ASHE | American Society for Healthcare Engineering | http://www.ashe.org |
| IAEM | International Association of Emergency Managers | http://www.iaem.com |
| NACCHO | National Association of County and City Health Officials, Bioterrorism and Emergency Response Program | http://www.naccho.org/project63.htm |
| NEMA | National Emergency Management Association | www.nemaweb.org |
| NOD | National Organization on Disability | http://www.nod.org |
| **Legal** | | |
| | General legal search engines<br>• FindLaw<br>• Cornell Law School<br>• General<br>• Government (general) | http://findlaw.com<br>http;//www.law.cornell.edu<br>http://www.law.com<br>http://www.firstgov.gov |
| | American Bar Association<br>• LAWLINK | http://w3.abanet.org/home.cfm<br>www.lawtechnology.org/lawlink/home.html |
| | *Federal Register* | www.gpoaccess.gov/fr/ |
| | Legislative search<br>• U.S. Congress<br>• U.S. House of Representatives<br>• THOMAS search engine | www.congress.org/<br>www.house.gov<br><br>http://thomas.loc.gov |
| Healthcare | *CEOExpress* newsletter (comprehensive search engine site for legal, news, business, all services) | http://www.ceoexpress.com |
| | *Preparing for a Bioterrorist Attack: Legal and Administrative Strategies*, 2003 | http://www.cdc.gov/ncidod/EID/vol9no2/02-0538.htm |
| Legal documents/acts/laws | Bioterrorism Act of 2002 | www.fda.gov/oc/bioterrorism/bioact.html |
| **Military Resources (multiple-link sites)** | | |
| USAMRIC | U.S. Army Medical Research Institute of Chemical Defense, Chemical Casualty Care Division | http://ccc.apgea.army.mil |
| USAMRIID | U.S. Army Medical Research Institute of Infectious Diseases | www.usamriid.army.mil/ |

| CATEGORY | AGENCY | WEB SITE |
|---|---|---|
| SBCCOM | U.S. Army Soldier and Biological Chemical Command | http://hld.sbccom.army.mil |
| **Electronic Texts** | | |
| U.S. Army | *Medical Aspects of Chemical and Biological Warfare*, 1997 | http://www.nbc-med.org /SiteContent/HomePage/WhatsNew /MedAspects/contents.html |
| USAMRIID | *Medical Management of Biological Casualties Handbook*, 4th ed., 2001 | http://www.nbc-med.org /SiteContent/HomePage/WhatsNew /MedManual/Feb01/handbook.htm |
| **Chemical, Biological, Radiological, Nuclear, and Explosive Weapons—Quick References** | | |
| CBRNE general | "National Homeland Security Knowledgebase" (a multi-link site) | http://www.twotigersonline.com /resources.html |
| Biological information | DHHS | www.bt.cdc.gov/ |
| Chemical | U.S. Army | http://ccc.apgea.army.mil |
| HAZMAT | DOT | http://hazmat.dot.gov |
| Nuclear, biological, and chemical (NBC) | "Medical NBC Online Information Server" (private site) | www.nbc-med.org |
| Public health emergency response | CDC | http://www.bt.cdc.gov |
| Radiological | Armed Forces Radiobiology Resource Institute | www.afrri.usuhs.mil |
| Smallpox | DHHS | www.hhs.gov/smallpox/ |

# RECOMMENDED READING

| CATEGORY | DOCUMENT TITLE | LOCATION AND DESCRIPTION |
|---|---|---|
| **Tools** | | |
| AHRQ | "Bioterrorism Emergency Planning and Preparedness Questionnaire for Healthcare Facilities," 2002 | www.ahrq.gov/about/cpcr/bioterr.pdf |
| APIC | Bioterrorism Readiness Planning Template for Healthcare Facilities | www.apic.org/bioterror/ |
| California | State of California, *HEICS III: Hospital Emergency Incident Command System*, 1998 | www.emsa.ca.gov/Dms2/heics3.htm |
| Hawaii | Healthcare Association of Hawaii, *Emergency Management Program*, 2003<br>• "Hospital Capability Assessment for Readiness" | https://www.hah-emergency.net/<br><br>Click on Public Library, then HAH Hosp Capability Assessment Readiness link |
| JCAHO | *Health Care at the Crossroads: Strategies for Creating and Sustaining Community-wide Emergency Preparedness Systems*, 2003 | http://www.jcaho.org/news+room/press+kits/em_intro.htm |
| OSHA | Technical links to health and safety | http://www.osha.gov/SLTC/index.html |
| **Emergency Management Guides** | | |
| AMA | American Medical Association See also:<br>• *Report 11: Medical Preparedness for Terrorism and Other Disasters*, Council on Scientific Affairs (1-00)<br>• *Report 26 of the Board of Trustees: AMA Leadership in the Medical Response to Terrorism and Other Disasters* (1-01)<br>• *Organizational Ethics in Healthcare: Toward a Model for Ethical Decision Making by Provider Organizations*, Institute for Ethics | http://www.ama-assn.org/ |

| CATEGORY | DOCUMENT TITLE | LOCATION AND DESCRIPTION |
|---|---|---|
| FEMA | *Emergency Management Guide for Business & Industry*, 2003<br><br>*Introduction to State and Local Emergency Operations Planning Guidance*, 2002 | www.fema.gov/library/bizindex.shtm<br><br>www.fema.gov/onp/introstate.shtm |
| Kansas City, Missouri, Health Department | *Bioterrorism Manual*, 2003 | www.kcmo.org/health.nsf/web /bioterrorism?opendocument |
| NACCHO | *Elements of Effective Bioterrorism Preparedness: A Planning Primer for Local Public Health Agencies*, 2001<br><br>"Bioterrorism Technical Assistance" | http://www.naccho.org/files /documents/Final_Effective _Bioterrorism.pdf<br><br>http://www.naccho.org/general621 .cfm |
| National Emergency Management Association | *If Disaster Strikes Today: A Governor's Primer on All-Hazards Emergency Management*, 2003<br><br>Emergency Management Accreditation Program (EMAP)<br><br>Emergency Management Assistance Compact (EMAC) | http://www.nemaweb.org/docs /Gov_Primer.pdf<br><br>www.emaponline.org<br><br>http://www.emacweb.org/ |
| National Governor's Association | *A Governor's Guide to Emergency Management*, vols. I and II | www.nga.org/cda/files /REPORTEMERGUIDE2001.pdf |
| National League of Cities | *Homeland Security: Practical Tools for Local Governments* | www.nlc.org/nlc_org/site/files /reports/terrorism.pdf |
| U.S. government | Federal WMD Contingency Plan, *U.S. Government Interagency Domestic Terrorism Concept of Operations Plan*, 2001 | www.fas.org/irp/threat/conplan.html |
| *Response Plans and Checklists* | | |
| AHA | Hospital Disaster Planning Resource List | http://www.aha.org/ |
| CDC | Bioterrorism Readiness Plan: A Template for Healthcare Facilities | www.cdc.gov/ncidod/hip/Bio /13apr99APIC-CDCBioterrorism.pdf |

| CATEGORY | DOCUMENT TITLE | LOCATION AND DESCRIPTION |
|---|---|---|
| DOT | *The Public Transportation System Security and Emergency Preparedness Planning Guide*, Federal Transit Administration, 2003 | http://transit-safety.volpe.dot.gov/publications/security/planningGuide.pdf |
| EPA | *Federal Radiological Emergency Response Plan*, 2000 | www.epa.gov/radiation/rert/docs/rerp-1-00.pdf |
| FEMA | Federal Response Plan | www.fema.gov/rrr/frp |
| MMRS | Metropolitan Medical Response System, *Field Operating Guide* and other documents | http://www.mmrs.hhs.gov |
| NACCHO | *Bioterrorism Emergency Response Plan*, 2003 | www.naccho.org/project63.cfm |
| NFPA | NFPA 473: Standard for Competencies for EMS Personnel Responding to Hazardous Materials Incidents, 1997 | www.nfpa.org/codes/codesandstandards/HazMat/HazMat.asp |
| VA | *Emergency Management Program Guidebook*, Hospital Planning Guide, 2002 | http://www1.va.gov/emshg/apps/emp/emp.htm |
| Washington, DC | *Planning Guidance for the Health System Response to a Bioevent in the National Capitol Region*, Metropolitan Washington Council of Governments, 2001 | www.mwcog.org/services/health/bioevent/ |
| | DC Emergency Management Agency | http://dcema.dc.gov/info/drp.shtm |
| | District of Columbia Disaster Response Plan | http://dcema.dc.gov/dcema/cwp/view.asp?a=1226&Q=533529&dcemaNav=\|31810\| |
| *Article Compendiums* | | |
| CDC | *Emerging Infectious Diseases*, various issues | http://www.cdc.gov/ncidod/EID/index.htm |
| JCAHO | *Health Care at the Crossroads: Strategies for Creating and Sustaining Community-wide Emergency Preparedness Systems*, 2003 | www.jcaho.org/news+room/press+kits/emergency+prep.htm |

| CATEGORY | DOCUMENT TITLE | LOCATION AND DESCRIPTION |
|---|---|---|
| JCAHO | *Joint Commission Perspectives*, Special Issue, December 2001, Vol. 21, No.12 | www.jcrinc.com/subscribers /perspectives.asp?durki=1122 |
| **Miscellaneous** | | |
| | *Why Can't We Talk? Working Together to Bridge the Communications Gap to Save Lives: A Guide for Public Health Officials*, National Task Force on Interoperability, 2003 | www.agilcprogram.org/ntfi/ntfi_guide .pdf |
| | Hazmat for Healthcare | www.hazmatforhealthcare.org /about_the_task_force.cfm |
| | Coalition for Partnership for Community Safety: Strengthening America's Readiness | http://www.hospitalconnect.com /partnershipforsafety |
| | OSHA Emergency Planning and Procedures "eTool" | www.osha.gov/SLTC/etools /evacuation/index.html |
| | *ATSDR: A Primer on Health Risk Communication Principles and Practices*, 2001 | www.atsdr.cdc.gov/HEC/primer.html |
| Training | ACEP, *Positioning America's Emergency Healthcare System to Respond to Acts of Terrorism*, 2002 | www.acep.org/download.cfm ?resource=741 |
| **Web Site Compilations** | | |
| Domestic Preparedness .com | Private site | www.domesticpreparedness.com |
| Rhode Island Department of Health | Selected web sites on bioterrorism and weapons of mass destruction | www.health.state.ri.us/environment /biot/resources.htm |

# Hospital Emergency Incident Command System Job Action Forms

## STAFF EMERGENCY REPONSE TEAM ROSTER
### (Responsiblities for each position attached)

| NAME | ADDRESS | PHONE | TITLE |
|------|---------|-------|-------|
|  |  |  | Owner |
|  |  |  | Administration |
|  |  |  | Incident Commanders |
|  |  |  | Operations Chief |
|  |  |  | Plans Chief |
|  |  |  | Logistics Chief |
|  |  |  | Finance Administration Chief |

## EMERGENCY INCIDENT COMMANDER

**Mission:** Organize and direct Emergency Operations Center (EOC). Give over-all direction for hospital operations and if needed, authorize evacuation.

Immediate

_____ Initiate the Hospital Emergency Incident Command System by assuming role of Emergency Incident Commander.

_____ Read this entire Job Action Sheet.

_____ Put on position identification vest.

_____ Appoint all Section Chiefs and the Medical Staff Director positions; distribute the four section packets which contain:
  • Job Action Sheets for each position
  • Identification vest for each position
  • Forms pertinent to Section and positions

_____ Appoint Public Information Officer (PIO), Liaison Officer, and Safety and Security Officer; distribute Job Action Sheets. (May be preestablished.)

_____ Announce a status/action plan meeting of all Section Chiefs and Medical Staff Director to be held within 5 to 10 minutes.

_____ Assign someone as Documentation Recorder/Aide.

_____ Receive status report and discuss an initial action plan with Section Chiefs and Medical Staff Director. Determine appropriate level of service during immediate aftermath.

_____ Receive initial facility damage survey report from Logistics Chief, if applicable; evaluate the need for evacuation.

_____ Obtain patient census and status from Planning Section Chief. Emphasize proactive actions within the Planning Section. Call for a hospitalwide projection report for 4, 8, 24, and 48 hours from time of incident onset. Adjust projections as necessary.

_____ Authorize a patient prioritization assessment for the purposes of designating appropriate early discharge, if additional beds needed.

_____ Ensure that contact and resource information has been established with outside agencies through the Liaison Officer.

Intermediate

_____ Authorize resources as needed or requested by Section Chiefs.

_____ Designate routine briefings with Section Chiefs to receive status reports and update the action plan regarding the continuance and termination of the action plan.

_____ Communicate status to chairperson of the Hospital Board of Directors or the designee.

_____ Consult with Section Chiefs on needs for staff, physician, and volunteer responder food and shelter. Consider needs for dependents. Authorize plan of action.

Extended

_____ Approve media releases submitted by PIO.

_____ Observe all staff, volunteers and patients for signs of stress and inappropriate behavior. Report concerns to Psychological Support Unit Leader. Provide for staff rest periods and relief.

_____ Other concerns:

_Source:_ California Emergency Medical Services Authority. 1998. _HEICS III: Hospital Emergency Incident Command System Update Project._ [Online report; retrieved 1/7/04.] http://www.emsa.ca.gov/Dms2/heics3.htm.

## LOGISTICS SECTION CHIEF

Positioned Assigned To:

You Report to: _____ (Emergency Incident Commander)

Logistics Command Center: _____ Telephone:

**Mission:** Organize and direct those operations associated with maintenance of the physical environment, and adequate levels of food, shelter, and supplies to support the medical objectives.

Immediate
_____ Receive appointment from the Emergency Incident Commander. Obtain packet containing Section's Job Action Sheets, identification vests, and forms.
_____ Read this entire Job Action Sheet and review organizational chart on back [not shown].
_____ Put on position identification vest.
_____ Obtain briefing from Emergency Incident Commander.
_____ Appoint Logistics Section Unit Leaders: Facilities Unit Leader, Communications Unit Leader, Transportation Unit Leader, Materials Supply Unit Leader, Nutritional Supply Unit Leader; distribute Job Action Sheets and vests. (May be preestablished.)
_____ Brief unit leaders on current situation; outline action plan and designate time for next briefing.
_____ Establish Logistics Section Center in proximity to Emergency Operations Center.
_____ Attend damage assessment meeting with Emergency Incident Commander, Facility Unit Leader and Damage Assessment and Control Officer.

Intermediate
_____ Obtain information and updates regularly from unit leaders and officers; maintain current status of all areas; pass status info to Situation-Status Unit Leader.
_____ Communicate frequently with Emergency Incident Commander.
_____ Obtain needed supplies with assistance of the Finance Section Chief, Communications Unit Leader, and Liaison Unit Leader.

Extended
_____ Ensure that all communications are copied to the Communications Unit Leader.
_____ Document actions and decisions on a continual basis.
_____ Observe all staff, volunteers, and patients for signs of stress and inappropriate behavior. Report concerns to Psychological Support Unit Leader. Provide for staff rest periods and relief.
_____ Other concerns:

*Source*: California Emergency Medical Services Authority. 1998. *HEICS III: Hospital Emergency Incident Command System Update Project*. [Online report; retrieved 1/7/04.] http://www.emsa.ca.gov/Dms2/heics3.htm.

## PLANNING SECTION CHIEF

Positioned Assigned To:

You Report to: _____ (Emergency Incident Commander)

Planning Command Center: _____ Telephone:

**Mission:** Organize and direct all aspects of Planning Section operations. Ensure the distribution of critical information/data. Compile scenario/resource projections from all section chiefs and effect long-range planning. Document and distribute facility Action Plan.

Immediate

_____ Receive appointment from Incident Commander. Obtain packet containing Section's Job Action Sheets.

_____ Read this entire Job Action Sheet and review organizational chart on back [not shown].

_____ Put on position identification vest.

_____ Obtain briefing from Incident Commander.

_____ Recruit a documentation aide from the Labor Pool.

_____ Appoint Planning Unit leaders: Situation-Status Unit Leader, Labor Pool Unit Leader, Medical Staff Unit Leader, Nursing Unit Leader; distribute the corresponding Job Action Sheets and vests. (May be preestablished.)

_____ Brief unit leaders after meeting with Emergency Incident Commander.

_____ Provide for a Planning/Information Center.

_____ Ensure the formulation and documentation of an incident-specific facility Action Plan. Distribute copies to Incident Commander and all section chiefs.

_____ Call for projection reports (Action Plan) from all Planning Section unit leaders and section chiefs for scenarios 4, 8, 24, and 48 hours from time of incident onset. Adjust time for receiving projection reports as necessary.

_____ Instruct Situation-Status Unit Leader and staff to document/update status reports from all disaster section chiefs and unit leaders for use in decision making and for reference in postdisaster evaluation and recovery-assistance applications.

Intermediate

_____ Obtain briefings and updates as appropriate. Continue to update and distribute the facility Action Plan.

_____ Schedule planning meetings to include Planning Section unit leaders, section chiefs and the Incident Commander for continued update of the facility Action Plan.

Extended

_____ Continue to receive projected activity reports from section chiefs and Planning Section unit leaders at appropriate intervals.

_____ Ensure that all requests are routed/documented through the Communications Unit Leader.

_____ Observe all staff, volunteers and patients for signs of stress and inappropriate behavior. Report concerns to Psychological Support Unit Leader. Provide for staff rest periods and relief.

_____ Other concerns:

*Source:* California Emergency Medical Services Authority. 1998. *HEICS III: Hospital Emergency Incident Command System Update Project.* [Online report; retrieved 1/7/04.] http://www.emsa.ca.gov/Dms2/heics3.htm.

## FINANCE SECTION CHIEF

Positioned Assigned To:

You Report to: _____ (Emergency Incident Commander)

Finance Command Center: _____ Telephone:

**Mission:** Monitor the utilization of financial assets. Oversee the acquisition of supplies and services necessary to carry out the hospital's medical mission. Supervise the documentation of expenditures relevant to the emergency incident.

Immediate
_____ Receive appointment from Emergency Incident Commander. Obtain packet containing Section's Job Action Sheets.
_____ Read this entire Job Action Sheet and review organizational chart on back [not shown].
_____ Put on position identification vest.
_____ Obtain briefing from Emergency Incident Commander.
_____ Appoint Time Unit Leader, Procurement Unit Leader, Claims Unit Leader, and Cost Unit Leader; distribute the corresponding Job Action Sheets and vests. (May be preestablished.)
_____ Confer with unit leaders after meeting with Emergency Incident Commander; develop a section action plan.
_____ Establish a Financial Section Operations Center. Ensure adequate documentation/recording personnel.

Intermediate
_____ Approve a "cost-to-date" incident financial status report submitted by the Cost Unit Leader every eight hours summarizing financial data relative to personnel, supplies, and miscellaneous expenses.
_____ Obtain briefings and updates from Emergency Incident Commander as appropriate. Relate pertinent financial status reports to appropriate chiefs and unit leaders.
_____ Schedule planning meetings to include Finance Section unit leaders to discuss updating the section's incident action plan and termination procedures.

Extended
_____ Ensure that all requests for personnel or supplies are copied to the Communications Unit Leader in a timely manner.
_____ Observe all staff, volunteers, and patients for signs of stress and inappropriate behavior. Report concerns to Psychological Support Unit Leader. Provide for staff rest periods and relief.
_____ Other concerns:

*Source*: California Emergency Medical Services Authority. 1998. *HEICS III: Hospital Emergency Incident Command System Update Project*. [Online report; retrieved 1/7/04.] http://www.emsa.ca.gov/Dms2/heics3.htm.

## OPERATIONS SECTION CHIEF

Positioned Assigned To:

You Report to: _____ (Emergency Incident Commander)

Operations Command Center: _____ Telephone:

**Mission:**   Organize and direct aspects relating to the Operations Section. Carry out directives of the Emergency Incident Commander. Coordinate and supervise the Medical Services Subsection, Ancillary Services Subsection, and Human Services Subsection of the Operations Section.

Immediate

___ Receive appointment from Emergency Incident Commander. Obtain packet containing Section's Job Action Sheets.

___ Read this entire Job Action Sheet and review organizational chart on back [not shown].

___ Put on position identification vest.

___ Obtain briefing from Emergency Incident Commander.

___ Appoint Medical Staff Director, Medical Care Director, Ancillary Services Director, and Human Services Director and transfer the corresponding Job Action Sheets. (May be preestablished.)

___ Brief all Operations Section directors on current situation and develop the section's initial action plan. Designate time for next briefing.

___ Establish Operations Section Center in proximity to Emergency Operations Center.

___ Meet with the Medical Staff Director, Medical Care Director, and Nursing Unit Leader to plan and project patient care needs.

Intermediate

___ Designate times for briefings and updates with all Operations Section directors to develop/update section's action plan.

___ Ensure that the Medical Services Subsection, Ancillary Services Subsection, and Human Services Subsection are adequately staffed and supplied.

___ Brief the Emergency Incident Commander routinely on the status of the Operations Section.

Extended

___ Ensure that all communications are copied to the Communications Unit Leader; document all actions and decisions.

___ Observe all staff, volunteers, and patients for signs of stress and inappropriate behavior. Report concerns to Psychological Support Unit Leader. Provide for staff rest periods and relief.

___ Other concerns:

*Source*: California Emergency Medical Services Authority. 1998. *HEICS III: Hospital Emergency Incident Command System Update Project*. [Online report; retrieved 1/7/04.] http://www.emsa.ca.gov/Dms2/heics3.htm.

# Index

Comprehensive emergency management (CEM), 159
Comprehensive Environmental Response, Compensation, and Liability Act (CERCLA), 82, 241
Concurrent review, 72
Confidentiality issues, 236–37
Consequence management, 153–54
Constitutional rights, 237–38
Contingency Hospital System, 221–22
Continuous quality improvement (CQI), 72–74
Controls, 53, 56
Cornell University, 9
Corrective controls, 56
Counseling services, 65
Countermeasures, 53, 239
CQI. *See* Continuous quality improvement
Crestpark Nursing Home, 121
Crisis management, 152–53
Critical services, 263–64
Cross, Jeannie, 11
Cuomo, J., 9
Cyanide, 31, 33

Damage assessment, 132
Daniell, W. E., 116
Dark Winter, 70, 197
Decontamination, 85–86
    biological exposure, 100
    case example, 102
    definition of, 108
    disposal issues, 114, 116
    effectiveness of, 108
    emergency operations plan, 63
    Israeli program, 290–91
    logistics, 112–14
    need for, 111
    plan diagram, 113
    radiological contamination, 100–101
    runoff issues, 240–41
    training for, 112
    types of, 109–11
Defense Against Weapons of Mass Destruction, Title XIV, 151
Defense, Department of (DoD)
    directives, 221
    Domestic Preparedness Program, 151
    medical personnel, 218
    military support requests, 216–17, 224, 225

response deployment, 187
sharing agreements, 221
weapons of mass effect, 27
Definitive care, 167
*Denton Regional Medical Center v. LaCroix,* 234
Detection
    CDC focus, 185
    controls, 56
    emergency operations plan, 63–64
    focus, 181
Deterrent controls, 56
DHHS. *See* Health and Human Services, Department of
DHS. *See* Homeland Security, Department of
Dimethoate, 102
Dioxin, 179
Direction and control functions, 132
Disaster. *See also* Emergency response
    assistance, 160–64
    culture, 5, 19
    death rates, 42
    declaration, 3, 160
    plan, 19, 142–43
    relief, 151
    statistics, 3
Disaster Mitigation Act, 263
Disaster preparedness program
    capability assessment, 57–58
    capacity assessment, 57–58
    checklist, 22–23
    development checklist, 76
    emergency operations planning, 58
Disaster Relief Fund, 256
DoD. *See* Defense, Department of
Domestic Preparedness Program, 88, 151
Donation coordination, 10, 66–67
Drills. *See* Exercises
Duty of care, 242

Education, 67, 153
EMA. *See* Emergency management agency
EMAC. *See* Emergency Management Assistance Compact
Emergency Alert System, 6
Emergency declarations, 250, 256–57
Emergency management
    all-hazards approach, 4, 129–30
    assistance coordination, 160–64
    community, 154

# About the Contributors

## ABOUT THE EDITOR

**K. Joanne McGlown, Ph.D., M.H.H.A., R.N., CHE**, is chief executive officer of McGlown-Self Consulting in Montevallo, Alabama; a medical consultant with Battelle Memorial Institute in Crystal City, Virginia; and adjunct professor at the University of Alabama at Birmingham. Dr. McGlown has more than 25 years' experience in prehospital emergency medical services (EMS), nursing, and healthcare administration and also has broad teaching experience in the areas of EMS, emergency and disaster management, and healthcare delivery issues in emergency and disaster environments. Her work has involved clinical and administrative management and consulting in the public, private, and government sectors. Dr. McGlown holds Associate of Applied Science degrees in emergency medical services and fire science administration, a bachelor's degree in sociology/psychology, and a Master of Science degree in hospital and health administration. Her doctorate is in administration of health services, with a major in strategic management. Dr. McGlown is a certified legal nurse consultant and a certified healthcare executive (CHE) and diplomate of the American College of Healthcare Executives. She serves on many national emergency management committees and participates in a number of task forces and think-tank meetings in these topic areas. Dr. McGlown is an officer of the board of the World Association of Disaster and Emergency Medicine and a frequent national and international speaker and lecturer on a variety of topics, including hospital preparedness for disasters and terrorism.

## ABOUT THE AUTHORS

**Ernest B. Abbott, Esq.**, is of the FEMA Law Associates in McLean, Virginia. Mr. Abbott is one of the nation's leading authorities on the legal aspects of federal disaster relief, flood, and emergency management programs. Recently ending a four-year term as general counsel for the Federal Emergency Management Agency (FEMA), Mr. Abbott specializes in all FEMA-program-related laws and regulations. Prior to his work at FEMA, he spent two decades specializing in regulated infrastructure industries in both the public and private sectors. He is chair of the American Bar Association's State and Local Government Law Section's Task Force on Emergency Management and Homeland Security. Mr. Abbott holds a law degree from Harvard Law School, a Master of Public Policy degree from Harvard's Kennedy School of Government, and a Bachelor of Arts degree from Swarthmore College. He is a member of the bar in the District of Columbia and in the states of Texas and Massachusetts.

**Jakov Adler, M.D.,** is emergency medical advisor for the Israeli Ministry of Health in Tel Aviv, Israel, and a colonel (ret.) in the Israeli Defense Forces. Dr. Adler heads medical emergency planning, training, and risk assessment for Israel's Ministry of Health. He has accumulated extensive experience in planning and organization of prehospital and hospital medical services in Israel and other countries as former deputy of the Medical Corps of the Israeli Defense Forces; head of the Medical Branch, Home Front Command (during the Persian Gulf War); director general of Magen David Adom (Red Cross Ambulance Services in Israel); and director of an emergency department in a large medical center in Jerusalem. An orthopedic surgeon and emergency physician with broad experience in trauma management, Dr. Adler has served several years as an adviser on disaster and emergency medicine to the Ministry of Health in Israel and in other foreign countries. He retired recently from his position as the head of the medical-support unit of the Department of Peacekeeping Operations at the United National Headquarters in New York. He has headed and operated in field hospitals during many humanitarian medical-assistance missions worldwide.

**Donna F. Barbisch, D.H.A., M.P.H., CRNA**, is chief executive officer of Global Deterrence Alternatives in Washington, DC, and a major general in the United States Army Reserve. Dr. Barbisch is among the nation's most distinguished experts in terrorism preparedness and response, developing and implementing comprehensive management programs that integrate critical infrastructure protection, preparedness, public health, and emergency services in the complex interagency context. With more than 25 years of leadership experience in the military, governmental, and private sectors, she is a leader, educator, facilitator, and change agent. She has previously been an advisor to the commander of the Soldier Biological Chemical Command (SBCCOM) for Weapons of Mass Destruction, Consequence Management, at Aberdeen Proving Ground, Maryland; a member of the 1998 original planning team for the Biological Warfare Improved Response Program; and the senior advisor on terrorism for the chief of the Army Reserve. Dr. Barbisch holds a Master of Public Health from the University of North Carolina at Chapel Hill and a Doctor of Health Administration from the Medical University of South Carolina. She is an adjunct professor at the U.S. Army War College, Strategic Studies Institute; the George Washington University; and the College of Health Professions, the Medical University of South Carolina. She sits on many national advisory boards and is a prolific national and international speaker in her areas of expertise.

**Connie J. Boatright, M.S.N., R.N.**, is director of education and research and deputy director of the Emergency Management Strategic Healthcare Group (EMSHG) in the Department of Veterans Affairs, and she is a colonel in the United States Army Reserve. EMSHG conducts research and learning-needs assessments for disaster-related issues and evaluates medical center capabilities to prepare for, respond to, and recover from catastrophic incidents. Ms. Boatright has held faculty positions at Indiana University Graduate School of Nursing and Indiana Wesleyan University. For the past 20 years, Ms. Boatright has been involved in initiatives in emergency, disaster, and weapons of mass destruction, particularly as related to healthcare systems and delivery. She has widely presented and published in the cited topics.

**Marjorie H. Brant, J.D.**, is an attorney and former general counsel for Columbia Gas of Kentucky in Lexington and Columbia Gas of Ohio in Columbus. Ms. Brant has 20 years of experience as an innovative legal counselor and leader for natural gas utilities serving more than 1.5 million customers. In this role, Ms. Brant served on the American Gas Association's

Security Committee and participated in the development of infrastructure security protocols for the natural gas industry following the attacks of 9/11. Ms. Brant is also an adjunct professor in the graduate Concentration in Emergency Management program at Jacksonville State University in Alabama. In addition to a Juris Doctorate from The Ohio State University, Ms. Brant holds master's degrees from the University of Pittsburgh and Purdue University and a graduate certificate in emergency management from Jacksonville State University.

**Peter W. Brewster** is area emergency manager for the Emergency Management Strategic Healthcare Group at the Veterans Health Administration in Indianapolis, Indiana. Mr. Brewster is responsible for the development, management, and linkage of federal medical and health contingency programs, such as the National Disaster Medical System (NDMS), with state and local government agencies and the Veterans Health Administration. He served as a program manager with VHA's Education, Research, Training, & Development section from 1990 to 2002. In that role, he was involved with various education and training projects for the VA as well as projects for external healthcare audiences through his work with the NDMS annual conference (1992–2003) and the 2001 Joint Commission on Accreditation of Healthcare Organizations emergency management standards committee, and other projects. Mr. Brewster is also a member of the National Fire Protection Association Technical Committee on Health Care Emergency Management. His background includes search, rescue, and emergency management with the city of Indianapolis, the National Park Service, and the U.S. Forest Service in Wyoming.

**John D. Hoyle, Sr., M.H.A., LFACHE**, is director of the Noble Training Center in Ft. McClellan, Alabama. Mr. Hoyle has been active in disaster medical preparedness and response for more than 30 years. He was a hospital executive for 31 years, including 22 years as president and chief executive officer of the three-hospital St. Luke's Hospitals system in northern Kentucky. He formed and led a disaster medical assistant team for the U.S. Public Health Service for 15 years and is a reserve officer in the Commissioned Corps of the U.S. Public Health Service, holding the rank of captain. Mr. Hoyle has responded to numerous major disasters and was part of the medical preparedness operation for the Olympic Games in Atlanta, Georgia, and Salt Lake City, Utah. He is also a FEMA-certified disaster mortuary team coordinator. Mr. Hoyle holds a master's degree in hospital administration, is a certified healthcare executive (CHE), and is a life fellow of the American College of Healthcare Executives (LFACHE).

**Jerry L. Mothershead, M.D., FACEP**, is physician advisor for the Medical Readiness and Response Division at Battelle Memorial Institute in Hampton, Virginia; senior medical consultant for the Navy Medicine Office of Homeland Security; and commander (ret.) of the Medical Corps of the United States Navy. Dr. Mothershead is an emergency medicine physician with more than 20 years of experience in operational medicine, emergency medical services, and emergency management. Prior to his retirement from the Navy in 2002, he served in a variety of positions, from the hospital setting to combat and humanitarian-support missions. He led the first medical response team to deploy to the Persian Gulf in 1990 and provided medical support to Kuwaiti refugees. During Operation Desert Storm, he served with special operations personnel. From 1996 until his retirement, he was the Navy specialty advisor for Emergency Medical Services, and in 2001, he was named senior medical advisor to the Navy Medicine Office of Homeland Security. Since 2002, he has continued to provide consultative services to federal, state, and local governmental agencies in emergency preparedness, homeland security, and consequence management operations against terrorism and weapons of mass destruction.

**Avagene Moore, CEM**, is president and coordinator of the Emergency Information Infrastructure Project and resides in Lawrenceburg, Tennessee. Ms. Moore is a certified emergency manager with 28 years of emergency management experience. She served as the local emergency program manager in her home county for 16 years and was responsible for comprehensive countywide planning and exercises that covered local hospitals, nursing and assisted-living facilities, public health agencies, day care centers, school systems, and local industries as well as the city-county governmental infrastructure. Ms. Moore worked for four years in the Emergency Management Laboratory of Oak Ridge Associated Universities prior to her affiliation with the Emergency Information Infrastructure Partnership (EIIP) and the EIIP Virtual Forum. She is a past-president of the National Coordinating Council on Emergency Management, the present-day International Association of Emergency Managers (IAEM). She is cochairperson of the IAEM Conference Committee and serves on the

International Disaster and Emergency Response Conference Committee as well as on the editorial board of the *Journal of Homeland Security and Emergency Management*.

**Eric K. Noji, M.D., M.P.H.**, is special assistant to the U.S. Surgeon General for Homeland Security and Emergency Preparedness and Response in the U.S. Public Health Service in Washington, DC. Dr. Noji is among the most well respected and experienced physicians and leaders in emergency preparedness and response in the United States and globally. He has served as senior medical advisor to the White House Office of Homeland Security in the Executive Office of the President and worked in the Department of Homeland Security, the Centers for Disease Control and Prevention, and the World Health Organization. He is also on the faculty of the Johns Hopkins Schools of Medicine and Public Health. Dr. Noji is the author or coauthor of more than 150 scientific articles and publications on disaster medicine, disaster epidemiology, natural and technological disasters, terrorism, refugees, and complex humanitarian emergencies.

**John H. Sorensen, Ph.D.**, is a distinguished researcher at Oak Ridge National Laboratory in Oak Ridge, Tennessee. Dr. Sorensen has been involved with research on emergency planning and disaster response for more than 25 years. He has been the principal investigator on more than 40 major projects for federal agencies, including the Federal Emergency Management Agency, the Department of Energy, the Environmental Protection Agency, the Nuclear Regulatory Commission, the Department of Defense, and the U.S. Chemical Safety and Hazard Investigation Board. Dr. Sorensen's research includes the Three Mile Island Public Health Fund Emergency Planning Project and the Second Assessment of Research on Natural Hazards, where he served as the subgroup leader for prediction, forecast warning, and emergency planning. Dr. Sorensen has authored more than 140 professional publications, including *Impacts of Hazardous Technology: The Psycho-Social Effects of Restarting TMI-1*. He has published extensively on response to emergency warnings, risk communications, organizational effectiveness in disasters, emergency evacuation, and protective actions for chemical emergencies. He holds a doctorate in geography from the University of Colorado at Boulder and was an assistant professor at the University of Hawaii.

**Barbara Vogt, Ph.D.**, is a sociologist on the research staff of the environmental sciences division at Oak Ridge National Laboratory in Oak Ridge, Tennessee. Since writing her doctoral thesis on the evacuation of nursing homes and hospitals, Dr. Vogt has focused her work on emergency preparedness and response, risk assessment, and issues of environmental justice. Many of the training publications, videos, and CDs available from the Federal Emergency Management Agency for the Chemical Stockpile Emergency Preparedness Program have been prepared under her guidance, including the recent *"Don't Be a Victim—Medical Management of Patients Contaminated with Chemical Agents."* Dr. Vogt also co-scripted a training CD on the medical management for biological warfare casualties for the U.S. Army Medical Institute for Infectious Diseases.

**William R. Wayland, Jr., J.D., M.S.H.H.A.**, is principal at the law firm of McKoon, Williams & Gold in Chattanooga, Tennessee. Mr. Wayland is a practicing attorney. He has served previously as general counsel or chief executive officer of hospital management companies, a physician/hospital organization, a managed care organization, and a reimbursement-compliance company. He is a current member of the American Health Lawyers Association and the Healthcare Financial Management Association. Mr. Wayland is a graduate of Vanderbilt University School of Law in Nashville, Tennessee, and the graduate program of healthcare administration at the University of Alabama at Birmingham.